# TRADE BOOKBINDING

## IN THE

# BRITISH ISLES

## 1660–1800

# TRADE BOOKBINDING

## IN THE

# BRITISH ISLES

## 1660–1800

### STUART BENNETT

OAK KNOLL PRESS

THE BRITISH LIBRARY

2004

First Edition, 2004

Published by Oak Knoll Press
310 Delaware Street, New Castle, Delaware 19720, USA
Web: http://www.oakknoll.com
Publishing Director: J. Lewis von Hoelle

and The British Library
96 Euston Road, St. Pancras, London NW1 2DB, UK


ISBN: 1-58456-130-0 (USA)
ISBN: 0-7123-4848-4 (UK)


Copyright: © 2004 Stuart Bennett


Library of Congress Cataloguing-in-Publication data is available upon request.
British Library Cataloguing-in-Publication Data is available from The British Library.

This work was printed and bound in China on archival, acid-free paper meeting the requirements of the
American Standard for Permanence of Paper for Printed Library Materials.

Designed and typeset by Katy Homans
Printed and bound by South China Printing Company

Frontispiece: see Fig. 4.35.
Lettering styles and spine decoration on London-printed duodecimo novels, 1737–1774,
from left to right: Alain René le Sage, *The Bachelor of Salamanca*, for A. Bettesworth [et al.], 1737, 2 vols.;
Claudine de Tencin, *The Siege of Calais*, for T. Woodward, 1740;
Francois Génard, *The School of Woman*, for J. Robinson, 1753;
Jean de Kerguette, *True Merit, True Happiness*, for F. and J. Noble, 2 vols., [1757];
Johann Bodmer, *Noah*, for J. Collyer, 1767, 2 vols.;
John Potter, *The Curate of Coventry*, for F. Newbery, 1771, 2 vols.;
Henry Brooke, *Juliet Grenville*, for G. Robinson, 1774, 3 vols.
Collection of William Zachs.

PRINTED IN CHINA

# CONTENTS

# A NOTE TO READERS

This book is set in Bell's Monotype, a font designed in 1788 by Richard Austin for the bookseller John Bell. It was not a success in England, but was copied in the United States as early as 1792. At the end of the nineteenth century it was a staple of the Riverside Press, who were unaware of its origin and simply called it "English copperplate." Stanley Morison discovered one of Bell's original specimen sheets in the 1920s, and restored Bell's name to this elegant typeface. Bell's bindings and publications are discussed in Chapter 3.

Illustration captions in the first two chapters only state places of publication outside London. They also omit imprint and edition information in order to concentrate, respectively, on historical background and the bookbinders' price lists. Captions in subsequent chapters consistently include full imprints and, less consistently, edition statements. All captions credit collections other than the author's. Paper sizes and formats are discussed in an appendix at the end of the book.

The illustration on this page is a copperplate engraving from Johann Amos Comenius, *Orbis Sensualium Pictus*, London, 1705.

# INTRODUCTION

Trade bookbinding in the British Isles in the seventeenth and eighteenth centuries has been a curiously neglected subject. In 1956 Graham Pollard wrote that retail booksellers could not sell their books "unless they were bound," but a consensus subsequently developed among scholars that books were mostly purchased in sheets, and "it was the task of the owner to have them bound."[1] As a result, researchers established important links between individual and institutional collectors and their bookbinders, but the broader, seemingly more anonymous connections between the bookselling and bookbinding trades were largely left behind.

Notwithstanding this scholarly consensus, late seventeenth- and eighteenth-century references, illustrations, catalogues, and advertising demonstrate that over eighty percent of the books in the British Isles were sold ready-bound, which means bound for booksellers *in trade bindings* either before wholesale distribution or retail sale. Among the most important of these historical sources are the catalogues of John Starkey and Robert Clavell, better known as the "Term Catalogues" from Edward Arber's compilation in 1903. From 1668 to 1673, these catalogues specifically described over eighty percent of their books as sold "bound," a percentage which turns up in other records with enough consistency to reveal an established practice in the book trade. The practice was settled in England by the early sixteenth century, and spread to Scotland and Ireland as printing became established in those countries. It continued at the same rate until mechanized processes began to supplant hand bookbinding in the 1820s. Concurrently with Starkey and Clavell's catalogues, and even as early as 1619, bookbinders published price lists for their standard trade styles. These price lists gave booksellers the security of fixed prices, and allowed them to advertise their ready-bound books accordingly.

A major development in trade bookbinding took place during the last half of the eighteenth century. Paper, which bound ephemeral publications as early as the fifteenth century, was increasingly used for more substantial books. Leather and part leather were advertised as "bound" and "half bound," paper as "sewed" and sometimes, more specifically, as "boards" (paper-covered pasteboard) and "paper" or "wrappers." By around 1800, boards and wrappers became sufficiently standard that prices for books in leather bindings ceased to be included in major trade catalogues.

These materials and more are the stuff of trade bindings, which John Carter defines in *ABC for Book-Collectors* as the

> *original binding as issued to the public.* . . . The only books which can qualify are those bound before issue by the retail or wholesale bookseller: in limp vellum, parchment, sheep or calf in earlier times, in the 18th century usually in calf or half calf. These are conveniently called *trade bindings*, and they are the bibliographical equivalent of the publisher's bindings of the past century and a quarter.[2]

Carter's definition, however, obscures an essential distinction between wholesale and retail binding. Trade bindings are, as he states, those commissioned by the "retail or wholesale bookseller," but

## BOOKS *lately printed for* F. and J. NOBLE.

1. **A**pparition ; or, Female Cavalier. A Story founded on Facts. 3 vols. 9s. bound.

2. Accomplish'd Rake ; or, Modern Fine Gentleman. 3s. bound.

3. Bubbled Knights ; or, Succefsful Contrivances. Plainly evincing, in two familiar Inftances lately tranfacted in this Metropolis, the Folly and Unreafonablenefs of Parents laying a Reftraint upon their Children's Inclinations in the Affairs of Love and Marriage. 2 vols. 6s. bound.

4. Child's Entertainer. Being a Collection of Riddles on the moft familiar Subjects, price 6d.

5. Emily : or, the Hiftory of a Natural Daughter, 2 vols. 6s. bound.

6. Fortune-Teller ; or, the Footman ennobled. Being the Hiftory of the Right Honourable the Earl of R***, and Mifs Lucy M—n—y. 2 vols. 6s. bound.

7. Fortunate Villager ; or Memoirs of Sir Andrew Thompfon. 2 vols. 6 s. bound.

8. Hiftory of Sir Harry Herald, with the Adventures of Mr. Charles Herald ; and Mifs Felicia Blanchman. 3 vols. 9s. bound.

9. Hiftory of a young Lady of Diftinction. In a Series of Letters, between a Mother and her Daughter. 2 vols. 6s. bound.

10. Hiftory of the great Plague in London. To which is added, a Journal of that at Marfeilles. 5s. in Boards and Marble Paper ; or 6s. bound in Calf, gilt and lettered.

11. Hiftory of My Own Life. Being an Account of many of the fevereft Trials impofed by an implacable Father upon the moft affectionate Pair that ever entered the Marriage State. 2 vols. 6s. bound.

12. Hiftory and Adventures of Frank Hammond. 3s. bound.

13.

A typical page from a catalogue of ready-bound novels printed for Francis and John Noble. This example appears at the end of their two-volume novel *True Merit, True Happiness, Exemplified in the Entertaining and Instructive Memoirs of Mr. S—*, [undated, but 1757], 12mo. Collection of William Zachs.

publishers' bindings, a subcategory of trade bindings, are exclusively wholesalers' bindings. They are an important part of the trade mainstream, as can be seen in the example of the Scottish bookbinder William Scott, who in 1787 received the commission to bind *in boards* much of the first Edinburgh edition of Burns's *Poems, Chiefly in the Scottish Dialect.*[3]

Carter's definition of trade binding may also be expanded to include more elaborate bindings in materials such as decorated vellum, russia leather, and goatskin. This last was usually called "turkey" in the seventeenth century, reflecting its Middle Eastern origin, and "morocco" in the eighteenth, as more and more skins were imported from North Africa. Even tortoiseshell has its place: in 1785 the prosperous bookseller John Stockdale advertised his one-volume edition of Shakespeare for sale in "boards, 15s.; calf, 17s.6d.; calf gilt, 18s.; russia, 19s.; vellum, 21s.; morocco extra ["extra" meaning "extra gilt"], 25s.; tortoiseshell, 63s."[4] Stockdale certainly displayed all these styles in his shop, and at three guineas the tortoiseshell binding must have incorporated the genuine article.

All of the bindings in Stockdale's advertisement clearly meet Carter's essential criterion for a trade binding: "bound before issue by the retail or wholesale bookseller." Stockdale was not unusual in having so many beautiful bindings for sale in his shop. As more examples are compared, and further records of the book trade emerge, increasing numbers of the fine bindings previously considered bespoke (which is to say privately commissioned in the way Samuel Pepys "bespoke" a binding from William Nott "the famous bookbinder"[5]) will be identified as trade bindings commissioned by booksellers.

Evidence of trade bookbinding appears both in historical sources and in the bindings themselves. This book assembles both types of evidence in order to provide the reader with proof of the primacy of trade bookbinding, and to show what these bindings looked like.

CHAPTER 1, "Bookbinders and Booksellers," begins with a brief discussion of the bookbinding and bookselling trades in the seventeenth and eighteenth centuries, and analyzes the way their interaction resulted in a wide variety of bindings. It goes on to argue the primacy of trade bookbinding in England.

CHAPTER 2, "The Bookbinders' Price Lists," considers those trade bindings, often the simplest, documented by the lists of prices agreed between major London bookbinders and booksellers. Illustrations display examples of trade styles, whenever possible on books named in the four surviving London lists of 1669–1760 and in the Dublin price list of 1743.

CHAPTER 3, "Publishers' Bindings," discusses the differences between early and modern publishers, and employs late eighteenth-century examples to define this sub-category of trade bindings. Subsequent sections deal with earlier leather, boards and printed paper labels, wrappers, and the variety of publishers' bindings used on children's books.

CHAPTER 4, "Common Trade Bindings: a Sampler," primarily illustrates calf and sheep bindings. The survey shows national styles, aesthetic developments and aberrations, and considers some of the problems, such as rebinding and redecoration, inherent in identifying and dating individual examples.

CHAPTER 5, "Deluxe Bindings," explores high-end trade bookbinding, with discussions of stylistic development, the persistence of certain patterns, and the difficulty of distinguishing ready-bound and bespoke bindings. The illustrations, mostly of goatskin bindings, show both basic and more elaborate forms of decoration, including those on authors' and publishers' presentation copies.

Most of the bindings shown in this book are on literary texts. Literary book production in general provides the book trade with a microcosm similar to that which Michael Sadleir describes in *The Evolution of Publishers' Binding Styles 1770–1900*. "What is true of novels," writes Sadleir, is also true both for "more dignified—certainly more bulky—books," and for "slighter, smaller works." Novels are "constructed with a keener eye for economy and utility and with less thought of eccentricity, elegance or embellishment than any other *genre* of published work," and at any given period probably represent "the norm of practical and cheap design."[6]

One caveat for the reader: there are no consistent guidelines for identifying the geographical origin of a binding. Throughout the seventeenth and eighteenth centuries, sheets were sent from London to provincial towns, then bound for local retailers. Some of these bindings can look like earlier, or even contemporary, London work. Similarly, provincially-printed sheets could be sent to London and given rough-and-ready bindings indistinguishable from crude provincial ones. At the other end of the scale, fine binding was always available in Oxford and Cambridge, as was the usual range of cheaper bindings for academic and other books; both university towns were important centers of the book trade even before the invention of printing. After about 1750, fine binding became more widespread, especially in the fashionable spa towns. Provincial bookbinders' tickets—small engraved or printed labels pasted into books—are extremely rare before 1800. Therefore, unless a book has at least one distinctive characteristic, usually the impression of an attributable binding tool, there is no hard and fast rule enabling us to tell an unsigned provincial binding from one executed in London.[7] From the mid-eighteenth century onwards, however, Irish and Scottish styles are more idiosyncratic, and it is generally possible to tell these bindings from each other and from English work of the period.

This book proposes a new way of looking at bookbindings produced in the British Isles before 1800. Simpler bindings of calf, sheep, and even goatskin have generally been neglected by scholars who, assuming such bindings were individually bespoke, paid little attention to the possibility that they might have categorizable features. By demonstrating that the overwhelming majority of these bindings were produced for booksellers, this study asks scholars to take a new look at them, to identify patterns which allow the inference of a common origin, and to associate bindings with individual wholesale and retail businesses and syndicates. Finding such patterns and associations will not be easy: the majority of pre-1800 books and bindings have perished, and although thousands remain, examples are so widely dispersed that re-assembling the record must be a slow and painstaking process. I have tried to show some of the possibilities available to researchers of trade bindings, but I make no claim that the visual record presented in this book is comprehensive.

Experienced collectors, librarians, and booksellers develop an instinct for identifying bindings based on years of handling them. Sometimes an expert can declare a binding to be from a certain area, of a certain period, or even by a particular bookbinder without immediately being able to say why. The following chapters provide a rationale for this instinctive process; they should help readers recognize the distinguishing features in the bindings they encounter, and provide tools for beginning the process of associating specific bindings with individual booksellers and syndicates. The examples shown here are unrestored, and even the simplest and most utilitarian can be beautiful objects. I hope some of their beauty will find its way to readers through the pages of this book.

## CHAPTER ONE

# BOOKBINDERS AND BOOKSELLERS

## I. TRADE RELATIONS

The bookbinder's lot in the 1660s was not an especially happy one, and for most of the next century there was little improvement.[1] Late seventeenth- and early eighteenth-century records, such as there are, show that bookbinders were poorly paid, with masters and journeymen earning significantly less than comparable positions in other trades.[2]

Although some binders seem to have made good livings up to the time of Henry VIII,[3] copyright practices of the late sixteenth and seventeenth centuries increasingly put power in the hands of those booksellers who were able to commission and acquire texts. As early as the 1620s, the poet George Wither complains that "the Bookeseller hath not onely made the Printer, the Binder, and the Claspmaker a slaue to him: but hath brought Authors, yea the whole Common-wealth. . . into bondage."[4] An eighteenth-century writer is more specific: "the bookbinder is a dependant on the bookseller. He receives the book in sheets from the bookseller, and his business is to bind it . . . as he is directed. . . . The profit of the trade is but inconsiderable in itself."[5]

Richard Head's *Proteus Redivivus: or, The Art of Wheedling* (1675) suggests that the binder's best hope is to abandon his craft and take up bookselling instead:

> Printing comeing in, broke the back of the writing Clerks, but yet gave a considerable life to the rising Book-binder, who not only bound for others but himself, and Printing his own Copies, had work enough to do to bind his own books, his stock encreasing by the benefit of Printing. . . . The Sonne after his Fathers Decease scornes the mean Title of a Bookbinder, and therefore employs others, and is henceforward stil'd a Bookseller; and the rest of his Brethren, who are able, follow his example.[6]

It was naturally in the booksellers' interest to pay as little as possible to those they employed. Although printers kept their earnings at a satisfactory level—there were fewer of them and their expensive equipment gave them greater negotiating power—the bookbinders suffered. The first surviving bookbinders' price list, dated 1619,[7] indicates that binders were attempting to regularize their incomes, and to present a united front to the booksellers who were the source of most of their work.[8]

The 1619 prices must have been the best the bookbinders could negotiate, but they were still remarkably low. Simple calf with a blind oval in the center of the covers was 2s. 6d. on a large folio like Sir Walter Raleigh's *History*, and 1s. 6d. on a smaller folio like *Purchas his Pilgrimage*. Even allowing for the greater cost of materials, larger bindings gave the bookbinding trade a better return than smaller ones. A simple sheep binding on an octavo New Testament cost the bookseller only 4d., about the price of a pound of butter, and on a sextodecimo (16mo) Psalter 2d., the same as two quarts of ale.[9] All of these prices had to include materials, and usually the additional labor of sewing the signatures onto cords, as the number of leaves that could be stab-sewn, or "stitch'd," was strictly regulated.[10] To make matters a little worse, it appears that bookbinders were bound by the Stationers' Company rule of the "quarterly book," which meant that for every twenty-five copies bound of the same edition, a twenty-sixth copy had to be bound for free.[11]

Such low prices meant that bookbinders were always under financial pressure. They were also treated by booksellers as inferiors, and used as porters and warehousemen, to fetch and carry between printers and booksellers.[12] It is easy to see why, in Head's phrase, they "scorned" the "mean Title of a Bookbinder," and were constantly attempting to find ways to improve their incomes, either by expanding their own businesses to include bookselling, printing, and miscellaneous sales,[13] or by trying to secure private commissions for fine binding, as many of the later binders' trade cards show.[14]

During the late seventeenth and much of the eighteenth century, a typical bookbindery was kept by a master binder who owned his own tools, bought his own materials, and employed a journeyman and an apprentice. There are no exact records showing what such a bindery produced on a daily basis, but it was probably on the order of fifteen to twenty-five books, depending on their size and the degree of decoration (known in the trade as "finishing"). Wives and daughters carried out the sewing, apprentices much of the unskilled labor like beating the folded leaves so that they lay flat, and masters and journeymen probably shared forwarding (the processes whereby the sewn and beaten sheets are turned into a book) and finishing operations, with the masters responsible for much of the gilt work. Twenty-five plain octavos in a day might produce, at 9d. each, an income of 6s. to 8s. per day over and above the cost of materials. A journeyman binder earned 10s.–12s. for a six-day work week (more towards the end of the eighteenth century, but prices were higher then too); an apprentice received room and board but no pay. The balance—for most binders rarely, if ever, as much as £2. 0s. per week—supported the master, his premises and equipment, and his family.[15]

Even the largest bookbinding operations seldom employed more than a dozen people, although by the last quarter of the eighteenth century a few had grown to twenty or more.[16] Booksellers also employed binders of their own. Some worked in retail shops; others bound and distributed books from nearby warehouses.

John Dunton's autobiography is the most important surviving record of London bookbinders' activities at the close of the seventeenth century. Dunton, a bookseller, noted that certain binders specialized: Edmond Richardson bound most of his "Calves Leather Books," and "had I not been pre-engaged," James Woodward "had bound all my Folio Books."[17] Dunton's deluxe bindings, probably mostly goatskin, were executed by John Baker, Thomas Knowles, and Robert Steel (fig. 1.1).[18] Given the low prices set in the bookbinders' price lists, deluxe bindings were one of the few ways bookbinders could hope to make money. Using goatskin instead of calf or sheep, and adding extra gilt decoration, a binder might double or triple the time and cost of materials he put into a commission, but he could charge a private customer seven or eight times more than the prices set by the bookbinders' price lists.[19] Retail commissions for deluxe bindings were few and far between, however. All but a tiny percentage of bindings executed between 1660 and 1800 were by craftsmen who never signed their work, whose bills

Fig. 1.1.
Trade goatskin by Robert Steel's bindery on Claudius Quillet, *Callipaedia*, for J. Bowyer, 1708, 8vo, showing several of Steel's characteristic tools. The delicate scrolls on the cover appear in a slightly different composition in Howard Nixon, *English Restoration Bookbindings* (1974), plate 39.

rarely survive, and whose livings were largely controlled by the price lists in which they probably had little say. It is no wonder that binders tried to expand their businesses into more lucrative areas.

The obvious way to a better living, as Head's *Proteus Redivivus* points out, was for binders to become booksellers by acquiring copyrights to texts and having them printed. Binders could then barter, or "exchange," copies through the trade, and obtain more books to bind and sell. Owning copyrights was also the way into the booksellers' syndicates, which shared the costs of purchasing copy from authors, printing, and possibly even binding, thereby reducing the financial risk for each participant. The largest and most powerful of these syndicates contained ten or more booksellers, and were called "congers," because of their tendency, like eels, to devour lesser creatures—in this case lesser booksellers.[20] Understanding these syndicates is essential to an appreciation of how books came to appear in different trade bindings.

With syndication, imprints varied according to the roles played by participants. A book might be "printed for" certain members who held the copyright, and "sold by" other members who contributed towards the cost of publication. Usually all of their names appeared in the imprint, but sometimes different title-pages were printed for booksellers who wanted their names to appear predominantly or exclusively.[21] Larger syndicates agreed on wholesale and retail prices in advance of publication. Once copies were distributed, syndicate members could sell them to other members at a set price, or sell them in the trade at a higher, but still wholesale, rate.[22]

Even with this system, booksellers could still end up with leftover copies. These could be distributed—and bound—many years after the original publication date. Advertisements make clear, for example, that copies of Shakespeare's 1685 Fourth Folio were still available during the first decade of the eighteenth century. The reissue of old sheets with new title-pages also shows booksellers using creative tactics to dispose of old stock. "Revised and Corrected," "A New Edition, with Additions," were printed on cancel title-pages, with new dates to make them look up-to-the-minute. Luke Meriton's *Pecuniae obediunt Omnia* (1698), describes the practice:

> . . . you must take special Care, and look
> You no new Title have to an old Book;
> For they new Title-Pages often paste
> Unto a Book which purposely is plac'd,
> Setting it forth to be th' Second Edition,
> Or Third, or Fourth, with 'mendments and Addition:
> . . . when a Book begins to fail,
>      This is their Trick to quicken up the Sale.

One of the more unscrupulous of such reissues appeared in 1700, a cancel title-page on the 1657 sheets of Henry King's *Poems*. The title, as shown in figure 1.2, declares the book to be by Ben Jonson.

Each of these practices affected how and when copies of books were bound. Over a period of years, or even decades, copies from a single edition of a book, whether domestically printed or imported in sheets from the Continent, could reach any number of different binders throughout the British Isles. These binders might be employed by (1) the commissioning booksellers, syndicate members, or their wholesale distributors, here collectively referred to as "publishers"; (2) a retail bookseller; (3) an independent bindery receiving its commission from a retail bookseller who received his copies in sheets; or, (4) an independent bindery receiving one or more copies from an individual for bespoke binding.

The transactions involved in the last three categories are straightforward and easily imagined. Many retail buyers probably chose their books ready-bound in the binding styles used by their favorite booksellers, and upscale booksellers may have wanted their shops to have a distinctive "look." Other buyers may have bespoke special bindings through their booksellers, or delivered sheets to their own binders.

Binding for the publishers, however, could be complicated. Here is how the system worked. Syndicates ordered copies from the printer to be delivered in sheets to their warehouses. These copies were distributed to the partners according to the terms of their agreement, and to other booksellers with advance orders. So far, so good. But the complication, about which woefully little information has survived, arises from the fact that these warehouses were operated by bookbinders who bound some

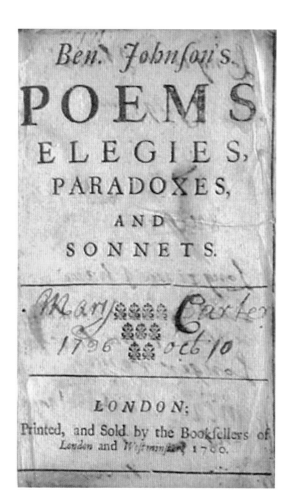

Fig. 1.2.
Henry King, *Poems, Elegies, Paradoxes, and Sonnets*, 1700, pot 8vo.

copies to order, and delivered others to retailers who employed their own binders.[23] The copies bound by the warehousemen were, as one scholar puts it, "early instances of edition binding."[24]

Distribution by bookbinder/warehousemen is confirmed by the ledgers of the printer William Bowyer, and the following example is typical of the process. In 1730 Bowyer printed Edward Harley's *An Abstract of the Historical Part of the Old Testament, with References to other Parts of the Scripture, especially to the New Testament.*[25] Bowyer printed 1500 ordinary paper copies on Dutch demy paper and thirty on large "Super Royal" paper,[26] and his entries show the binders and binder/warehousemen to whom he delivered copies. The deluxe bookbinder Thomas Elliott received eighteen of the large paper copies.[27] "Auditor" Harley, as he was known, received the other twelve directly, and over the next couple of years the majority of the ordinary paper copies were distributed to two bookbinder/warehousemen. Most went to "Mr. Chulmley" (probably Philip Cholmondeley) and a smaller number to "Mr. Matthews."[28] A few others went to Elliott, apparently for fine bindings commissioned by a bookseller,[29] and in 1732 Bowyer cleared out most of his remaining sheets, delivering 655 copies to Harley, who reissued them in 1735, with other tracts, through the booksellers Ward and Wicksteed.[30]

Harley's *Abstract* was printed "for the Author," rather than for a bookseller or syndicate, but the distribution practices were essentially the same. This entry shows how one binder, Thomas Elliott, was employed for the fine bindings, and how at least one known bookbinder/warehouseman was used for most of the remaining stock. Elliott bound dozens rather than hundreds of copies, and probably had specific instructions for their delivery, both to booksellers for resale and to individuals as gifts. "Chulmley" and Matthews delivered copies to the trade, bound if required, and collected payments. Normally warehousemen rendered their accounts to a bookseller or syndicate, but because Harley's *Abstract* was printed at the expense of the author, "Chulmley" and Matthews probably accounted directly to him.

## II. THE PRIMACY OF TRADE BOOKBINDING

If the previous section gives an idea how the organization of the book trade resulted in many different bindings on copies of the same book, it only peripherally addresses the question of "trade" versus "bespoke" binding. It is traditionally argued that booksellers were reluctant to go to the expense of having books bound in advance of retail sale, and that they might prefer to deal with the irritation of a customer forced to wait until a bespoke binding was completed than go to the expense of binding a book which might take a long time to sell.[31] Among the bases for this argument are (1) the wide variety of bindings which survive, and (2) the few surviving English illustrations showing bound books offered for sale in bookshops.

Johann Amos Comenius's *Orbis Sensualium Pictis*, first published in Nuremberg in 1657 or 1658, has been proposed as evidence of what an English bookshop looked like at that time. The illustrations in this Nuremberg edition were copied and engraved for the first edition of the work in English, published in London in 1659, and these plates were used in successive reprints through 1729 (fig. 1.3). One authority, Graham Pollard, infers from this illustration that the vertical half-title sometimes seen in mid-seventeenth century English books was used "to label the bins for the bookseller's unbound stock."[32] Geoffrey Wakeman goes much further and concludes that "in the seventeenth century booksellers kept most of their stock in sheets."[33]

Wakeman's statement will not stand up to close investigation, at least with respect to the English book trade. First, we must look at the Comenius illustration itself. It is German; the 1659 English copperplate is an exact copy.[34] In the 1756 Nuremberg edition of Comenius's work, and possibly earlier, the bookshop engraving is replaced by a woodcut with the same image, suggesting the interior of a German bookshop had not much changed. Joseph Richter's *Bildergallerie*, Vienna, 1785 (fig. 1.4), confirms the *status quo*, showing the same open shelves with stacks of unbound sheets. But in 1777 a London edition of Comenius appeared with new, English woodcuts, one of which shows an entirely different bookshop interior (fig. 1.5). This is clearly intended to depict more accurately an English shop of the time, and shows a shop entirely shelved with bound books, ready for purchase.

In England the large-scale sale of ready-bound books at the end of the eighteenth century is supported not only by this 1777 illustration to Comenius, but also by such other illustrations of trade premises as survive from that period (figs. 1.6–1.9).[35] The accuracy of these illustrations is confirmed by the circa 1800 statement of a German observer in London, that "booksellers sell all books ready bound," with many of the standard texts "often stocked in fine bindings,"[36] and by surviving booksellers' advertisements.

Having said this much about the English 1777 Comenius woodcut, I will go further. I believe it also more accurately depicts the interior of a *seventeenth-century* English bookshop, much more so than a 1650s Nuremberg engraving. Why? The Oxford bookseller John Dorne's 1520 day-book survives, and its sales records show that Dorne sold ready-bound books roughly six times as often as those in sheets.[37]

Fig. 1.3.
"The Booksellers Shop," copperplate engraving from Johann Amos Comenius, *Orbis Sensualium Pictus*, 1705. This image first appeared in the German edition of 1657 or 1658, and was copied for the first London edition of 1659. The plates were then reused for successive London editions, including this one, through 1729.

Fig. 1.4.
Joseph Richter, *Bildergallerie.* Vienna, 1785. The image at the top is a library, at the bottom, a bookshop. Courtesy of Department of Special Collections, Stanford University Libraries.

Fig. 1.5.
"The Booksellers Shop," woodcut illustration from the London edition of Johann Amos Comenius, *Orbis Sensualium Pictus*, 1777. Courtesy of Robin de Beaumont.

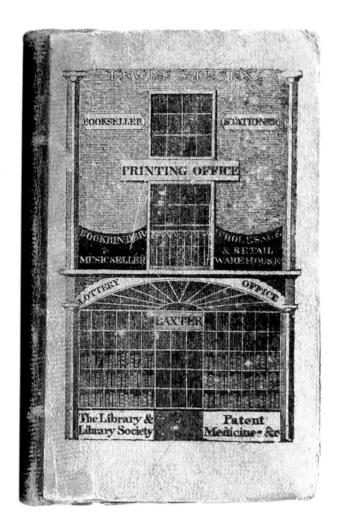

Fig. 1.6.
"The Elephant and the Bookseller," engraving by Van der Gucht after William Kent, as it appeared in John Gay's *Fables*, 1727. The bookseller's stock may be somewhat idealized, but it is all ready-bound. Courtesy of Department of Special Collections, Stanford University Libraries.

Fig. 1.7.
"Saml. James, Bookseller," trade card, engraved by Samuel Sympson, circa 1770. This interior scene seems very grand for a bookshop, and may represent James's circulating library; he appears to have owned both. Nevertheless, it is unlikely James would show these shelves of bound books if his primary sales were of unbound sheets. British Museum Print Department, Heal

Collection, no. 17.77. By permission of the Trustees of the British Museum.

Fig. 1.8.
The exterior of John Baxter's bookshop in Lewes, Sussex, from the pictorial paper onlays on the covers of his *The Sister Arts*, 1809, pot 8vo (trimmed and bound as an 18mo), showing ready-bound books in the window. Although this view is after 1800, the window display is similar to those in Sigfred Taubert, *Bibliopola* (Hamburg, 1966), Vol. II, plates 84 and 99, the latter showing the windows of Hamilton & Co.'s Wholesale and Retail "Shakspeare Library," circa 1790. Plate 103 in the same volume depicts ready-bound books for sale in an interior scene at James Lackington's "Temple of the Muses," circa 1795.

Fig. 1.9.
Thomas Rowlandson,
"Dr. Syntax & Bookseller,"
from William Combe,
*The Tour of Dr. Syntax*,
1812, an image strikingly
similar to a 1784 colored
aquatint by H. Wigstead.
Both are set in a book-
seller's room displaying
shelves of ready-bound
books. Wigstead's aquatint
is plate 88 in Taubert,
*Bibliopola*. Courtesy of
Department of Special
Collections, Stanford
University Libraries.

His shop would not have looked like Comenius's 1650s illustration with its stacks of rough sheets; as early as 1520 retail bookselling in England had clearly evolved in a manner quite different to that on the Continent.[38] In 1496 the bookseller John Russhe sued the London printer/bookseller Richard Pynson in a dispute over books Russhe expected to receive "redy bound the piece," and what is known of the Cambridge bookseller Garret Godfrey in the 1520s indicates that his business also operated on lines similar to John Dorne's.[39] Anecdotes from the later sixteenth and early seventeenth centuries suggest that large numbers of books continued to be sold ready-bound in England. Letters between a Cambridge academic and a country gentleman around 1630 include lists of books supplied for the gentleman's library. One of these, a church Bible, was sent for bespoke binding and caused no end of trouble. The rest of the books, many of them new publications, were transmitted without comment. One can only conclude that these latter books were bought ready-bound, and that only the expensive folio Bible received special, bespoke, treatment.[40]

Although this kind of anecdotal evidence is far from conclusive, it does support the premise of large-scale selling of ready-bound books in England from 1520 through 1777. Furthermore, the short-hand terminology of the bookbinders' price lists strongly suggests they are intended for traders, and one eighteenth-century list states that the general public were charged higher prices.[41]

One additional piece of evidence is determinative, categorically demonstrating the extent to which ready-bound books were sold in Restoration England. That evidence is John Starkey and Robert Clavell's *Mercurius Librarius* (1668–71), and the subsequent catalogues published by Clavell alone, all of which contain specific details of books offered for sale "price bound." These important catalogues irrefutably show that, once established in the sixteenth century, the sale of ready-bound books was the mainstay of the English retail book trade.

Trade practices, especially in pre-industrial society, are slow to change. Often such practices evolve only under outside economic or social pressure. The book trade is no exception. The sudden advertising of prices for bound books in 1668 is a startling change from earlier practice, and collective lists like Starkey and Clavell's suggest that the trade was pulling together under some external strain. One does not have to look far to see what the strain was: the Great Fire of London in 1666.

The Great Fire caused staggering losses to the London book trade; Pepys's bookseller Joshua Kirton was not alone in being completely ruined by it.[42] Lord Clarendon vividly describes these losses, which "in books, paper, and the other lesser commodities . . . amounted to no less than Two Hundred Thousand Pounds." Clarendon specifically recounts the tragedy of the spontaneous combustion of all the books and papers the trade had rushed for safekeeping to the great vault in St. Paul's Cathedral at the onset of the fire. After the fire died down, the booksellers, anxious to see if their property had survived, rushed to open the vault, but "the air from without fanned the strong heat within . . . first the driest and most combustible matters broke into flame," and then "consumed all of what kind soever that till then had been unhurt there."[43]

In the aftermath of the Great Fire, Starkey and Clavell successfully promoted *Mercurius Librarius* as an advertising tool for the book trade. General catalogues existed before *Mercurius Librarius*, but these were unpriced and with no mention of bindings;[44] it is not known whether the compilers of these earlier catalogues charged booksellers for entries in them. Starkey and Clavell did charge, as we know from complaints that appeared in a rival publication,[45] but they included details about the books published and where they could be purchased, including their prices, when these were supplied by the booksellers.

These priced catalogues reveal the retail selling practices of the Restoration book trade, and conclusively demonstrate the extent to which books were sold ready-bound, especially in the more common octavo and smaller sizes. The first and shortest number of *Mercurius Librarius*, published in 1668, sets the standard. Apart from two pamphlets published at 6d., and five plays at 1s. each, twenty-nine of the remaining thirty books are published "price bound." A similar proportion of books in the remaining seven numbers of *Mercurius Librarius* are also offered "price bound," even some inexpensive books like John Milton's *Accidence commenc'd Grammar*, advertised in the Trinity 1669 list as "Price, bound, 8d." The last number contains a listing for a Latin prayer book, *Liturgia, seu Liber precum Communium*, offered for sale by Samuel Mearne, "Price, bound, 4s." This edition was a smallish octavo, and at 4s. it was priced a full shilling more than the next most expensive octavo in the "Divinity" category of the list. Mearne certainly sold copies bound in colored turkey, just as he did with later editions of the same work (fig. 1.10).[46]

The most substantial single catalogue in the series containing details of books offered "price bound" is Robert Clavell's *A Catalogue of all the Books Printed in England since the Dreadful Fire of London, in 1666. To the End of Michaelmas Term, 1672* (1673) (fig. 1.11).[47] This catalogue collects the material in the eight issues of *Mercurius Librarius* and adds many new publications. The poetry section is a representative sample, and gives some idea of the catalogue's extent:

POETRY IN FOLIO. Seven titles are given. Two, Cowley's *Works*, and Katherine Phillips's *Poems*, are printed for Henry Herringman (one of Pepys's favorite booksellers), and are, respectively, "Price bound 14s" and "Price bound 8s." Two others, Ogilby's *Fables of Esop*, and Ogilby's *Virgil* are "Sold by Robert Clavel," and are both offered "in quires," the Aesop at £3. 0s., and the Virgil at 40s. A pamphlet, *Severall copies of Verses on the death of Mr. Abraham Cowley*, is offered by Herringman at 6d., and two works by the Duchess of Newcastle, *Plays*, and *Poems, or Severall Fancies in Verse*, are listed with no bookseller or price.

POETRY IN QUARTO. Seven titles are given, five of them pamphlets, including Dryden's *Dramatick Poesy, an Essay*. This is offered by Herringman at 1s. with no binding stated—its format, length,

 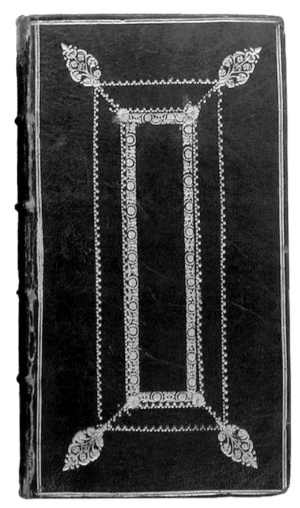

Fig. 1.10.
*Liturgia, seu Liber precum Communium,* on the left "Apud Sam. Mearne, Bibiopolam Regium, 1681," and on the right "Apud Car. Mearne, Bibliopolam, 1685," respectively foolscap and crown 12mo. The simple decorated goatskin bindings are almost certainly by the Mearne bindery. The pot 8vo edition advertised in Clavell's list would have been a similar size to the crown duodecimo. Courtesy of the William Andrews Clark Library, University of California, Los Angeles.

Fig. 1.11.
A page from Robert Clavell, *A Catalogue of all the Books Printed in England since the Dreadful Fire of London, in 1666. To the End of Michaelmas Term, 1672, 1673.*

### Poetry in Quarto, and Octavo. 13

#### Poetry in Quarto.

Querer per Solo querer; to love only for Love sake; a dramatick Romance, Represented at Aranjuez before the King and Queen of Spain, to celebrate the birth-day of the King: By the Meninas, &c. Written in Spanish, by don Antonio de Mendoza 1623. paraphrased in English. 1654. Together with the Festivall of Aranwhez; price bound 3 s. printed for Moses Pitt in Little-Brittain.

Youths Tragedy, a Poem drawn up by way of Dialogue, between Youth, the Devil, Wisdome, Time, Death, the Soul, the Nuncius; for the caution and direction of the younger sort: price stitch 6 d. Printed for J. Starkey, and Fr. Smith, in Fleet-street, and without Temple-bar.

A Satyr against Hypocrites, price stitch 6 d printed for Nath. Brook in Cornhil.

The Souls warfare Comically digested into Scenes. Acted between the Soul and her Enemies: wherein the cometh of Victria, with an Evangelical Theodia, price stitch 6 d. printed for Allen Banks, at the West end of St. Pauls.

A Dramatick Poesy, an Essay; by John Dryden Esq; price 1 s.

The dreadful burning of London, described in a Poem, by J.G.M.A. Both printed for H. Herringman in the New-Exchange.

Paradise lost, a Poem in 10 Books, by J. Milton, price bound 3 s. sold by Thomas Helder in Little Brittain.

#### Poetry in large Octavo.

AN Antidote against Melancholly, made made up in Pills, compounded of witty Ballads, jovial Songs, and merry Catches, collected by John Playford, price bound 2 s. printed for John Playford near the Temple Church.

The Remains of Sir Fulk Grevil Lord Brook, being Poems of Monarchy and Religion, never before printed, price bound 2 s. printed for H. Herringman in the New-Exchange.

Scarronides, or Virgil Travestie, a mock-Poem, on the first and fourth Books of Virgils Eneiads in English, Burlesque, price bound 1 s. 6 d.

The Poems of Horace, consisting of Odes, Satyrs and Epistles, rendred into English, and Paraphrased by several Persons, price bound 3 s. 6 d. both printed for H. Brome at the West end of St. Pauls.

The whole Book of the Psalms of David, and other Hymns in Meeter, to be sung to the common Tunes used in Parish Churches; set forth by the right Reverend, Henry King late Lord Bishop of Chichester, price bound 2 s. printed for John Playford.

Poems, Songs and Sonnets, together with a Masque, by Thomas Carew Esq; The Songs set in Musick by Mr. Henry Laws Gentleman of the Kings Chappel, and one of his Majesties late private Musick.

Steps to the Temple, the delights of the Muses, and Carmen Deo nostro, by Richard

Crashaw, price bound 2 s.

The Brittish Princess, an Heroick Poem, written by the honourable Edward Howard Esq; price bound 2 s.

Poems, by J. Donne, &c. late Dean of St. Pauls, with Elegies on the Authours death.

Poems and Translations, with the Sophy, written by Sir John Denham Knight of the Bath: all five printed for Henry Herringman in the New Exchange.

ΚΡΙΣΤΟΛΟΓΙΑ, or a Metrical Paraphrase on the History of our Lord and Saviour Jesus Christ, dedicated to his universal Church, price bound, 1 s. 6 d. printed for Peter Parker in Cornhil.

A Collection of Poems upon several occasions; written by several Persons of Quality, never before in Print, price bound 1 s. 6 d. printed for Hobart Kempe in the New Exchange.

The Wits, or Sport upon Sport, in select Peices of Drollery; digested into Scenes by way of Dialogue, together with variety of Humours of several Notions, fitted for the pleasure and content of all Persons, price bound 1 s. 6 d. printed for F. Kirkman.

Paradise regained, a Poem in four Books; to which is added, Sampson Agonistes, a Dramatick Poem, the Authour John Milton, price bound 2 s. 6 d. printed for John Starkey in Fleet-street.

Annus Mirabilis, the year of Wonders, 1666, an Historical Poem, containing the progress

D

and price were the same as for Dryden's plays, which were also sold unbound. Another Herringman pamphlet, *The Dreadful Burning of London, described in a Poem*, is offered with no price stated. Three other pamphlet poems are offered by three different booksellers, each "price sticht 6d." *Paradise Lost*, sold by Thomas Helder, is offered "price bound 3s." Helder's imprint was on one of the 1669 title-pages of the poem, and he probably had a bookbindery as part of his business. A "dramatick Romance" called *Querer por Solo querer: to love only for Love Sake* is offered by Moses Pitt, "price bound 3s."

POETRY IN LARGE OCTAVO. Seventeen titles are given; of which fourteen are offered "price bound" as follows: 1s. 6d. (six items, including Dryden's *Annus Mirabilis*, and Henry King's *Poems*); 2s. (five items, including Richard Crashaw's *Steps to the Temple*); 2s. 6d. (two items, including Edmund Waller's *Poems*, and Milton's *Paradise Regained*[48]); and the highest "price bound" of 3s. 6d. for Brome's *Horace*, which was unusually thick for an octavo and graced with two engravings. The three unpriced items were all printed for Henry Herringman and include volumes of poetry by Thomas Carew, John Denham, and John Donne. The three were grouped in a list of five, "all five printed for Henry Herringman in the New Exchange."

POETRY IN SMALL OCTAVO. Eighteen titles are given, only one (Denham's *Cato Major*) a pamphlet, is offered "price 6d." with no binding stated. Of the other seventeen, fifteen are offered "price bound" from one to five shillings. Perennial favorites of the time, such as Thomas Randolph and Francis Quarles (both of whose poems were popular enough to be named specifically in the bookbinders' price lists) command unusually high prices bound, 3s. each for Randolph's *Poems* and Quarles's *Divine Poems*. Quarles's slighter *Divine Fancies*, which unlike the previous two titles has no frontispiece, is 1s. 6d. bound. The highest "price bound" of 5s. is for Quarles's *Divine Emblems and Hieroglyphicks*, which has engravings throughout the text.

POETRY IN LARGE TWELVES. Eight titles are given, six of them offered "price bound," with the highest price, 2s., commanded by Sandys's translation of Ovid's *Metamorphoses*. The two unpriced titles are George Herbert's *The Temple*, and *The Psalter of David, with Titles and Collects*. While these two were regularly sold in standard trade bindings, they were often bound in goatskin.

POETRY IN SMALL TWELVES. Three titles are given, all of them "price bound." Another Psalter, *The Psalms, Hymns, and spiritual Songs of the Old and New Testament*, is offered "price bound 1s, 6d." It declares its audience to be "Christians . . . especially in *New England*," which suggests a number of bound copies intended for export.

A review of the other sections of Clavell's catalogue reveals a similar pattern, with a significantly smaller percentage of folios offered "price bound" than books in the smaller formats, and with the overwhelming majority, over eighty percent, of octavos and duodecimos offered for sale ready-bound.

The overall proportion of titles offered ready-bound is startling in its correspondence to the percentage of bound books sold in John Dorne's Oxford shop of 1520, roughly six books sold bound for every one sold in sheets. This correspondence indicates that selling ready-bound books was a settled trade practice, and confirms that the primary purpose of the bookbinders' price lists was to allow booksellers to order books bound for them at fixed prices, to sell ready-bound both wholesale and retail. What is unusual about the 1660s and '70s is the sudden *advertising* of prices, caused by the tremendous economic pressure of the Great Fire. Similar advertising of books "price bound" appears in individual

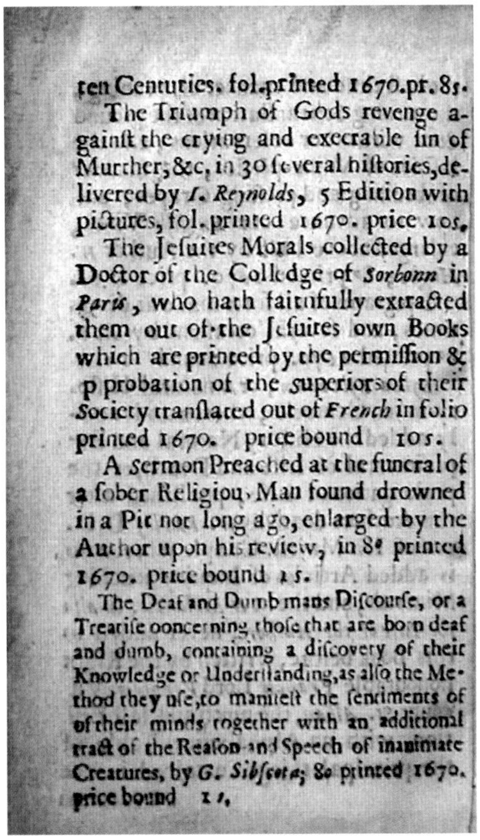
ten Centuries. fol. printed 1670. pr. 8s.
The Triumph of Gods revenge against the crying and execrable sin of Murther, &c, in 30 several histories, delivered by *J. Reynolds*, 5 Edition with pictures, fol. printed 1670. price 10s.
The Jesuites Morals collected by a Doctor of the Colledge of *Sorbonn* in *Paris*, who hath faithfully extracted them out of the Jesuites own Books which are printed by the permission & probation of the superiors of their Society translated out of *French* in folio printed 1670. price bound 10s.
A Sermon Preached at the funeral of a sober Religious Man found drowned in a Pit not long ago, enlarged by the Author upon his review, in 8° printed 1670. price bound 1s.
The Deaf and Dumb mans Discourse, or a Treatise concerning those that are born deaf and dumb, containing a discovery of their Knowledge or Understanding, as also the Method they use, to manifest the sentiments of their minds together with an additional tract of the Reason and Speech of inanimate Creatures, by *G. Sibscota*; 8° printed 1670. price bound 1s.

Fig. 1.12.
A page from the bookseller William Crook's advertisements printed at the end of George Sibscota, *Deaf and Dumb Man's Discourse*, 1670. The two folios at the top of the page are not offered "price bound."

booksellers' lists of the period, the type of list often printed at the end, and occasionally the beginning, of books (fig. 1.12).

In view of the wide variety of bindings surviving on the very titles and editions listed in Clavell's catalogues, it is not exactly obvious what "price bound" meant. Most likely it was a base price, at which the most simply bound copy in a bookseller's stock would be sold or, to approach the matter slightly differently, the price that included the charge for a simple binding as set forth in the bookbinders' price lists. Gilt lettering and other decoration would usually cost extra, but a retail bookseller intent on attracting business might sell a more elaborate binding at the advertised price, and encourage customers to return for similar bindings on other books. Syndicate members might also keep better gilt bindings in their shops, and supply undecorated ones when wholesale discounts were required. "Price bound" almost certainly did not mean that no copies were available in sheets, although warehouses containing more flammable and less portable stacks of unbound sheets may have suffered more in the Fire than retail shops where most bound copies were kept. Conceivably, "price bound" meant that no discount was allowed a customer who chose to buy a copy in sheets, either hoping to save money or to commission a bespoke binding.

The booksellers' sudden revelation of their trade practices did not last long. Clavell's next catalogue, published in 1675, grouped titles under headings showing their respective prices, and deleted the term "bound."[49] The 1675 catalogue took the sale of ready-bound copies for granted, as is shown by the fact that the overwhelming majority of prices were unchanged from 1673. By the late 1670s, priced books in Clavell's catalogues were a distinct minority, and by the early 1680s, well under ten percent. The same trend can be seen in booksellers' advertisements in individual books.[50] From the 1680s

Fig. 1.13.
Engraved book inserts of
Paul and Isaac Vaillant,
James Crokat, and Cesar
Ward and Richard Chandler,
circa 1740, and also James
Wallis's printed book insert,
circa 1780. These were
placed in ready-bound
copies sold in these booksellers' shops, in the same
way some modern book-
shops insert their own
printed bookmarks. Their
long-term survival rate, not
surprisingly, was low, and
examples are now rare.

on, the appearance of prices in booksellers' lists waxed and waned, possibly according to how well the bookbinders kept to their published price lists, but more probably according to the whim or determination of individual booksellers.[51] As newspapers proliferated during the eighteenth century, books were increasingly advertised, usually with prices, and sometimes with styles of ready-binding. Throughout these lists and advertisements, the prices stated for "bound" copies are invariably the same as prices for copies when no binding is specified: the presence of a simple leather binding is taken for granted.

Booksellers also developed other methods of advertising their wares. One of these, shown in figure 1.13, further demonstrates the widespread sale of ready-bound books. During the latter half of the eighteenth century, booksellers like William Bent published general catalogues with thousands of priced entries. These catalogues follow the practice of individual booksellers' advertisements: all entries refer to copies ready-bound in calf or sheep unless otherwise stated.

If the economic pressures of the Great Fire were the reason for the sudden illumination of established trade practice, why did the lights go off so quickly? Economic pressure of a different kind is probably the answer. The booksellers no doubt quickly learned that having once advertised a price for a book, bound or otherwise, there was nowhere for those prices to go but down. Wholesale customers would expect trade terms; retail customers would want discounts, or would expect a fancier "extra" binding for the advertised price of a plain one, and so on. The time-honored trade practice of slipping a little premium onto the prices charged the gentry would also no longer be sustainable. In one of his catalogues, published in 1680, Clavell entirely omitted prices, lamenting that "no direction to the Buyer can herein be given; the various fortune that Books are subject to, in respect to the Fame of some, Repulse of others, Time, Plenty, Scarcity, &c. render the Prizes of most Books uncertain."[52]

Evidence that most books were sold ready-bound can also be found in surviving libraries of the period, and I would like to close this chapter with a glance at what is now perhaps the most famous private library of the time, that of Samuel Pepys. Howard Nixon's *Catalogue of the Pepys Library at Magdalene College, Cambridge*, Vol. VI (1984) describes Pepys's fine bindings, most of which he received as gifts. Nixon also documents the "common bindings" in the library, suggesting that Pepys commissioned "a very high proportion" to order from individual bookbinders.[53] I disagree. There is no question that the young Pepys had a desire "to see my whole study almost of one binding,"[54] but the diversity of decoration on Pepys's books indicates that his concept of "one binding" was more relaxed than Nixon would have us believe.

Pepys regularly referred to bookbinding in the *Diary*. One particularly evocative entry, on January 2, 1664/5, shows Pepys arriving at Joshua Kirton's bookshop after a day of good food, music, and sexual intrigue. Kirton's binder had copies of "Hookes book of the Microscope" in the final stage of production, "so pretty that I presently bespoke it."[55] By this Pepys means he bespoke the book itself (the point is important because elsewhere this book regularly refers to "bespoke binding"), and before the month was out he took a number of his own books to the same binder. Not surprisingly, when they were finished they looked like the Hooke volume, and prompted Pepys' satisfied comment about the appearance of his study.

When Pepys refers (in the *Diary* and elsewhere) to commissioning, or "bespeaking," bindings, he means rebinding and decorating books and manuscripts he *already owns*. Among Pepys's special collections—old plays, early classical and literary texts, and manuscripts—we find specific binders doing bespoke work during the *Diary* period and beyond. They bound up pamphlets and manuscripts, and rebound books bought second-hand. If Pepys were commissioning bindings for any of the books he bought new during the *Diary* period, it seems inconceivable that he would not somewhere have mentioned the process.[56] Instead, the evidence of the *Diary* and Pepys's books themselves confirm regular visits to bookshops such as those of Joshua Kirton, John Martin, and Henry Herringman, where Pepys bought ready-bound books and took them home. In one well-known *Diary* entry, Pepys records a visit to John Martin's shop, where he "bought that idle, roguish book, *L'escholle des Filles;* which I have bought in plain binding (avoiding the buying of it better bound) because I resolve, as soon as I have read it, to burn it. . . ." He read it right through in a state of what can discreetly be called high excitement, and duly burned it the next day.[57]

When Pepys ordered titles as they were announced for publication or in the course of production, his booksellers supplied copies bound in trade calf with extra gilt (fig. 1.14). "Hooke's book of the Microscope" has already been noted, and the same process occurred later, in 1702, when the bookseller John Nutt was finishing Charles Le Cène's *Essay for a New Translation of the Bible*. Like Kirton with Hooke's *Micrographia* in 1665, Nutt had copies "now a-bindeing," as Pepys put it in a letter to Humfrey Wanley, one of which Pepys bespoke for his library.[58] Pepys also had standing orders for gilt calf bindings on periodicals. Over several years these volumes were bound to match by the booksellers who supplied them; later volumes occasionally show small variations in the tooling as the booksellers' binders changed.

Only a small percentage of the books in Pepys's library can be identified as the result of such standing orders. The diversity of bindings, from the *Diary* period until Pepys's death in 1703, shows large

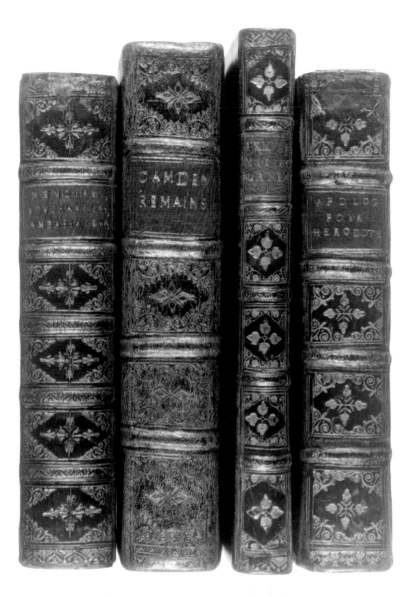

Fig. 1.14.
Four bindings from Samuel
Pepys's library, in the style
"F" identified by Howard M.
Nixon, *Catalogue of the Pepys
Library at Magdalene College,
Cambridge*, Vol. VI (1984),
plate 11. The binding on the
far right was almost certainly
bespoke by Pepys; it is on H.
Estienne, *L'Introduction au
Traité . . . preparatif à l'apologie
pour Hérodote*. Antwerp, 1568.
The other three volumes are,
from left to right, A. van
Wicquefort, *Memoires*. The
Hague, 1677; W. Camden,
*Remains*, 1674; and Sir W.
Temple, *Miscellanea*, 1680.
By permission of the Pepys
Library, Magdalene College,
Cambridge.

numbers of them in standard, but by no means uniform, ready-bound styles "entirely typical of the bind-ings which were being turned out in countless workshops."[59] And why not? By the late 1660s trade bindings were commonly available with extra gilt on the spines and covers, and with gilt-lettered, colored goatskin labels. This is the "common" binding to which Nixon refers, and which was bespoke by Pepys on the overwhelming majority of the books he had rebound: each spine compartment gilt with French cor-ners and a central fleuron or cross, the label in the second compartment from the top. These were among the binding styles Pepys saw when he visited London bookshops; these were the ones he chose. Only with a book destined for the fire, like *L'escholle des Filles*, would Pepys avoid "the buying of it better bound." Even though Pepys had more of his books rebound, relabeled, and gilded during his retirement,[60] the majority of them, English and foreign, survive just as they came, ready-bound from the bookshops.

If the fastidious Pepys was willing to have scores of different trade bindings in his beloved library, it is surely evidence that the less demanding had at least as much diversity. What David Pearson says of the sixteenth century is therefore equally true of the post-Restoration: that new books were on the whole bought ready-bound from the booksellers, and that "such an explanation of the general set-up of the retail trade would certainly accord with the mass of evidence to suggest that individuals showed little concern for consistency among the decoration of their books."[61]

## CHAPTER TWO

# THE BOOKBINDERS'
# PRICE LISTS

The last chapter described the prevalence of ready-bound books, and the link between their sale and the bookbinders' price lists. The price lists were clearly intended for the book trade, not private customers, and their contents, although expressed in a sometimes obscure shorthand, show what booksellers could expect to pay for standard trade bindings. Because binding was one of book production's primary expenses, removing the element of uncertainty was a major step forward in relations between bookbinders and booksellers. By relying on the lists, booksellers could confidently advertise their books at "prices bound."

The price lists were printed as folio broadsides; almost all surviving copies are unique. The earliest is *A generall note of the prises for binding all sorts of bookes* (London, 1619). Subsequent London lists appeared in 1646, 1669, 1695, 1744, and 1760. The Dublin bookbinders published their own lists in 1743, 1766, and 1791; and around 1620 the King's printer for Ireland, Thomas Downes, published a list of books sold bound, with the different prices charged in London and Dublin. Except for the 1766 and 1791 Dublin lists, all of these have been published with a commentary by Mirjam Foot in *Studies in the History of Bookbinding* (1993).[1]

The lists give the prices bookbinders charged for simple trade bindings, and the higher prices charged for bindings with standard embellishments. Bibles, not surprisingly, receive the most detailed descriptions, especially in the 1619 list, but over the years secular books appear more frequently, and by the 1760 list are in the majority. Mirjam Foot's commentary explains many of the arcane terms.

Professor Foot, however, states that "these lists cannot be used to establish the original binding price for a specific seventeenth- or eighteenth-century book."[2] Provided we can identify the kinds of bindings called for by the lists—one of primary goals of this chapter—I think we *can* use the price lists for that purpose. We must keep in mind, however, that some binders may have charged extra for lettering-pieces, or the kind of gilt work an individual bookseller desired to give his shelves a particular look, whereas other binders may have supplied these things as a courtesy to attract and keep a bookseller's business.

How consistent were the bookbinders' prices? In 1630, the Cambridge academic Joseph Mede took a large folio church Bible to a local binder and complained bitterly about the 15s. quoted to do a full-scale job. Yet with gilt decoration, metal cornerpieces, and such, the binder was in fact proposing to charge the exact price set by the bookbinders' price list of 1619.[3] The same consistency occurs with the 1669 price list (fig. 2.1), which was issued near the time that Robert Clavell "won his battle with Starkey and was including prices as well as imprints in the Term Catalogues."[4] How effectively Clavell's (and by implication the bookbinders') pricing system worked even outside London can be seen in examples such

# A General Note of the Prices of Binding all sorts of Books;

## Agreed on by the Book-binders, whose Names are under-written.

As it was presented to the Master, Wardens, and Assistants of the Worshipful Company of Stationers, *August*, the 2d, 1669.

### Ogilby's Bibles in Folio, or the like.

| | l. | s. | d. |
|---|---|---|---|
| Gilt Edges in one Volumn | 01 | 00 | 00 |
| Fillets only | 00 | 12 | 00 |
| Plain Ovals | 00 | 08 | 00 |

### Bibles in small Folio, London, or the like.

| | | | |
|---|---|---|---|
| Edges and Fillets | 00 | 06 | 06 |
| Fillets | 00 | 03 | 06 |
| Ovals | 00 | 02 | 06 |

### Bibles in Quarto, Cambridg, or the like.

| | | | |
|---|---|---|---|
| Edges Extraordinary | 00 | 05 | 00 |
| Edges Ordinary | 00 | 03 | 06 |
| Fillets | 00 | 02 | 06 |
| Ovals | 00 | 01 | 06 |

### Bibles in Octavo, Brevere, or the like.

| | | | |
|---|---|---|---|
| Edges Extraordinary | 00 | 03 | 00 |
| Edges Ordinary | 00 | 02 | 04 |
| Fillets | 00 | 01 | 06 |
| Ovals | 00 | 01 | 00 |

### Bibles in Octavo, Nonperil, or the like.

| | | | |
|---|---|---|---|
| Edges Extraordinary | 00 | 02 | 10 |
| Edges Ordinary | 00 | 01 | 10 |
| Fillets | 00 | 01 | 02 |
| Ovals | 00 | 01 | 10 |

### Bibles in 12.

| | | | |
|---|---|---|---|
| Edges Extraordinary | 00 | 02 | 06 |
| Edges Ordinary | 00 | 01 | 06 |
| Fillets | 00 | 01 | 00 |
| Ovals | 00 | 00 | 08 |

### Bibles in 24.

| | | | |
|---|---|---|---|
| Edges Extraordinary | 00 | 02 | 06 |
| Edges Ordinary | 00 | 01 | 06 |
| Fillets | 00 | 01 | 00 |
| Ovals | 00 | 00 | 08 |

### Service-Book, Testament, and Psalms, Brevere, Octavo.

| | | | |
|---|---|---|---|
| Edges Extraordinary | 00 | 02 | 10 |
| Edges Ordinary | 00 | 01 | 10 |
| Fillets | 00 | 01 | 02 |
| Ovals | 00 | 01 | 10 |

### Service Brevere in 12. & Psalms, or otherwise.

| | | | |
|---|---|---|---|
| Edges Extraordinary | 00 | 01 | 08 |
| Edges Ordinary | 00 | 01 | 02 |
| Fillets | 00 | 00 | 09 |
| Ovals | 00 | 00 | 06 |

### Service in 24. with Psalms, &c.

| | | | |
|---|---|---|---|
| Edges Extraordinary | 00 | 01 | 02 |
| Edges Ordinary | 00 | 00 | 10 |
| Fillets | 00 | 00 | 08 |
| Plain | 00 | 00 | 06 |

### Books in Folio, Latin.

| | l. | s. | d. |
|---|---|---|---|
| Atlas Major, 3 Vol. or the like, Rolls | 1 | 10 | 00 |
| Aristot. 2 Vol. Rolls | 0 | 11 | 00 |
| Lexicon Poliglott, or the like, 2 Vol. | 0 | 12 | 00 |
| Item, in one Vol. Rolles | | 18 | 00 |
| Plutarchi Opera, 2 Vol. or the like, Rolls | 0 | 08 | 00 |
| Lipsius in Senecam ⎫ | | | |
| Lipsius in Tacitum ⎬ or the like | 0 | 03 | 06 |
| Buxtorph. Heb. Bib. ⎭ | | | |
| Corpus Juris Civ. one Vol. | 0 | 04 | 00 |
| In 2 Vol. or the like | 0 | 06 | 00 |
| Critici Sacri, 9 Vol. or the like, Rolles | 1 | 10 | 00 |
| Scapula Lexicon, Grotius in ⎫ Vet. Test. or the like ⎬ | 0 | 03 | 00 |
| Ravanella. S. 3 Vol. | 0 | 09 | 00 |
| Estius in Epist. or the like, one Vol. | 0 | 02 | 06 |
| Brennius in Bib. Gerardi Loci Com. ⎫ 4 Vol. or the like ⎬ | 0 | 03 | 00 |

### Books in Quarto, Latin.

| | l. | s. | d. |
|---|---|---|---|
| Sculteti Medulla ⎫ | | | |
| Mellificium Hist. ⎬ Rolls | 0 | 01 | 04 |
| Vossi Gram. or the like ⎭ | | | |
| All Latin Books in Quarto, large & thick | 0 | 01 | 02 |
| If not thick | 0 | 01 | 00 |
| All Latin Books, Pot-paper, Rolls, Thick, | 0 | 01 | 00 |
| If not thick | 0 | 00 | 10 |

### Books in 8. 12. and 24.

| | | | |
|---|---|---|---|
| Servelius Lexicon, Octo. large | 0 | 00 | 10 |
| Virgil, Horatius vel Paterculius, ⎫ and the like ⎬ Rolls | 0 | 00 | 10 |
| All thick Octo. Latin, Rolls. | 0 | 00 | 08 |
| All thin Octo. | 0 | 00 | 07 |
| All Twelves and Sixteens | 0 | 00 | 06 |
| All Twenty fours | 0 | 00 | 05 |

### Books in Folio, English.

| | | | |
|---|---|---|---|
| Ogilby's China, Virgil, all his other ⎫ Books, or the like, in single Vol. ⎬ Marble Fillets ⎭ | 0 | 08 | 00 |
| Æsop compleat in one, Iliads and Odysses ⎫ in one, or the like, Marble Fillets ⎬ | 0 | 10 | 00 |
| The same Books plain | 0 | 07 | 00 |
| The same Books single | 0 | 05 | 00 |

### Kings Works, or the like

| | l. | s. | d. |
|---|---|---|---|
| Kings Works, or the like | 0 | 03 | 06 |
| Hammond on N. Testament ⎫ Poultons Stat. or the like, Rolls ⎬ | 0 | 03 | 00 |
| Davile's Hist. ⎫ Raoleighs Hist. ⎬ or the like | 0 | 03 | 00 |
| Plutarchs Lives ⎫ or the like Heylins Cosmog. ⎬ | 0 | 02 | 06 |
| Cotgraves Dict. Bakers Chronicle, ⎫ Taylors Cases of Conscience, Rolls ⎬ | 0 | 02 | 00 |
| Life of Christ, Rolls | 0 | 01 | 10 |
| Hammond on Psalmes ⎫ Spotswood Hist. or the like ⎬ | 0 | 01 | 08 |
| Cassaudra, and the like | 0 | 01 | 06 |

### Small Folio.

| | | | |
|---|---|---|---|
| Fullers Holy War ⎫ Hubbards Reports ⎬ Baxalin, and the like ⎭ All Pot Folio's small | 0 | 01 | 04 |

### Books in Quarto, English.

| | | | |
|---|---|---|---|
| Goldman, or the like, Rolls | 0 | 01 | 06 |
| Hughs Grand Abridgment, being ⎫ 3 Vol. Rolls ⎬ | 0 | 04 | 00 |
| Wests Presidents, Thomas Dict. or the like | 0 | 01 | 02 |
| Cokills twelfth part, or the like | 0 | 01 | 00 |
| Baxters Saints Rest | 0 | 01 | 02 |
| Baxters Reasons, Rolls. And ⎫ all such English Quarto's thick ⎬ | 0 | 01 | 00 |
| All small Pot-paper Quarto's Rolls | 0 | 00 | 10 |

### Books in Octavo, English.

| | | | |
|---|---|---|---|
| All large Octo. Decay of Piety, or the like | 0 | 00 | 09 |
| Taylors Living and Dying, or the like | 0 | 00 | 08 |
| All thin Crown Octavo's | 0 | 00 | 07 |
| All Pot Octavo's, Quarles Poems, &c. | 0 | 00 | 06 |

### Books in 12. and 24.

| | | | |
|---|---|---|---|
| All large Twelves | 0 | 00 | 06 |
| All small Twelves and Twenty-four's | 0 | 00 | 05 |

### Sheeps Leather, Folio's.

| | | | |
|---|---|---|---|
| Ottaman Empire, or the like, Rolls | 0 | 01 | 02 |
| Noyes Reports, or the like, Rolls | 0 | 01 | 00 |
| All thick Pot Follio's | 0 | 01 | 00 |
| All thin Pot | 0 | 00 | 10 |

### Large Quarto, Sheep.

| | l. | s. | d. |
|---|---|---|---|
| Placita Rediviva, or the like, Rolls | 0 | 00 | 10 |
| All thin Crown Rolls | 0 | 00 | 09 |
| All Fools-Cap, or the like, Rolls | 0 | 00 | 08 |

### Quarto's Pot-paper, Sheep.

| | | | |
|---|---|---|---|
| Stillingfleets Origines Sacra, or the like, rolls | 0 | 00 | 08 |
| All thick Pot | 0 | 00 | 06 |
| All thin Pot | 0 | 00 | 05 |

### Octavo's Large.

| | | | |
|---|---|---|---|
| Decay of Piety, or the like | 0 | 00 | 05 |
| Gent. Callings, or the like | 0 | 00 | 04 |
| Records Arithm. Erasmus Colloq. ⎫ Testaments Octo, Rom, or the like ⎬ | 0 | 00 | 04 |
| All thin Crown, and all Fools-Cap | 0 | 00 | 03½ |

### Octavo Pot.

| | | | |
|---|---|---|---|
| Test. Octo. Com. Quarles Poems. ⎫ Randolphs Poems. Hools Cor- ⎬ derius, or the like ⎭ | 0 | 00 | 03 |
| All thin Pot | 0 | 00 | 02½ |

### Large Twelves.

| | | | |
|---|---|---|---|
| Present State of Eng. Pr. of Piety, or the like | 0 | 00 | 03 |
| Meads almost a Christ. Ac. of Com. the like | 0 | 00 | 02½ |
| Redemption of Time, or the like | 0 | 00 | 02 |

### Pot Twelves.

| | | | |
|---|---|---|---|
| Baxters Call, Doct. Bible, or the like | 0 | 00 | 02½ |

### Twenty-four's.

| | | | |
|---|---|---|---|
| Practice of Piety, or the like | 0 | 00 | 03 |
| Gerrards Meditat. Crums of Comf. the like | 0 | 00 | 02½ |
| All thin Twenty-four's | 0 | 00 | 02 |

### All sorts of Thin Books, Sheeps-Leather Fillets.

| | | | |
|---|---|---|---|
| As Grammars, Psalters ⎫ Small 12s, 24s, and 32s. ⎬ | 0 | 00 | 04½ |
| Primmers Gilt, the Grofs | 1 | 00 | 00 |
| Primmers Plain, the Grofs | 0 | 10 | 00 |

| | | | |
|---|---|---|---|
| Thomas Hunt. | William Terry. | William Stephens. | John Grover. |
| Samuel Mearn. | Joseph Cater. | William Willis. | William Charles. |
| Thomas Raw. | John Homersham. | Walter Davis. | Richard Sympson. |
| George Eversden. | Nathan Brooker. | Martin Barnham. | William Hilliard. |
| George Calvert. | Edward Eccleston. | Langlie Curtis. | Richard Janua. |
| William Richardson. | Christopher Lingerd. | Robert Cox. | Gregory Pool. |
| Edward Powel. | John Cope. | Jonathan Adams. | George Bale. |
| Robert Cutler. | Richard Olliffe. | Richard Littleton. | William Bishop. |
| Hilliam Harris. | Thomas Allsop. | John Hewet. | Adam Winch. |
| William Rands. | William Potter. | John Shepherd. | Thomas Brown. |
| Humphry Toy. | Thomas Lammar. | Richard Barnes. | James Parkhurst. |
| William Branch. | William Redmayne. | William Baker. | John Shrimton. |
| Edward Gough. | Peter Scarlet. | Thomas Hartley. | John Spicer. |
| Francis Hyarne. | Robert Smith. | Samuel Freeman. | Richard Hewes. |
| Henry Evans. | John Fletcher. | William Curtis. | Robert Finnis. |
| Joseph Moore. | Thomas Kequick. | William Veery. | John Major. |
| John Donne. | Richard Dew. | Samuel Cook. | Nathaniel Oldfield. |
| William Sherington. | John Bishop. | Joshua Mitchel. | Daniel Barber. |
| Robert Deevs. | Walter Dunn. | Joshua Conuiers. | James Hatton. |
| Thomas Hodyson. | William Mason. | Samuel Sprint. | William Goff. |
| Thomas Cooper. | John Mendey. | | |

Licensed, *September* 23. 1669. ROGER L'ESTRANGE.

Fig. 2.1.
The 1669 Bookbinders' Price List.
By permission of the Houghton
Library, Harvard University.

as the Trevelyan family copy of Sir Richard Baker's *Chronicle of the Kings of England* (1674), which was purchased in Newcastle-upon-Tyne. The binding is original "nondescript sprinkled calf" and the book contains the buyer's manuscript note "Bought of Mr. Richard Randell in Newcastle a° 1677 . . . Pretium 20/s."[5] The 1669 bookbinders' price list gives "*Bakers* Chronicle" as an example of folios to be bound in calf for 2s., and the style would have been just the "nondescript sprinkle" seen on the Trevelyan copy. Twenty shillings is the price at which Clavell advertised the *Chronicle*, bound, in the 1670 Midsummer *Mercurius Librarius*, so it is logical to infer that not only the price of the book, but also the price of the binding (wherever the book was bound) were as consistent in 1677 Newcastle, or in 1630 Cambridge, as they were in London. Surviving binders' bills of the eighteenth century also show consistent charges. Mirjam Foot "looked through a large number of bills for binding work . . . in the 1720s and 1730s," and also through "a quantity of bills of work done for George Hawkins, the bookseller, dating from the 1740s, 1750s, and 1760s."[6] For the former group she found the prices charged, so far as comparison was possible, were the same or slightly lower than the prices on the 1744 list. For the latter group she found a number of bills that "quoted the same titles, bound and decorated in the same way as those mentioned in the 1760 list, charging the same price."[7]

Between 1619 and 1669 there were a few minor developments, such as a reduction in the detail specified for certain types of work, and a few slight changes in the pricing. Between 1619 and the second London price list of 1646, the fashion for "cross-binding," or as it is more commonly known, *dos-à-dos* binding, had largely ended and ceased to be included in the list, and between 1646 and 1669 the mysterious distinction between "double lac'd" and "single-lac'd" Bibles, almost certainly referring to degrees of gilding, came and went.[8]

The terms used throughout these lists are a shorthand so compressed as to be almost a code. By 1669, the date of the first surviving list from the period of this study, these abbreviated terms allowed the entire list—137 different prices in twenty-seven categories—to be contained on a single-sided broadside along with the names of the eighty-one bookbinders who subscribed. Specific prices are given for books bound both in calf and sheep. The difference in the prices is dramatic, with sheep never more than half the price of calf, and in the larger formats considerably less.[9] Goatskin and other binding materials are never specifically mentioned in the London price lists. There are several possible reasons: more expensive materials might have been priced as bespoke bindings, one at a time; there might have been set premiums for more expensive skins; or customers, especially booksellers, might have provided special materials themselves (in the same way they provided their printers with paper), and received an appropriate credit against their binding bills.

The 1669 list, *A General Note of the Prices of Binding all sorts of Books*, begins with Bibles,

| Ogilby's Bibles in Folio, or the like. | l. | s. | d. | Bibles in Quarto, Cambridg, or the like. | l. | s. | d. |
| --- | --- | --- | --- | --- | --- | --- | --- |
| Gilt Edges in one Volumn | 01 | 00 | 00 | Edges Extraordinary | 00 | 05 | 00 |
| Fillets only | 00 | 12 | 00 | Edges Ordinary | 00 | 03 | 06 |
| Plain ovals | 00 | 08 | 00 | Fillets | 00 | 02 | 06 |
| | | | | Ovals | 00 | 01 | 06 |

And so on through successively smaller sizes, the Bible binding column ending with "Service in 24. With Psalms, &c."

What are we to make of all this? Clearly "Gilt Edges" is a far more elaborate treatment than "Fillets only" or "Plain ovals." But what do "Gilt Edges" signify, not to mention (in the quarto and all smaller sizes) "Edges Extraordinary" and "Edges Ordinary?"

All the decoration listed for Bibles probably involved gilt work, except perhaps the "Plain ovals," which are the large center tools so often seen, sometimes gilt and sometimes blind, on otherwise minimally-decorated calf Bibles of the period. One argument in favor of even "Plain ovals" being gilt, apart from the fact that gilt is how they are seen on many surviving examples, is that the cheapest binding on a quarto Bible, "Ovals," is priced 1s. 6d., four pence more than "All Latin Books in Quarto, Large & thick." "Edges Extraordinary" and "Edges Ordinary" involve too great a price differential—1s. 6d. in quarto— to refer simply to the gilding of the page edges, so we must look to the degree of tooling on the books themselves. In so doing we can interpret "edge," in one of its common seventeenth-century usages, to mean furnishing with a border.[10] Figures 2.2–2.3, although goatskin bindings rather than calf, are intended to give an idea of these two styles. "Extraordinary" involves multiple panels, with elaborate interlacing ornaments made up of small decorative tools (the term probably evolved from the "double lac'd" of the 1646 list).[11] These small tools were used to create versions of the elaborate patterns characteristic of the golden age of English bookbinding. "Ordinary" might be a single or double panel, less elaborately decorated, but with more gilt than one would see on the less expensive "Fillets" style. The important thing to remember is that decoration of this period tended towards panels within panels; as the English "cottage roof" style became increasingly widely used, it too could be seen as another "edge." (For an example of the cottage roof style, see fig. 5.34.)

It must be said, however, that the remainder of the bindings specified in the 1669 price list bear no hint of the style that we associate with this golden age. A couple of the folio specifications, for "Ogilby's *China, Virgil*, all his other Books, or the like," allow for "Marble Fillets" at 8s. per volume, or 10s. if the two-volume sets are bound in one. This must mean both marbled calf, a recent introduction to England (the price differentials are too great to mean marbled leaf edges), and gilt fillets, a combination probably made popular by Samuel Mearne, who began to use it in the early 1660s, and who in 1669 was one of the price list's subscribers.[12] But the remaining bindings are plain indeed, and provide an excellent introduction to the most basic of trade binding styles.

All of the lists include specific titles, chosen under their format headings—folio, small folio, quarto, etc.—for their relative size and thickness. The seventeenth-century lists have separate sections for books in Latin, whose titles include not only books printed in England, but also many standard academic texts printed on the Continent and imported in sheets. One of the entries for a thicker folio is "Rawleighs Hist." (fig. 2.4), grouped with Davila's *History of the Civil Wars of France*, another folio of about the same thickness, with the note "or the like," and priced 3s. "Rawleighs Hist." is Sir Walter Raleigh's *The Historie of the World*, and the 1666 edition illustrated here is the edition to which this price list refers (the next folio edition did not appear until 1677).

Further down the list, under the heading "Books in Octavo, English," are "All large Octo. *Decay of Piety*, or the like" at 9d. It is safe to say that "the like" included the rest of Richard Allestree's

Fig. 2.2.
This lovely goatskin binding
is on a duodecimo King James
Bible, 1679, and is by the
Oxford binder William Cox.
It gives some idea of what I
believe the price lists meant
by "Edges Extraordinary,"
with borders made up of
small interlacing tools, and
including a central panel. The
binding is also highly unusual
in that it is signed by the
binder on the fore-edge. By
permission of the British
Library, Shelfmark c109r2.
See also Mirjam M. Foot,
"A Binding by William Cox,
1684" in *Studies in the History
of Bookbinding*, pp. 202–03.

Fig. 2.3.
Another goatskin binding on
a King James Bible, Oxford,
1697, together with *The Whole
Book of Psalms*, Cambridge,
1696, 4to, by the Oxford
binder Richard Sedgley. The
less elaborate double gilt panel
is probably what the price lists
meant by "Edges Ordinary."
According to the 1695 price
list, a similar binding in calf
cost 3s. 6d. By permission of
the British Library, Shelfmark
c108k9.

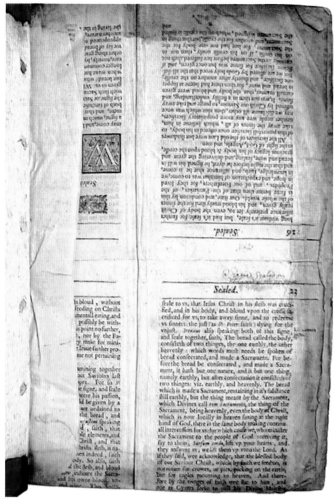

Fig. 2.4.
Sir Walter Raleigh, *Historie of the World*, 1666, folio, calf. This edition was advertised in Clavell's 1673 catalogue at 30s. bound. A 1674 ownership inscription on the title shows the binding is not later than that date, and its simple style, with small corner fleurons, and a double-line fillet at the edges repeated about a third of the way in from the spine, is characteristic of the period, as is the use of the printer's waste as flyleaves. The blind-tooling on the covers is a carry-over from the previous two decades; during the 1670s it gave way to more symmetrical panels. Courtesy of the William Andrews Clark Memorial Library, University of California, Los Angeles.

Fig. 2.5.
Francis Quarles, *Emblems*, 1684, pot 8vo, calf. This simple binding was priced "All Pot Octavo's, *Quarles* Poems &c" at 6d. The head of the spine shows an early paper manuscript lettering piece. The only gilt on the binding is the edge-roll on the covers, not shown here because much of it has rubbed away.

Fig. 2.6.
Richard Allestree, *The Gentleman's Calling*, 1660, 8vo, sheep with a blind fillet on the covers and spine, stained to an almost somber darkness. There seems to have been a coat of varnish or glaire applied, which has now largely dissolved or flaked away. In the section "Sheeps Leather" under "Octavo's Large," the 1669 list refers to this title as "Gent. Callings, or the like," binding price 4d. Courtesy of the Lilly Library, Indiana University, Bloomington, Indiana.

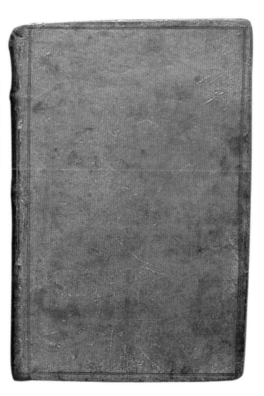
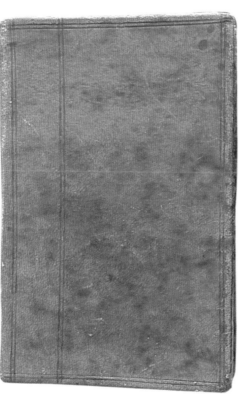

Fig. 2.7.
Left to right: Edmund Waller, *Poems &c.*, 1664; and Thomas Carew, *Poems, Songs, and Sonnets*, 1670, both foolscap 8vo, sheep. Both were pub-lished by Henry Herringman; these may have been his warehouseman's cheap bind-ings for distribution around the trade.

immensely popular devotional works. At the end of the octavo section are "All Pot Octavo's, *Quarles Poems, &c*" at 6d. (fig. 2.5).[13]

The remainder of the 1669 price list goes on to dispose of "All large Twelves" and "all small Twelves and Twenty-four's" with two prices for calf bindings, and then proceeds to "Sheeps Leather" (fig. 2.6). As noted above, these prices are dramatically lower than calf bindings on the same sizes: Quarles in "Octavo Pot" is 6d. in calf, but only 3d. in sheep. The Waller and Carew volumes illustrated here (fig. 2.7), though not specifically named on the price list, would have come under the heading "Octavo's Large" at "All thin Crown, and all Fools-Cap." These two are both foolscap, and would have cost in these simple unlettered bindings 3½d. each.

The next extant list, printed in 1695, is titled *A General Note of the Prices of Binding All Sorts of Books in Calves-Leather: Agreed on by the Bookbinders, Freemen of the City of London, And by them Presented to the Master, Wardens and Assistants of the Worshipful Company of Stationers, at a Court holden March, 1694/5.*[14] It is much shorter than its 1669 counterpart, probably because it was intended to revise only certain prices contained in the 1669 list, and to leave the rest as they stood. Confirmation of this hypothesis may be found in the last section of the list, which declares "The antient allow'd Rate of Binding *Bibles* in *Calf,*" and sets forth an abbreviated version of the exact prices contained in the 1669 list.

The Pepys Library contains a unique broadside titled "The *Bookbinders* Case Unfolded: or, A *Duty of Man*, 12°; Rate for Binding, *Six Pence*" (fig. 2.8). The author was probably John Baker, Dunton's bookbinder who bound "so extraordinarily well."[15] This broadside—without Pepys it would have been lost to posterity—is, as Bernard Middleton writes, "the earliest detailed description of bookbinding in England."[16] More important for my purposes, it is a meticulously detailed description of pre-1695 *trade* bookbinding.

The point of Baker's broadside is that trade binders are woefully underpaid for their work. He lists no fewer than 66 separate operations required for binding in calf a duodecimo copy of Allestree's *The Whole Duty of Man*, from "folding, quiring, and beating" to tooling, gilding, polishing, and "lastly Pressing the Book." For the sum total of these 66 operations, plus the various materials, the binder was paid 6d. This price dates the broadside between 1669, when the price for a duodecimo in calf was set at 6d. (it had been 5d. with "rolles" in 1646), and 1695, when the new price list raised a duodecimo in calf to 8d. The typography of the broadside is consistent with an early 1690s date, and Middleton suggests it may be "connected with the 1695 move for higher prices."[17] This is more than likely, considering that the bookbinders' petition for the 1695 rate increase was, as they stated, based on "the lowe condition they were brought by the lownesse of prices and the dearenesse of Lether."[18]

Baker's detailing of the bookbinder's tasks clarifies a couple of important points about trade binding processes. The previous chapter noted the regulation dating from Elizabethan times that only books up to a certain size could be sold "stitch'd," or stab-sewn before binding. This broadside makes it clear that the 6d. paid for binding a substantial duodecimo like *The Whole Duty of Man* included proper "Sowing, with Appendices," in other words that the gatherings were sewn onto "Packthred" (either cords or, conceivably, recessed thongs), and that these appendices of packthred were subsequently opened or frayed out, scraped soft, pasted, drawn through small holes in the book's boards to secure the boards to the text block, then flattened out and trimmed.

# The *Bookbinders* CASE Unfolded:

## O R,

A *Duty of* MAN, 12º; Rate for BINDING, Six Pence.

The Particulars are as follows.

Folding
Quiring
Beating
Preſſing
Collating
Putting Paper thereto
Sowing, with Appendices
Glewing
Drying
Opening the Packthred
Scrapeing the Packthred
Backing the Book
Cutting out Paſtboards
Beating Paſtboards
Marking the Paſtboards
Holing the Paſtboards
Paſting the Packthred
Drawing it into the Boards
Knocking the ſlips down
Cutting off the Packthred
Preſſing the Book in Boards
Cutting the Book 3 times,
   or more

Squaring the Fore-edges
Rounding the Paſtboards
Sprinkling the leaves 3 times
Making Headbands
Headbanding the Book
Glewing the back
Paring the Calf-Skin
Cutting out the Cover
Grinding Plow-Knives
Grinding Squaring-Knives
Fetching Imperfections, and
   changing of Sheets
Paring the Cover
Paſting the Cover
Covering the Book
Clipping the Corners
Tying up the Book in Boards
Cording each ſide the Bands
Nipping the Bands
Melting the Back at the Fire
Setting the Headband
Rubbing the Back
Drying the back

Untying the Boards
Opening the Papers
Drying the ſides
Rubbing the ſquares
Preſſing when dry
Colouring with Copperas-water
Paſting over the Cover
Sprinkling with Ink
Drying the Cover
Rubbing the ſcurf off the Ink
Burniſhing three times
Tearing off the firſt Paper
Paſting down the ſecond Paper
Preſſing the Book
Filletting the Back
Filletting the ſides
Tooling at the Corners
Glearing the Book
Rolling with Gold
Sweeping off the Gold
Poliſhing the Book
Laſtly Preſſing the Book

*Beſides Workmanſhip, there are uſed theſe following* Materials.]

Paper
Thred
Packthred
Glew
Paſte

Paſtboards
Colour Red
Colour Green
Calves Leather
Copperas

Ink
White of Eggs
Fire
Gold
*Nota Bene,* alſo Tools of div. ſorts

Fig. 2.8.
The only surviving copy of this broadside, the first detailed account of bookbinding—and *trade* bookbinding—to be printed in England. Samuel Pepys preserved it in his copy of Joseph Moxon's *Mechanick Exercises.* By permission of the Pepys Library, Magdalene College, Cambridge.

At least as important, and more obvious to the naked eye, is a second series of operations noted at the end of the broadside's list. These are the "finishing" processes, and they include "Filletting" the back and sides, "Tooling at the Corners" and "Rolling with Gold" (fig. 2.9). A fillet is a wheel, normally rolled on the covers to create a frame or panel, and on either side of the bands on the spine, or at regular intervals on the spine if the book has been sewn on recessed thongs and no false bands have been inserted. A fillet produces a line or, more often in the 1690s, a double line, and it is the most commonly seen decoration on bindings of this period. "Tooling at the Corners" is described by Middleton as "the impression of a floral tool in each corner of the covers." He says this is "a comparatively rare embellishment for retail bindings,"[19] but this is not true in my experience of 1690s calf bindings. Floral corners even begin to appear on sheep bindings around this time (fig. 2.10).

"Rolling with Gold" means gilding with a wheel, in this context clearly a patterned wheel rather than a fillet; "roll" was sometimes used generically to include both.[20] Not all sixpenny bindings necessarily included gilding—the broadside's author was, after all, making his case for better pay—but many did. According to Middleton, "apparently the only parts that were gilt on a sixpenny binding" were "the edges of the boards;"[21] but in fact a slow shift was occurring, and as early as the 1660s and '70s some booksellers were ordering gilding on the spine in addition to, or instead of, on the edges (fig. 2.11). The reason must be that more and more people were shelving their books in the new fashion, with spines facing outwards instead of fore-edges. Gilt board edges for decorative purposes became less important as they became less visible, but they remained in use for more elaborate bindings, and even on simple trade work throughout the eighteenth century. Any significant amount of gilt finishing was an extra for which the bookseller, and usually the retail customer, paid. By the early eighteenth century, however, gilt spine rules and volume numbers, and in some cases even labels (fig. 2.12), were standard features on most trade bindings, including sixpenny or, after 1695 eightpenny, duodecimo calf bindings (fig. 2.13).

Needless to say, the broadside's title, *Duty of Man*, has a double edge to it. On the one side it refers to the binder's duty in carrying out so many tasks for such small compensation, and on the other it alludes to the fact that Richard Allestree's *The Whole Duty of Man* was one of the most popular, often-reprinted, and thus regularly bound books of the era, from its first publication in 1659 until well into the eighteenth century. Many finely bound octavos survive, but the simply-bound duodecimo editions were so popular that they were read to pieces. I was unable to locate a copy of a 1680s or '90s duodecimo edition in a well-preserved original binding, with or without floral tools in the corners. These floral corners consistently appear in octavo and larger sizes as well (fig. 2.14); by the time of the 1695 price list the old fillet style, illustrated here on a 1680s set of Plutarch's *Morals* (fig. 2.15), was definitely out of fashion, although—as always in such a conservative trade as bookbinding—this does not mean it was extinct.

Figure 2.16 shows a "gilt backs" set of Plutarch's *Lives*, and speculates on how such gilding was priced, but there is little hard evidence to support any specific arrangement other than that there must have been a scale of extra charges determining whether only the spine was gilt, or both spine and covers. From the similarities of so many bindings from different workshops, the obvious inference is that whatever the scale was, it resulted in a fairly standard trade gilt "look" (fig. 2.17). The Pepys Library has any number of examples.

Fig. 2.9.
Giles Rose, *A Perfect School of Instructions for the Officers of the Mouth*, 1682, 12mo, calf, a sixpenny binding showing every detail called for in *The Bookbinders Case Unfolded*, including the floral corners on the cover panels and the gilt roll on the edges. Courtesy of the Lilly Library, Indiana University, Bloomington, Indiana.

Fig. 2.10.
John Bunyan, *The Pilgrim's Progress*, 1702 [–1702–1705], pot 12mo, an inexpensive binding combining various editions of all three parts (the third part was not by Bunyan) in sprinkled sheep, paneled and with the usual floral cornerpieces, which by the turn of the eighteenth century began to be seen on sheep as well as calf. Binding a single volume of Bunyan's popular book—curiously enough never specifically named in any of the price lists—would have cost 2½d. by the 1669 price list (the 1695 list did not revise any of the prices for sheep). No doubt there was an extra charge for binding all three together, but probably no more than another penny altogether, to include the extra sewing and leather.

Fig. 2.11.
Christopher Harvey, *The School of the Heart*, 1675, pot 12mo. According to the 1669 price list, calf bindings on "all small Twelves and Twenty-four's" were 5d. This gilt spine, typical of the 1670s and 80s, is too elaborate to have been anything but an extra, but both covers and edges have only the most minimal blind decoration, showing the incipient change-over in fashion from gilt edge-rolls to gilt spines.

Fig. 2.12.
Samuel Parker, *The Ecclesiastical Histories of Socrates, Sozomen, & Theodorit, Faithfully Abridg'd from the Originals*, 1707, 8vo, simple calf with a contemporary, probably original, morocco label, but no other gilt at all, not even on the cover edges. According to the 1695 price list, this is an "Octavo, *Large*, English" (the same heading covers the octavo edition of "Duty of Man"); the binding price in calf was 10d.

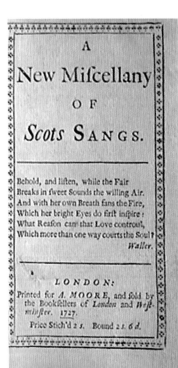

Fig. 2.13.
Allan Ramsay's *A New Miscellany of Scots Sangs*, 1727, pot 12mo, calf, showing the simple spine gilding and label which became increasingly common in the early eighteenth century. The title-page shows the cost of the binding: "Stich'd 2s. Bound 2s. 6d." From the 1695 price list, which gives 6d. as the price for calf bindings on "All small Twelves and Twenty Fours," it appears that the bookseller made no additional profit on the sale of ordinary bound copies. Not all would have had a gilt spine, and it is even conceivable that this copy was bought "stich'd" and given a bespoke binding. It is most likely a retail binding, however, and although a bookseller might have added a small premium for the extra gilt, I believe many

retail booksellers used some of their greater profit margins on retail sales to absorb the extra cost of the gilding that made their books, and their shop displays, more attractive to customers.

Fig. 2.14.
Hermann Hugo, *Pia Desideria: or, Divine Addresses . . . Englished by Edm. Arwaker*, 1690, calf. This is the edition contemplated by the 1695 price list, which names it under "*All* Fools Cap Octavo's," price bound in calf 8d., the same price as for "*All Large* Twelves." No other edition, English or Latin, was printed in England between 1690 and 1700, although Latin editions in octavo appeared in 1677 and 1685, and were probably still available. Whether this copy was bound pre-1695 for 6d., or in 1695 or after for 8d., the style, although a little crude, is typical unlettered trade work of the 1690s. Courtesy of the William Andrews Clark Memorial Library, University of California, Los Angeles.

Fig. 2.15.
Plutarch, *Morals: Translated from the Greek by Several Hands*, 3 vols., 1684–85, 8vo, calf. By 1695 this translation had been completed in five volumes, and was sufficiently popular to be named among "Octavo, *Large*, English." Binding all five in calf cost 4s. 2d. Because Volumes IV and V were not published until 1690, the binding of this three-volume set can be fairly safely dated before then. Note the absence of volume numbers on the spines, and the older style of cover filleting, which by 1695 had almost entirely given way to the blind panel with floral corners seen in the other illustrations here. Courtesy of the William Andrews Clark Memorial Library, University of California, Los Angeles.

Fig. 2.16.
Plutarch, *Lives. Translated from the Greek*, 5 vols., 1693, 8vo, in a fine calf binding, the covers blind-paneled with a floral cornerpiece containing the initials "I.W.," and the spines fully gilt in typical 1690s style. Gilt spines like this probably cost the bookseller 4d.–6d. each over and above prices stated in the list. The 1695 price list gives a collective price of 5s. for the five volumes of the *Lives*, 10d. more than the price for the five volumes of Plutarch's *Morals* or for binding five individual volumes in "Octavo, Large, English." This is a substantial charge for a comparatively small amount of additional sewing and leather; the bookbinders may simply have been capitalizing on a popular, recently-published set, or perhaps the extra charge included volume numbering and labels. Courtesy of the William Andrews Clark Memorial Library, University of California, Los Angeles.

Unlike the English price lists, the Dublin bookbinders' list of 1743 actually gives a scale of prices for what it calls "gilt work." This Irish list—chronologically the next survival after 1695—is titled *Whereas the Bookbinders of the City of Dublin at a Meeting the 15th Day of September 1743, then held, did Unanimously Agree. . . .* It is a broadside of three columns.[22] There is a certain charm to the language of this price list; it is not quite the dry recitation of its London counterparts. It even begins with a little note allowing binders to charge extra to retail customers: "Octavos shall be charg'd Ten Pence, Twelves Eight Pence (at least) . . . to all Gentlemen, Authors, or others."

The price list opens with "the Gilt Work," the highest prices for bindings on various sizes of Bibles and prayer books. The cheapest bindings on the list are sheep, and in between are "Books bound in Calve's Leather and Letter'd only" (fig. 2.18). But the list allows for more elaborate treatment of these calf bindings, with extras specified and priced, than is seen on the earlier London lists. These extras are quoted under two headings: "Gilt Back only," and "Filleted on the Back only with a Tool added thereto" (fig. 2.19). For both, the list is fairly casual about size differences. An "Imperial Folio" is significantly larger than a "Super-Royal ditto," which in its turn is larger than a "Royal ditto," but gilt backs on all three are 2s. Quartos of the same three gradations are all 1s., medium and smaller quartos are 10d., with

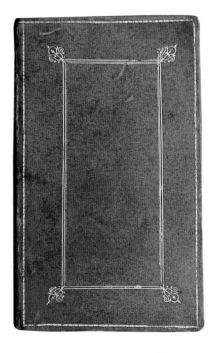

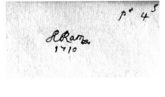

Fig. 2.17.
Delarivier Manley, *Secret Memoirs and Manners of several Persons of Quality, of Both Sexes, from the New Atalantis*, 2 vols., 1709, 8vo, showing a probable price scale for additional gilt work on standard trade bindings. The two volumes were published at different times, and this contemporary owner helpfully noted his purchase price in each volume in 1710. For the first volume, with spine and covers simply gilt, he paid 4s.; for the second, blind-paneled and sprinkled, and with only the spine label gilt, he paid 3s. 6d. According to Edward Arber, *The Term Catalogues* (1903–06), III, 643, the first volume was published in May, 1709 at 3s. 6d., and doubtless the second volume appeared at the same price. The additional 6d. must have been for the extra gilt, and the 1743 Dublin price list gives rough confirmation: it offers "gilt back only" on a medium octavo at 5d. Courtesy of the William Andrews Clark Memorial Library, University of California, Los Angeles.

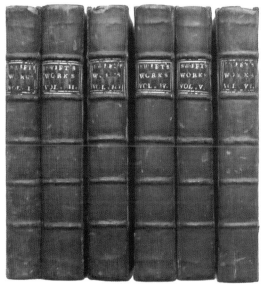

Fig. 2.18.
Jonathan Swift, *Works*, 6 vols., Dublin, 1738, 12mo, an edition its publisher George Faulkner advertised in six "neat pocket volumes" at 16s. 3d. the set, little more than half the price of the same text in grander octavo format, which was £1. 10s. for the six volumes. This binding is typical of simple Irish calf of the period, and were it not for the statement of an extra charge "For lettering the Volume in Black" in the 1743 Dublin price list, this would seem to be the exact binding contemplated by the heading "Books bound in Calve's Leather and Letter'd only." There is no gilt anywhere on these bindings apart from the lettering, which is on a painted black background. The covers show the light, fine sprinkle and glossy surface seen on a large number of different bindings for Faulkner; perhaps this workshop may be called "Faulkner's smooth calf bindery." Courtesy of the William Andrews Clark Memorial Library, University of California, Los Angeles.

Fig. 2.19
Two types of "gilt back,"
from left to right: (a) Richard
Allestree, *Whole Duty of Man*,
1735, 8vo, calf with the spine
as shown and a simple gilt
double fillet framing the covers. This seems more likely
to be standard decoration
than an "extra." (b) Matthew
Pilkington, *Poems on Several
Occasions*, Dublin, 1730, 8vo,
shown here with the binder's
spine title "Miscellany
Poems." This binding also
has a simple gilt fillet on the
covers, but the elegant spine
is well worth the extra 5d.
the Dublin price list allowed.
The Allestree photograph
is courtesy of the William
Andrews Clark Memorial
Library, University of
California, Los Angeles;
the Pilkington, courtesy of
the Lilly Library, Indiana
University, Bloomington,
Indiana.

"Royal Octavo 7d., Medium ditto 5d." and "Twelves of all Sizes 4d." Decoration with the book "Filleted on the Back only with a Tool added thereto" is much cheaper: the largest folios are 6d., dropping to a penny for both octavos and duodecimos.

The "Calve's Leather and Letter'd only" heading on the price list confirms my earlier sugges-tion as to how the gilding included with the simplest bindings shifted from the cover edges to the spine: simple Irish bindings of this period are not normally gilded on the edges, but they do quite consistently include gilt spine titles. Curiously enough, Irish spines are rarely seen lettered direct, as this price head-ing implies; even Irish goatskin bindings are more likely to have separate, contrasting spine labels than their English counterparts. It appears that "gilt back" bought a red morocco label (fig. 2.19b), but there may not have been a set rule for simpler bindings. The price list is ambiguous, and although "Calve's Leather and Letter'd only" implies that lettering is included, it apparently means that lettering, although included, is charged extra (figs. 2.20–2.22). The simplest calf bindings, however, are more likely to be lettered in a spine compartment first painted black, and from which the black often chips and peels (fig. 2.22). This, the price list declares, is an extra, at least on books "Filleted on the Back only with a Tool added thereto," and so, presumably, also on the more simple "Calve's Leather and Letter'd" bind-ings. The statement of the charge is quite specific: "For lettering the Volume in Black on the second Pannel of Folios and Quartos, each Book 2d. For all Octavos and Twelves ditto 1d." Still another extra under the same heading as "lettering in Black," is one that only applies to smaller sizes: "For Filleting and Rolling all Octavos and Twelves each 3d." This implies fancier treatment than the filleting "on the

Fig. 2.20.
Thomas Parnell, *Poems on Several Occasions*, Dublin, 1744, calf, in the format the 1743 price list calls "Medium Octavo." This copy was given as a Trinity College prize to one John Roberts in 1762. It is a standard binding "in Calve's Leather and Letter'd only," but of course the gilt college arms were an extra. College records show that it paid the binder Joseph Leathley 9d. for standard calf bindings in 1732, which is what the 1743 price list shows as the trade rate;the gilt label may have been an extra. (Perhaps after 1743 the College paid a little more, or perhaps it received trade terms as such a large customer.) Leathley could well have bound this book, as he did so many other prize books for the College. Alternatively, he or another binder could have added gilt arms to the covers of a book already ready-bound; for this Leathley's standard charge was 8d.

Fig. 2.21.
Henry Fielding, *The History of Tom Jones, a Foundling*, 3 vols., Dublin, 1749, 12mo, the first Irish edition, with spine lettering and volume numbering on single morocco labels. This Dublin edition reduced the English first edition of the same year from six volumes to three. Its binding is simple sprinkled calf, entirely undecorated except for the red morocco labels. These quite efficiently eliminate the need for any other gilt-work on the bindings, by incorporating the volume numbers, usually stamped directly on the spines, into the labels themselves. If lettering in a blacked compartment was an extra, it seems likely these more expensive goatskin labels were as well. Courtesy of the Lilly Library, Indiana University, Bloomington, Indiana.

Fig. 2.22.
Matthew Prior, *Miscellaneous Works*, 2 vols., Dublin, 1740, 8vo, another set bound by Faulkner's "smooth calf binder," here showing especially well the "blacked" compartments of the spines with their gilt lettering. Courtesy of the Lilly Library, Indiana University, Bloomington, Indiana.

Back only with a Tool added thereto," which is offered at a penny. It seems likely that the 3d. buys a gilt fillet and roll on both the spine and covers.

All of these extras bring us back to the first section of the price list, "For the Gilt Work." Mirjam Foot writes that the "Gilt Work" list for binding Bibles is "on the whole comparable with those for 'Edges Ordinary' on the 1669 and 1695 London price lists."[23] Similar prices must have applied to "gilt work" on other books in these formats, but unlike the London price lists, this Irish one gives no specific book titles other than Bibles and "Common-Prayers."

There are, however, some dramatic differences in the prices for the "Gilt Work" and the more ordinary bindings on this list. If we look at the price of a royal folio Bible in the "Gilt Work," it runs 16s. 3d. A royal folio simply bound in calf and lettered is 5s., with an additional 2s. for a gilt back, a total less than half the price of the full "Gilt Work." This is an enormous difference, even allowing for the greater thickness of Bibles. Clearly the full treatment implied not only gilt edges, but quite a lot of tooling. Finishing was the best paid work in bookbinding, and fine work consumed both a great deal of time and of gold leaf.

It is tempting to speculate that this large price differential might mean that the "Gilt Work" prices also include goatskin, making it an entirely distinct category from the simpler bindings in "Calve's Leather." Yet surviving bills from Joseph Leathley's and other Dublin binderies make clear that this was not the case. Goatskin was simply too expensive to be included in any set list of prices; the binder James Coghlan's 1750s memorandum book shows his small calfskins at a shilling each, and his single "½ Skin of Red Morocko" at 3s.[24] Furthermore, a receipt from Leathley showing the prices charged for binding large paper copies of Plato's *Dialogues* in 1738 demonstrates just how much more expensive the additional gilt was: ten copies in "blew Turky Gilt over" with splendid Harleian patterns were 10s. each, whereas copies in "Red Lether Gilt" (goatskin, less elaborately prepared) with a much simpler gilt panel were 6s. 6d.[25]

Sheep binding in the Dublin price list is divided into three groups. The first is "Banded," which means fully sewn on cords that become the raised bands of the spine. For fully sewn and bound books in banded sheep, the prices are, on the whole, one-half to three-fifths the cost of calf, with the smallest difference in the octavo format. In calf a royal octavo is 1s. 2d., a medium octavo 9d.; in sheep there is only one price for an octavo, 7d., and unlike all other formats in this section it carries the statement, "if Letter'd." This may have been a way for binders to make a slightly better profit on bindings in the most common of all formats.

The second, cheaper, group is "Plain Sheep," a binding style with the *highest* price, for "Testaments," set at 2½d. each, but with specified discounts for orders by the hundred.

The third group, and cheapest of all, is "Grains," which are almost half the price of plain sheep on the same titles, hardly more than a penny a volume. "Grains" was the outer split part of sheepskin, the cheapest available leather; the term was later supplanted by "roan."[26] The use of grains shows the relentless drive on the part of the booksellers towards cheaper and cheaper bindings for quantity sales. The only way binders could get the cost per volume down to just over a penny per volume (12s. 6d. per hundred for "Testaments Saw'd," as opposed to £1. 0s. 10d per hundred for "Plain Sheep") was by using this cheaper sheepskin, and by abandoning sewing. Plain sheep bindings, although not sewn on raised

bands, would at least have had some minimal sewing on recessed cords (fig. 2.23). "Saw'd," as Mirjam Foot notes, means that the backs of the sections were sawn in, cords pressed into the grooves and onto the boards, and the whole glued up with no sewing at all—"an early form of 'perfect binding.'"[27]

Another section of the 1743 Dublin list for quantity binding includes "Lacquerd Work," which calls for "Common-Prayers and Manuals per Hundred, whereof one Quarter to be Shagreen" at £2. 10s. At 6d. per volume, this is far and away the highest price for quantity binding, and must imply both better materials and a more elaborate style. Mirjam Foot suggests some possible interpretations for "Lacquerd," including varnishing, marbling, and sprinkling.[28] She does not specifically discuss "Shagreen," which almost certainly refers to leather, usually sheep, dyed green and varnished to resemble, as closely as possible, goatskin (figs. 2.24–2.25). Figure 2.24 shows a particularly elegant example, which would never have been part of any kind of bulk binding price, unless it was for a group of presentation copies. But this binding shows how fine the "lacquerd" style could be, at least on shagreen.

Three other sections of this list respectively offer prices for binding in "Vellum plain," "Russia Bands," and "Forril" (unsplit sheepskin)—all three are binding styles for account ledgers. This kind of work was not included in the London price lists, probably because, as later London trade directories show, such binding was a fairly specialized practice there and did not require inclusion in price lists circulated around the general book trade. Both this Dublin list and the London list of 1744 contain prices for various sizes of "Gilt Paper and Black," and "Rul'd Paper."

Because rising commodity rates affected both London and Dublin markets in the same way, the new prices in the 1743 Dublin list must have resulted from the same problems with calfskin that caused the London bookbinders to issue a revised list the next year. On May 14, 1744, the London bookbinders forwarded their new rates "To the Booksellers of London & Westminster. &c," noting "the exorbitant prices that Leather now Bears by the Scarceness of that Commodity."[29] Generally speaking, the price rises are on the order of twenty percent over those of the 1695 price list, reducing to nearer ten percent

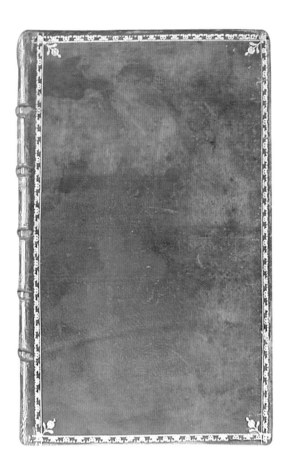

Fig. 2.24.
Francis Hutcheson, *An Enquiry into the Original of Our Ideas of Beauty and Virtue*, 1753, 8vo, in a fine binding of sheep stained green and varnished—probably "lacquerd"—to resemble goatskin, which it does but for the obvious grain underneath. If this is part of what the Dublin binders meant by "shagreen" in their 1743 price list, it is handsome work indeed, complete with gilt edges and Dutch marbled endpapers. The binding is highly unusual in having the place and date of publication gilt in the second spine compartment from the bottom. It seems likely to be the work of an Irish bookbinder, but there are no marks of provenance to help further. Hutcheson himself was Irish, and his son, who may have overseen this posthumous edition, lived in Dublin.

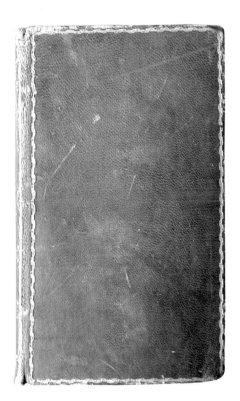

Fig. 2.25.
A later and more obvious example of Irish shagreen, less highly lacquered and with the sheep grain more clearly visible, on James Hurdis, *The Village Curate*, "third edition, corrected," Dublin, 1790, 12mo.

with smaller formats; but in keeping with the new fashion for lettering books, many of the prices for the larger sizes include that cost in the binding price. No printed copy of the price list survives, only a manuscript in the contemporary bookbinder James Coghlan's memorandum book. If his transcript is complete, as seems likely, this list is frustratingly short of individual titles. Most of the entries concern devotional books, with specifications for binding the *Book of Common Prayer* such as

> folio Demy plain 2s. 6d.
>
> Ditto Edges 5s. 0d.
>
> 4to Royal plain 2s. 6d.
>
> Small 4to plain 1s. 3d.
>
> Ditto Edges 2s. 6d.
>
> 8vo Large Letter Edges 1s. 6d.
>
> 8vo pica Edges 1s. 1d.

"Edges" clearly means a degree of gilt work, just as in the earlier lists, but at double the price of "plain." "Plain" does not mean entirely undecorated, but rather a less elaborate type of gilding, like the "plain ovals" in the 1669 price list (figs. 2.26–2.27).

The 1744 London list, like its Dublin companion of the previous year, includes a section of "Sheep Binders prices p C neat," *i.e.* bindings by the hundred (fig. 2.28). These are for duodecimo and smaller sizes, but include a few oddities, such as the Hoppus *Measuring* in figure 2.29, which is among the most expensive of books bound at prices per hundred. A helpful catch-all is also offered in this section for titles not specified: any book of 12 sheets or fewer is 16s. per hundred; more than 12 sheets is 18s. For the first time in any binders' list, there is a note of "Sowing & Folding Prices." Folios cost a farthing per alphabet (i.e. a run of signatures) for folding, and apparently the same again for sewing, and so on through the various formats. "Common Sowing 1 penny halfpenny p C sheets: for Sowing only two sheets at a time three half pence." All of this suggests the different kinds of sewing economies that could be attempted, and all show just how cheap this labor was. And if these sewing prices do not seem low enough, the section ends with the following note: "NB: that the Above is the very full price. Some women will work Cheeper."

The last of the available price lists is dated London, June 2, 1760, again addressed "To the Booksellers of London and Westminster" and this time raising both calf and sheep prices "In Consideration of the great Advance on both Sorts of Leather."[30] This list gives far more individual titles than its predecessor, including prices for binding in calf such works as the Imperial Paper folio of "Catesby's Carolina, per Vol. Lettered" (16s.), Royal Paper quartos of "Smollett's Don Quixote, lettered" (3s. 3d.), and so on through Royal Paper, Demy, and Crown Octavos, and Demy and Small Twelves (figs. 2.30–2.34). Each size, after specifying various titles (no fewer than twenty-one in the "Demy Octavo" category), adds the line "All Books on the same Paper, &c. the like Price."

The list ends with bindings in sheep, followed by a short section of Bibles and prayer books. Each section for sheep bindings is specified to be "Sheep, Rolled," *i.e.* with a wheel tool, which seems normally to have been no more than a fillet on either side of the spine bands (fig. 2.35). Octavo is the largest size given for sheep binding, unlike earlier lists which begin with "Pot Folios," and there is one section, akin to the "Grains" section of the Dublin list, which gives prices even cheaper than the usual sheep. This

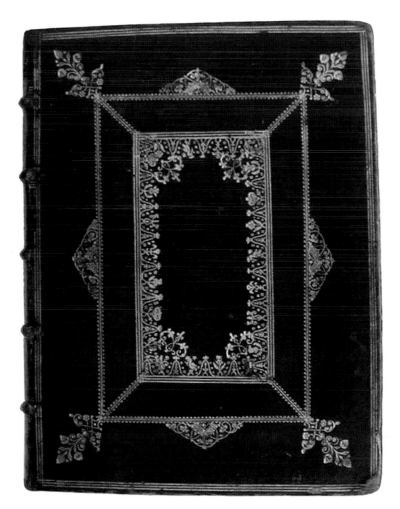

Fig. 2.26.
*The Book of Common Prayer*,
1730, 4to. The price on the
title-page is *"Four Shillings,
Unbound."* This elegant
binding, which also has an
elaborately gilt spine, is a distinct step up from the more
simple "edges" and gilt oval
on the smaller *New Week's
Preparation* and Bible in figure 2.27. The "Unbound" on
the title-page suggests that,
as with many books in larger
formats, this was intended
both for bespoke bindings,
and for booksellers to sell at
different prices according
to how finely bound it was.
Courtesy of the William
Andrews Clark Memorial
Library, University of
California, Los Angeles.

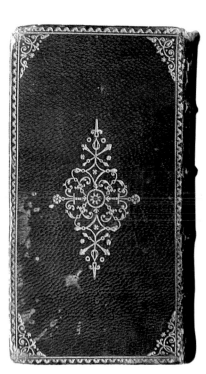

Fig. 2.27.
Left to right: (a) *The New
Week's Preparation Compleat*,
1746, 12mo, goatskin. The
London price list of 1744
has an entry pricing "All
Sacrament Books Black Calf
Under the Size of the new
Week's preparation" at 6d.,
and "Size of the New" at 7d.
(b) The Bible. Oxford, 1739,
pot 12mo, goatskin. The
similarity of the gilt patterns on these two books, a
traditional style akin to the
one called "Ovals" in the
1669 list, suggests that this
may be the style contem-
plated by the term "Edges"
in the 1744 price list. Both
bindings are too fine to be
those contemplated by the
7d. entry in the list.

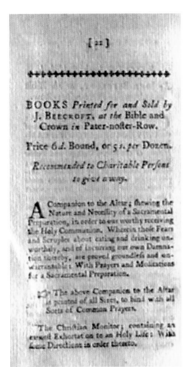

Fig. 2.28.
A page of the bookseller John Beecroft's advertisements, printed at the end of his "nineteenth edition" of John Norris, *Spiritual Counsel: or, the Father's Advice to his Children*, 1761, 24mo. This book is included in Beecroft's list at "6d. Bound, or 5s. per Dozen. Recommended to Charitable Persons to give away." Another title on Beecroft's list, *The Countess of Moreton's Daily Exercise*, is among those specifically named in the 1744 price list to be bound in sheep at 13s. per hundred.

Fig. 2.29.
Edward Hoppus, *Practical Measuring Made Easy*, 1738, narrow 8vo, listed as "Hoppus Meshuring" in the 1744 price list. Copies bound like this in simple sheep could be had for 18s. per hundred. At these bulk binding prices, even end-papers were not required, as can be seen in the illustration of the inside front cover. Courtesy of the William Andrews Clark Memorial Library, University of California, Los Angeles.

Fig. 2.30.
Nathaniel Bailey, *An Universal Etymological English Dictionary*, 1749, 8vo. This title is cited in the 1760 list as "Bailey's Dictionary" under "Octavo's, Demy, Calf." This edition is stated to be the thirteenth; by 1760 four more editions had also appeared. The price is stated on the title-page as "Six Shillings," certainly for bound copies. This shabby but original binding was the standard issue; the price list's 1s. 2d. would have included the gilt fillet on the covers and spine. Courtesy of the William Andrews Clark Memorial Library, University of California, Los Angeles.

Fig. 2.31.
*The Works of Shakespear in Nine Volumes*, 1747, pot 12mo. This is Thomas Hanmer's edition of Shakespeare; the 1760 price list specified "Theobald's Shakespear, per Vol" in the larger "Demy Twelve" size at 9d. per volume. This set was a "Small Twelve," and a calf binding cost 7d. per volume, probably including the gilt fillet on the covers and spines. The labels may have been an extra. Courtesy of Department of Special Collections, Stanford University Libraries.

Fig. 2.32.
*The Works of Virgil . . .
Translated in to English Verse;
By Mr. Dryden*, 3 vols., 1748,
12mo, listed in the 1760
price list: "Dryden's Virgil"
under "Demy Twelves, Calf"
at 10d. per volume. The
calf covers are entirely plain
except for a light sprinkle.
The extra charge for each
gilt spine, including the

labels and the "blacked"
compartment with the vol-
ume number, was probably
the same 4d. as in the Dublin
list for "Gilt Back only"
in "Twelves of all Sizes."
Courtesy of the William
Andrews Clark Memorial
Library, University of
California, Los Angeles.

Fig. 2.33.
The spines of the last six
volumes of *The Works of
Alexander Pope, Esq. In Ten
Volumes Complete*, 1757,
foolscap 12mo. This set
appears in the 1760 list
under "Small Twelves, Calf"
as "Rasselas, Shandy, and
Pope's Works," at 7d. per
volume; Pope's works also
appeared in nine vols., 8vo,

and the price list includes
an entry for them under
"Crown Octavo's, Calf" at
9d. per volume The covers of
the illustrated set have the
same fillet as the spines; this
simple gilding was no doubt
included in the binding price.
Courtesy of the William
Andrews Clark Memorial
Library, University of
California, Los Angeles.

Fig. 2.34.
Two copies of the 1760 first
edition of Laurence Sterne's
*Tristram Shandy*, listed
under "Small Twelves, Calf"
as "Shandy" (along with
Johnson's "Rasselas"), binding price 7d. per volume.
*Tristram Shandy* is the only
novel so successful that it
was specifically named in a
bookbinders' price list the
same year it was published.
On the left is a copy bound
in calf, a standard trade binding with gilt fillets and red
morocco labels, which are
original to the book as can be
seen from the absence of the
gilt fillet in the spine compartment of Vol. II, where
the red morocco is slightly

chipped. Note the slip by the
finisher, who put the wrong
volume numbers on the
spines, and had to go back
and correct his mistake.
Collection of William Zachs.
The second copy is of the
same first edition, but bound
in trade sheep, "tree" style,
which is to say stained by the
finisher with a mix of pearl-
ash and copperas to give the
tree-shaped pattern on the
covers. "Tree" staining was
more common on calf than
sheep; this binding has been
given a little extra treatment,
including the single gilt fillet
frame on the cover. Courtesy
of Department of Special
Collections, Stanford
University Libraries.

Fig. 2.35.
Mme. de Beaumont, *The Young Ladies Magazine, or Dialogues between a Discreet Governess and Several Young Ladies*, 4 vols. in two, 1760, 12mo. This title is listed under "Small Twelves, Sheep, Rolled" as "Young Lady's Magazine, per Vol." Sets are almost always seen with the four volumes bound as two; in this illustration the first part of the gilt spine number "1–2" is almost obliterated. The price was 5d. per volume, which raises the question whether these two slender volumes counted as one when bound together.

"Rolled" often means no more than a simple fillet, as on this binding, but there is usually also some kind of decorative acid sprinkle or stain on the covers, as can be seen here and in other bindings of the period. Courtesy of Department of Special Collections, Charles E. Young Research Library, University of California, Los Angeles.

Fig. 2.36.
"Red Sheep, Rolled," also known as "Bassil Red," on Sarah Trimmer, *A Series of Prints of Ancient History . . . in which Children receive the first Rudiments of their Education*, 1788, 16mo. This volume, containing the engravings, was offered in sheets, marbled paper, and, as here, "neatly Bound in Red Leather, 2s. 4d."

section is headed "Red Sheep, Rolled," and gives some titles intended to indicate the octavo and smaller sizes. Howard Nixon identifies this "red sheep" from James Coghlan's memorandum book. Coghlan calls it "Bassil red," which a nineteenth-century writer defines as "sheepskin tanned, used for common bindings."[31] Surviving examples retain an orange tinge, as can be seen in figure 2.36.

One casual mention in this 1760 list reveals a style that had become common by the middle of the eighteenth century: half binding (fig. 2.37). The single reference is in the first entry under "Imperial Folio," the largest size in the list. At roughly 30 x 22 inches, Imperial Folio is nearly twice as large as the circa 15 x 12½ inch "Pot Folio." The Imperial Folio "Albinus's Tables, Calf, lettered"—a reference to the mammoth *Tables of the Skeleton and Muscles of the Human Body*, published in both Latin and English

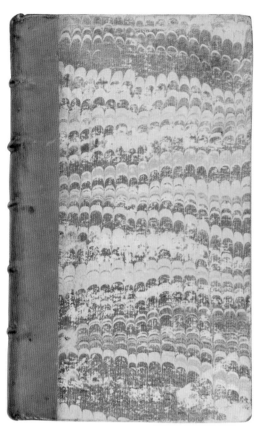

Fig. 2.37.
Henry Fielding, *Miscellanies*, 3 vols., 1743, 8vo, a typical "half binding." The spines are sheep, with volume numbers in the second compartment where, if the buyer chose, they could be covered by title labels. The covers are pasteboard overlaid with Dutch marbled paper. Probably introduced in the late seventeenth century, this type of binding became increasingly popular in the 1740s, and remained a standard for the rest of the century, with calf or sheep spines, and either plain grey or blue, or marbled paper on the covers. Variations on the style included gilt spines, leather or vellum corners, and after about 1770 different marbling patterns on the paper were introduced. A version of this binding for circulating libraries left the edges of the sheets untrimmed, so that the book could later be rebound and given a bright new look with its freshly-cut edges. Courtesy of the Lilly Library, Indiana University, Bloomington, Indiana.

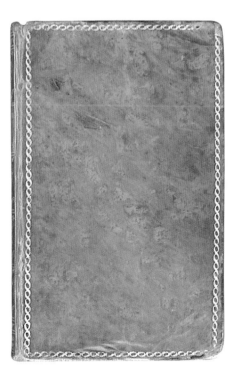

Fig. 2.38.
An Irish "gilt back" on the third Dublin edition of Henry Mackenzie's popular sentimental novel *The Man of Feeling*, 1780, 12mo, in marbled tree calf, the covers framed by a simple gilt rope. The spine, which has been treated (probably "lacquerd") to give a darker, highly polished surface before the application of gilt tooling, is in the Chippendale style typical of the decade.

in 1749—is £1. 2s., but "Ditto, half bound, lettered" is exactly half the price, or 11s. This price difference shows just how expensive calf had become—there is actually slightly more labor involved in a half than a full binding (assuming one is dealing with an already pared calfskin)—and although the price differential diminishes as the format of the book reduces, clearly there were significant cost savings to be had.

Although the "Edges" and "Gilt Work" categories in the price lists demonstrate that decorated bindings were part of the daily practice of bookbinders, the lack of more specific detail in the price lists is their most frustrating feature. Most frustrating of all, in view of the large number of surviving examples, is the absence of any reference in the lists to goatskin. Lord Harley's librarian supplied his binders with morocco skins, and it is quite likely that booksellers followed the same practice. It is also logical to infer that binders with large quantities of upscale commissions, like the Mearnes, the Steels, Baumgarten, and others, would have stocked as much goatskin as they could afford, and made upward adjustments in binding prices.

The progression of the price lists from 1669 to 1760 demonstrates one aspect of the book trade most clearly, and that is the pressure to produce cheaper and cheaper bindings. Vast quantities of bindings were produced with sheep, unlettered and practically undecorated, at prices per hundred, and sold by the dozen. By 1760 even calf bindings were often virtually undecorated: completely plain boards were normal, and spines had only the minimal gilt fillet and labels, if that. John Jaffray's manuscripts refer to this period as having "very few Finishers then, little or no finishing, except the lettering being required."[32] By the 1780s the general state of trade bookbinding had improved somewhat, probably because the proliferation of cheaper paper bindings meant that the higher-priced leather received additional finishing. The elegant neoclassicism of the period, which inspired Chippendale and other craftsmen, found its way into bookbinding styles (fig. 2.38), and the 1781 *Master Bookbinders' Memorial to the Booksellers* referred to "the Degree of Perfection" which bookbinding had achieved "in the Course of the last sixteen Years." By the 1790s, the export trade was bringing even more work to the London bookbinders and, as the binder James Watson put it, "the Booksellers' orders were . . . in general done up in an extra manner. In addition to this a very general practice prevailed of preparing immense numbers in a superficial and showy style. . . ."[33]

As with so many commonplace features of daily life, no writer has recorded the bookbinders' routine working and accounting practices, but the bookbinders' price lists and the examples illustrated paint a detailed and compelling picture of the range of bindings booksellers acquired in the ordinary course of business.

## CHAPTER THREE

# PUBLISHERS' BINDINGS

In 1903, Edward Arber, editor of *The Term Catalogues*, wrote that "the habit of Publishers of binding books in whole leather *before publication* evidently originated in the Commonwealth period. When? And by whom?"[1] Pre-publication binding in fact began in England at least as early as 1496, when Richard Pynson was supposed to deliver books "redy bound the piece," and it expanded throughout the sixteenth and seventeenth centuries.

Arber's question addresses a subtle, but critical, distinction between trade bindings and publishers' bindings. Trade bindings include all bound books sold to retail customers. Publishers' bindings, a subcategory of trade bindings, include only books which are already bound *before* they reach the retailer. Publishers' bindings were executed for the commissioning bookseller or syndicate, or by a wholesale distributor, which in the early days was often, but not always, the same entity.[2] The concept of publishers' bindings meant that retailers, whether shopkeepers or itinerant chapmen, received their copies ready-bound at a wholesale price that included the cost of the binding.

Attempting to identify early publishers with specific bindings is no easy task. Beginning in the mid-1760s, some readily-identifiable styles appeared, notably Newbery's vellum-backed boards (fig. 3.1), and boards and wrappers with printed labels: all authorities accept these as publishers' bindings. With respect to bindings before that time, scholarly opinion can fairly be described as both conflicting and confused.

In 1930 Michael Sadleir, in *The Evolution of Publishers' Binding Styles*, made an enormously influential statement:

> The bookseller-publisher of the decades from 1730 to 1770 issued his books either in loose quires, or stitched, or at most in a plain paper wrapper. . . . It is difficult to see how the organization of the trade (such as it then was) could make any greater completeness of book-issue conceivable.[3]

Before Sadleir, cataloguers often used the term "original" to describe simple period bindings in calf or sheep. So powerful was Sadleir's influence, however, that by the time I began to train as a book cataloguer in the early 1970s, the settled rule was that, for pre-cloth books, only wrappers and boards were "original," and the best one could hope to call any other kind of binding was "contemporary."

Although it is accurate to say that trade and publishers' bindings are indeed contemporary with their dates of publication, Sadleir's assertion does an injustice to the sophistication of the pre-1770 book trade. Starkey and Clavell's catalogues of the late 1660s and 1670s show many publisher-booksellers advertising their books as ready-bound in leather. Beginning in the early eighteenth century, some booksellers stated bound prices on title-pages (fig. 3.2). Catalogue, title-page, and periodical advertising continued throughout the eighteenth century. Most advertisements specified the bookseller with whom

Fig. 3.1.
John Newbery, *Arithmetic*, and four other volumes from *The Circle of the Sciences*. London, for T. Carnan, and F. Newbery, 1776–78, 18mo, various editions, bound in the "vellum manner," with the spines stained green, printed paper labels, and the boards covered with Newbery's characteristic dark blue paper. Courtesy of Department of Special Collections, Charles E. Young Research Library, University of California, Los Angeles.

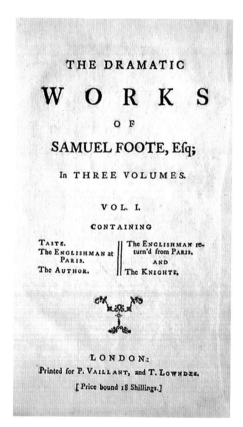

THE DRAMATIC
WORKS
OF
SAMUEL FOOTE, Efq;

In THREE VOLUMES.

VOL. I.

CONTAINING

| TASTE. | The ENGLISHMAN re- |
| The ENGLISHMAN at | turn'd from PARIS. |
| PARIS. | AND |
| The AUTHOR. | The KNIGHTS. |

LONDON:
Printed for P. VAILLANT, and T. LOWNDES.
[ Price bound 18 Shillings.]

Fig. 3.2.
Samuel Foote, *The Dramatic Works*, a made-up collection of thirteen separate plays printed between 1754 and 1774, 8vo, each with its original title and price. The aggregate of the thirteen plays alone is about 18s., the price stated on the title-page —buyers, in effect, got this very simple calf binding for free.

retailers and other purchasers were supposed to place orders. When that bookseller or his agent supplied a bound copy, it was in a publisher's binding.

As bookselling syndicates developed towards the end of the seventeenth century, and more and more booksellers' names appeared in imprints during the first half of the eighteenth century, publishers' bindings became increasingly diverse, even on copies of the same book. The Bowyer printing ledgers show that most editions, whether published by an individual or a syndicate, were placed with multiple binders, a practice which allowed retailers to receive their bound copies more or less simultaneously.

Some retail shopkeepers, chapmen, and other itinerant booksellers, did not want to go to the time and expense of commissioning bindings, and preferred to receive books ready-bound from their suppliers. Thus many of the simplest generic bindings, such as the common calf and sheep on chapmen's books, are among those usually commissioned by publishers. Edition binding these popular books allowed publishers to take advantage of bulk rates, such as the "Sheep's Leather Books at 14s. the hundred" offered to John Dunton,[4] and to meet the retailers' demand for the cheapest possible ready-to-sell books (figs. 3.3–3.4).

In order to make the case for a variety of publishers' bindings, this chapter is divided into sections. Sections I and II discuss publishers and offer a definition of a publisher's binding. Section III begins to explore how to identify specific examples. Although we know from Starkey and Clavell's catalogues that publishers' bindings were widespread as early as the 1660s and '70s, the most distinctive types, such as those of the Newbery and John Bell firms, appear at the close of the eighteenth century. These are considered first in order to establish the nature of the genre. Section IV continues with some earlier examples of publishers' leather. Section V considers paper bindings of the mid-eighteenth century and later, with separate discussions of boards, paper labels, and wrappers. Section VI concludes with a survey of the wide variety of publishers' bindings used on children's books.

## I. PUBLISHERS

A modern publisher produces and distributes books and periodicals, either as the copyright owner or as an agent, usually for the author. This kind of publisher—commissioning printing and binding, and distributing copies in bulk at wholesale—became increasingly established in the last half of the eighteenth century, and had largely taken over the London book trade by the middle of the nineteenth.

In the seventeenth and eighteenth centuries, however, "publisher" meant something quite different. "Bookseller" was the term used by all traders, wholesale and retail, but at the top of the ladder were those booksellers who owned copyrights and could participate in private copyright auctions. The very uppermost rung was occupied by the powerful men who led the syndicates, or congers. At this time, "publishers" were wholesale distributors. They could also be retailers, but that was a separate part of their business. Most operated "on a lower rung of the trade ladder."[5] According to one 1740 dictionary, a publisher was the kind of bookseller "who has his name put at the bottom of pamphlets, newspapers, &c."[6] In the law courts they were sometimes called "mere publishers," because they had no control over the nature of the texts they distributed.

For a copyright-owning bookseller to make a profit on an edition, he had to sell far more copies wholesale than he could ever expect to sell retail in his own shop. Publishers looked after the details

Fig. 3.3.
Archibald Campbell,
Marquis of Argyle,
*Instructions to a Son*. London,
Printed and Sold by Richard
Baldwin, 1689, pot 12mo,
sprinkled sheep, a 2½d. binding according to the 1669
price list, but here almost
certainly a publisher's bulk
binding. This was probably
produced in-house; John
Dunton specifically says that
Baldwin operated a bindery
at this time.

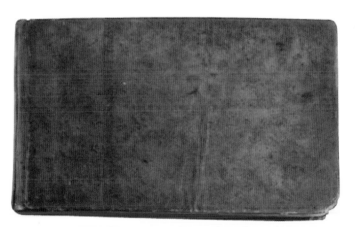

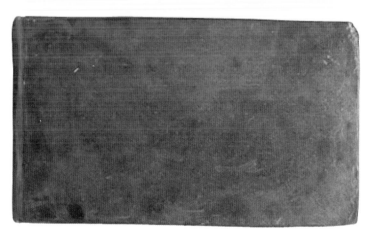

Fig. 3.4.
Three popular books of
country dances. Top to
bottom: John and Henry
Playford, *The Dancing-
Master*. London, J.
Heptinstall for H. Playford,
1698, tenth edition; John
and Henry Playford, *The
Dancing-Master*. London,
W. Pearson, 1721, 2 vols. in
one, seventeenth edition, the
title stating "Price Bound
3s. 6d."; and, at right, *The*

*Compleat Country Dancing-
Master*. London, I. Walsh,
1735, the title stating "Price
3s. 6d. Bound." All are in
the oblong duodecimo for-
mat standard for such books,
approximately 4¼ x 8 inches,
and bound in publishers'
sprinkled sheep. Courtesy
of the William Andrews
Clark Memorial Library,
University of California,
Los Angeles

of wholesale distribution. The smallest operations did little more than deliver newspapers, broadsides, and pamphlets—lightweight objects never intended to be bound. The largest operations were owned by prosperous merchants. These operations sometimes included binderies of their own, but their main focus was moving editions of a thousand or more books quickly and efficiently throughout the British Isles and abroad. In the middle were warehouses run by bookbinders, who bound and delivered copies to order.

As publishers, these bookbinder/warehousemen not only bound books, but also collected wholesale subscriptions from the trade in advance of printing, and delivered printed copies once the edition was finished (these copies could be bound or unbound according to the individual retailer's requirements). Large publishing operations employed several different bookbinder/warehousemen at a time to insure that sufficient copies of a new book would be available; this also, of course, guaranteed that such editions appeared in diverse bindings. John Dunton makes clear that another, crucial, aspect of the publisher's job was to keep exact accounts of the number of copies subscribed and delivered, the prices charged and money collected, and also of any extra copies that might be included free as incentives to encourage larger subscriptions.[7] Every reference Dunton makes to a publisher includes some mention of his accounts; he describes the large, and perhaps arrogant, publishing firm of Awnsham and John Churchill as "two Booksellers (and Brothers) of an universal Wholesale Trade . . . exact in their accompts, and . . . well furnished for any *great Undertaking*."[8]

Large publishers like the Churchills probably distributed both syndicated publications and those of smaller booksellers like Dunton. Some booksellers with large-scale binding requirements also operated their own bookbindery/warehouses. John Dryden's bookseller Jacob Tonson had a bindery, as did later eighteenth-century publishers like John Murray.[9] Booksellers like Tonson may have acted as their own publishers, distributing ready-bound copies around the trade and keeping their own wholesale accounts, or they may have produced only their own retail bindings. More likely they produced a combination of both wholesale and retail bindings to keep their employees fully occupied, and used publishers for distribution and accounting and, when needed, additional binding. What is clear from Starkey and Clavell's catalogues is that individual booksellers controlled their most profitable, retail, sales. From 1668 to 1711, these catalogues always included the name and address of the bookseller with whom customers (and also booksellers) could place orders. As discussed in the caption to figure 2.13, I believe that many booksellers used some of their greater profit margins on retail sales to absorb the expense of the more decorative bindings that made their shops attractive to customers. Provincial booksellers, who received discounts, and customers ordering from a distance probably received more basic bindings similar to those distributed in London wholesale trade. That most provincial orders were filled with bound copies can be seen, for example, in the records of the Durham Cathedral library, which received about eighty percent of its books ready-bound between 1675 and 1705, the same percentage as was offered ready-bound in Clavell's catalogues.[10]

As the eighteenth century progressed, some well-established provincial booksellers became wholesale distributors of books printed in London, Scotland, and Ireland, allowing the commissioning booksellers, as one writer puts it, "to achieve deep penetration of the provincial market."[11] Sometimes title-pages carried the names of these provincial booksellers;[12] a few were even part-owners of

Fig. 3.5.
John Trusler, *The Works of Mr. Hogarth Moralized.* London, [no printer, 1768], 8vo, engraved throughout, including the title which states "Price Bound, One Pound Eighteen Shillings." Although this may well be a bespoke binding, the price of the book was sufficiently high that an Irish bookseller may have had enough of a profit margin to allow the commissioning of a fine binding. This one is in the style of the Dublin binder William McKenzie. One roll appears to correspond to no. 15 in Joseph McDonnell and Patrick Healy, *Gold Tooled Bookbindings Commissioned by Trinity College Dublin* (1987), plate XCV. Other tools are similar but not identical to those illustrated elsewhere in McDonnell and Healy, and in Maggs Bros. Ltd. *Bookbinding in the British Isles*, Catalogue 1075 (1987), items 210–11, and Catalogue 1212 (1996), item 167. Collection of William Zachs.

copyrights and participated in syndicates. These provincial distributors also employed bookbinders to operate their warehouses and bind their books. Some of these provincially-trained binders later found their way to London.[13]

One result of these developments was an increasing distribution of books in sheets from London to provincial, and even Scottish and Irish, booksellers (fig. 3.5). There was also a steady market in North America and elsewhere for books printed and bound in the British Isles, even after the end of the American Revolution.[14] Until the last quarter of the eighteenth century, however, there was a major obstacle for booksellers outside London, preventing free trade in both directions. Many London booksellers asserted perpetual copyright for their publications, which naturally included the works of the most popular authors. In the 1730s and later, this monopoly was increasingly threatened by large-scale importation, to London but especially to the provinces, of editions printed in Scotland and Ireland.[15] This issue was finally resolved by the 1774 landmark House of Lords decision in *Millar v. Donaldson*, which abolished the perpetual copyrights on which the London trade had insisted. Provincial, Scottish, and Irish booksellers were then free to print and sell copies of Shakespeare, Milton, Bunyan, and the other profitable authors of the seventeenth and early eighteenth centuries. Once the Donaldson case was resolved, London booksellers increasingly acted as distributors and agents for provincial, Scottish, and Irish publications.[16]

Widespread wholesale distribution required a dependable system of trade discounts and payment terms, whether for large quantities of books sent in sheets to provincial distributors, or for a few ready-bound books sent to a small retailer. As early as the sixteenth century there existed what Samuel Johnson, in a letter written in 1776, describes as "the usual Allowance to sell again" in the book trade.[17]

When Starkey and Clavell published their catalogues in the 1660s and '70s, the usual allowance from the London bookseller or syndicate to the retailer was probably a straightforward discount of around twenty percent, with no middle-man.[18] Until at least the middle of the eighteenth century, syndicate members themselves got preferential terms on copies subscribed for in advance, and if they needed to replenish their stock of a book printed for their syndicate, they could do so at rates between the subscription price and the wholesale price charged traders outside the syndicate.[19]

By 1776, the year of Johnson's letter, the old bookselling syndicates had lost much of their control over the trade, although working partnerships remained and continued to form. Provincial and foreign booksellers played a larger role in sales, which meant more middle-men could be involved in transactions. As the son of a country bookseller as well as an author, Johnson had first-hand knowledge of book trade matters. His letter was written to the Master of University College, Oxford, and concerned publications of Oxford's Clarendon Press. It describes the workings of the book trade in precise and masterly prose, much too fine to paraphrase:

> It is perhaps not considered through how many hands a book often passes, before it comes into those of the reader, or what part of the profit each hand must retain as a motive for transmitting it to the next.
>
> We will call our primary agent in London Mr. Cadel[20] who receives our books from us, gives them room in his warehouse and issues them on demand. By him they are sold to Mr. Dilly a wholesale Bookseller[21] who sends them into the Country, and the last seller is the Country Bookseller.[22] Here are three profits to be paid between the Printer and the Reader, or in the stile of commerce between the Manufacturer and the Consumer; and if any of these profits is too penuriously distributed the process of commerce is interrupted. . . .
>
> Mr. Cadel who runs no hazard and gives no credit will be paid for warehouse room and attendance by a shilling profit on each Book. . . .
>
> Mr. Dilly who buys the Book for fifteen shillings . . . will sell it to his country customer at sixteen and sixpence by which at the hazard of loss and the certainty of long credit, he gains the regular profit of ten per cent. which is expected in the wholesale trade.
>
> The Country Bookseller buying at sixteen and sixpence and commonly trusting a considerable time gains but three and sixpence, and if he trusts a year, not much more than two and sixpence. . . . With less profit than this, and more you see he cannot have, the Country Bookseller cannot live, for his receipts are small, and his debts sometimes bad.[23]

Johnson's account makes no mention of binding, appropriately enough, as the Clarendon Press was unusual in issuing its books only in sheets.[24] In 1776, however, Johnson's "last buyer" would not have received his copy entirely unbound; at some point it would, at the very least, have been sewed in wrappers or put up in boards (*i.e.*, sewn into paper-covered pasteboards), and in the majority of cases it would have had a retail binding of part or full leather. For Johnson's description to have included the cost of binding would have unnecessarily complicated matters for his correspondent. But the distributorship and profit-sharing Johnson describes bear as directly on bookbinding matters as the bookbinder/warehouseman arrangements discussed earlier in this chapter.

In fact bookbinding arrangements in Johnson's time were not much different from John Dunton's. The sheets sent to London by the Clarendon Press may have added one stage to the process, with both Cadell and Dilly acting some part of the role of the earlier publishers. Probably Cadell filled the subscription orders of larger booksellers who had agreed to take multiple copies in sheets, acting as a warehouseman and no more. It was left to Dilly to have copies sewn in wrappers and boards, as well as bound in leather, before filling smaller orders from country booksellers and other retailers. Cadell would certainly have bound copies for his own shop, however, and perhaps for others as well. Both he and Dilly were well equipped to organize large-scale binding, and are known to have used the services of some of the best London bookbinders.[25] They may also have employed full-time journeymen, as did John Murray at about this time, with their employees operating the warehouses and carrying out edition binding, with finer work going out to independent high-class binderies.[26]

Bookbinding businesses offered quantity discounts for large orders, at least for simpler work, as both John Dunton and the 1743 and 1744 price lists testify. If such discounts followed the pattern of the "usual Allowance," they would have allowed the wholesale distributor to keep parallel accounts for his expenses and receipts. If Dilly arranged the binding, his ledger would have had multiple entries for copies sold in different bindings, something along the lines of an advertisement quoted earlier in this book, John Stockdale's for his 1785 edition of Shakespeare. Such entries would have included columns for copies of the same book in, *e.g.*, "boards, 15s.; calf, 17s.6d.; calf gilt, 18s.; Russia, 19s.; vellum, 21s.; morocco extra, 25s.; tortoiseshell, 63s."[27]

## II. DEFINING A PUBLISHER'S BINDING

Michael Sadleir defines a publisher's binding as "the form of envelope (be it of paper wrappers, paper boards, cloth or what not) in which any book was first issued by its publisher."[28] If we add to Sadleir's "envelope" all the different bindings described in Stockdale's advertisement, quoted above, and expand the term "publisher" to include its seventeenth- and eighteenth-century meaning, this is a perfectly adequate definition.

Surviving retail booksellers' accounts show their reliance on receiving copies from publishers in various bindings at fixed prices.[29] These included not only the simple leather denoted by the term "bound," but also boards and wrappers, and the wide variety of publisher's bindings advertised by Stockdale in 1785. But what guidelines are we to follow, and how are we to distinguish a publisher's binding from a trade binding?

I suggest there are two ways to identify a publisher's binding:

(1) Distinctive and consistent, preferably uniform, features in a group of bindings with the same bookseller's imprint; and/or,

(2) A clear link between the bindings and the commissioning bookseller or distributor, whether integral to the book, as in a printed paper label, or external, as in newspaper advertisements, the publisher's own catalogues, or other documentation.

One strong indication that a group of bindings was not bespoke (*i.e.* privately-commissioned) is the survival of multiple copies of one edition in the same binding. As paper bindings proliferated, beginning in the 1760s, boards and labels provide both consistent features and links to publishers. In the

Fig. 3.6.
Bindings for Charles Cooke
on two works by William
Dodd, *Thoughts in Prison*, and
*Reflections on Death*. London,
for C. Cooke, [no dates, but
the frontispieces are captioned,
respectively, 1796 and 1800],
18mo, tree calf, spines gilt
with red and green morocco
onlays including, at the foot,
"Cooke's Edition," a neat little
advertisement that appeared
on many of Cooke's bindings.

decades before boards and labels, however, links between bindings and publishers can usually be found only in the less reliable recurrence of distinctive binding features. Generally speaking, there is a greater likelihood of linking a binding to a single publisher. Books issued by syndicates were more likely to be distributed in sheets to multiple warehousemen. The result was that books appeared simultaneously in so many different bindings that attempting to distinguish publishers' from retail trade bindings will often be unproductive.[30]

As a trial run, let us employ these two criteria on 1790s bindings for Charles Cooke, shown in figure 3.6.

(1) Many of Cooke's bindings have uniform features: tree calf with double labels (the dark middle ones contained volume numbers when necessary). The spine ornaments are not always the same, but this ornamental circle often recurs.

(2) "Cooke's Edition" appears on a separate spine onlay, definitively linking the bindings to the publisher. No third-party retailer, let alone private customer, would incur the additional expense of such labels.

(3) Charles Cooke is a single bookseller, and these bindings are clearly his alone.

Publishers' bindings as readily identifiable as Cooke's are common enough in the nineteenth century, but rare before 1800. Nevertheless, samples of some other publishers' books, especially those from the last half of the eighteenth century, show similar recurring features.

## III. PUBLISHERS' BINDINGS OF THE
## LATER EIGHTEENTH CENTURY

The previous chapter showed how, by the mid-eighteenth century, common binding styles in calf and sheep employed less and less decoration, reaching a low point around 1760 when there were "very few Finishers . . . little or no finishing, except the lettering being required."[31] As publishers' paper boards became more common in the last quarter of the century, the alternative, more expensive, leather bindings began to receive additional decoration again, and continued to do so through the end of the century and after. John Stockdale's catalogue shows the range of materials publishers were willing to use to produce distinctive styles for upmarket bookshops.

John Bell's editions of Shakespeare, other British poets and playwrights, and what he called his "classics" are immediately recognizable from their bindings (fig. 3.7). Bell was one of the major beneficiaries of the 1774 House of Lords decision abolishing perpetual copyright. As one scholar puts it, Bell "seized the initiative" by immediately undertaking the publication of major series of works by earlier authors who had been released from copyright restrictions. Between 1776 and 1778 Bell issued a total of twenty-one volumes of *The British Theatre* in 6d. weekly parts. His *Poets of Great Britain Complete from Chaucer to Churchill*, published in partnership with the Martins of Edinburgh, began in 1777 and by 1792 had reached 109 1s. 6d. volumes.[32]

These two publications, along with Bell's Shakespeare (fig. 3.8), were enormously successful. Bell featured all three on his trade card, on which he declared that "Gentlemen *for their Libraries*, Merchants *and* Captains *of* Ships *for Exportation*, Booksellers *and* Shopkeepers *to sell again, may be*

Fig. 3.7.
"Bindings by John Bell,"
an illustration from
Stanley Morison's *John Bell,
1745–1831* (1930), following
p. 113. Reprinted with the
permission of Cambridge
University Press.

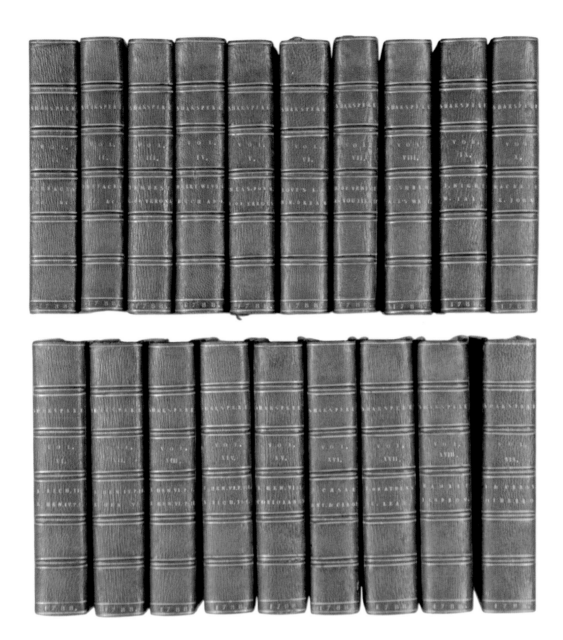

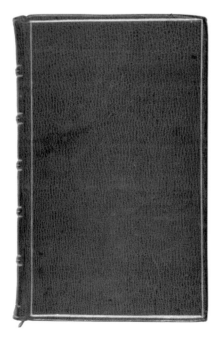

Fig. 3.8.
*The Dramatick Writings of Will.
Shakspere.* London, for, and
under the direction of, John
Bell, 1788, 20 vols., 12mo. The
unusual form of the imprint
shows how strongly Bell
wanted to identify himself
with the printing of this edition, and the bindings are
fine examples of Bell's austere
morocco. Courtesy of the Lilly
Library, Indiana University,
Bloomington, Indiana.

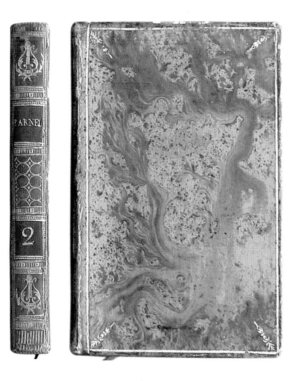

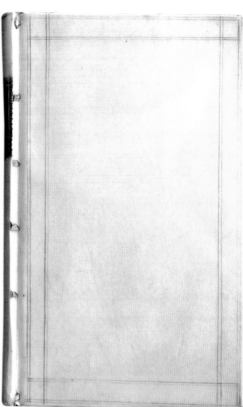

T. CARNAN and F. NEWBERY Jun. 5

19. A DESCRIPTION of ENGLAND and WALES. Containing a History of each County, with a particular Account of its Antiquities, Curiosities, Situation, Rivers, Soils, Cities, Towns, Seats, Sieges, Battles, and the Lives of the Illustrious Men each County has produced. Embellished with Two Hundred and Forty Copper-plate Cuts of Palaces, Castles, the Ruins of Roman and Saxon Buildings, Abbies, Monasteries, and other Religious Houses. Besides a Variety of Cuts of Urns, Inscriptions, and other Antiquities. In Ten Volumes. Price 1l. 15s. bound in the Vellum Manner, or 2l. in Calf and Lettered.

20. Elementary PRINCIPLES of the BELLES LETTRES. By M. Formey, Secretary to the Royal Academy at Berlin. Price 3s. bound.

21. Certain Ancient TRACTS concerning the Management of Landed Property re-printed. By Sir Anthony Fitzherbert. Price 4s. 6d. bound.

22. A GENERAL HISTORY of the WORLD, from the Creation to the present Time. Including all the Empires, Kingdoms and States; their Revolutions, Forms of Government, Laws, Religions, Customs, and Manners; the Progress of the Learning, Arts, Sciences, Commerce and Trade; together with their Chronology, Antiquities, Public Buildings, and Curiosities of Nature and Art. By William Guthrie, Esq. John Gray, Esq. and others eminent in this Branch of Literature, in Thirteen Vols. Price 3l. 10s. bound.

23. INTEREST TABLES, on an Improved Plan; shewing by Inspection, the legal Interest on every Sum from 1l. to 1000l. and from 1000l. to 10,000l. for 1 Day, to 30, 40, and 50 Days, and for 3, 6, 9, and 12 Months. Tables for 3, 3½, 4, 4½, 5, 5½, 6, 6½, 7, 7½, and 8 per Cent. per Annum, from 1l. to 10,000l. for 3, 6, 9, and 12 Months. A Table for 100l. at 3 per Cent. per Annum, from 1 Day to 365 Days, particularly useful to the Dealers in East India Company's Bonds. A Table of Discount at 6½ per Cent. the Allowance made by the East India Company to the Purchasers of Goods at their Sales, for Prompt Payment; calculated to the One Hundredth

Fig. 3.9.
Specimens of Bell bindings: tree calf gilt on a volume of *The Poets of Great Britain*, 1778, pot 12mo, "Bell's Edition," published in collaboration with the Martins of Edinburgh; and vellum, gilt-lettered on a painted label, on a volume of *Bell's Classical Arrangement of Fugitive Poetry*, 1789, pot 8vo.

Fig. 3.10.
*A Dictionary of the Bible*. London, for T. Carnan, and F. Newbery, 1777, 12mo. The calf binding is standard Newbery, and this work was advertised at 2s. 6d. bound. The page from the publishers' catalogue printed at the end of the volume shows the various bindings available on other publications, including, at the top, the "vellum manner" and calf options on *A Description of England and Wales*, shown in figure 3.11. Courtesy of the William Andrews Clark Memorial Library, University of California, Los Angeles.

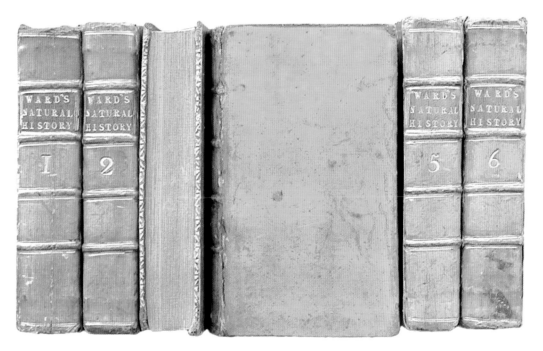

Fig. 3.11.
*A Description of England and Wales, with a Description of each County.* London, for Newbery and Carnan, 1769, 10 vols., 12mo. This set was advertised at "1£. 15s. bound in the Vellum Manner, or 2£. in Calf and Lettered." It is half-bound, with calf corners and marbled boards; binders economized on their use of leather whenever possible during times of shortage. The binding is typical Newbery, and was probably sold at the calf price of £2. 0s. Courtesy of the Lilly Library, Indiana University, Bloomington, Indiana.

Fig. 3.12.
Samuel Ward, *A Modern System of Natural History.* London, for F. Newbery, 1775–76, 12 vols. in six, pot 12mo, calf. This set was advertised at 18s. sewed, £1. 1s. in the "vellum manner," and £1. 4s. in calf, with the advertisements making clear that the twelve volumes of the set were bound in six, as shown here. They have been photographed with one volume turned edges outwards. The gilt edge-roll is quite distinctive, and may in due course help identify the work of some of Newbery's individual binders, all of whom, however, worked in this generic style.

*supplied on the most reasonable Terms, with* Books *in* Quires *or in the various Plain and Ornamental Bindings*."[33] Bell owned a large bookbindery, responsible for the "plain and ornamental bindings" he refers to in his advertisement. We even know the name of his head finisher in the 1780s, Thomas Fairbairn, who must have been largely responsible for the elegance of the best of these bindings. Fairbairn was one of the organizers of the 1786 bookbinders' strike, but he never had to go out, nor did any of Bell's employees, because Bell granted the requested work-hour reduction without argument.[34]

One of Bell's binding innovations was setting type in pallets in order more quickly to letter the spines on his many multi-volume sets; the regularity of the lettering is visible on the selection of bindings in figures 3.7–3.8.[35] Figure 3.9 shows a standard calf gilt and a more expensive vellum; decorated vellum reached its apogee at about this time in the work of the Edwards of Halifax bindery.

Charles Cooke and other booksellers followed Bell's lead. Bindings such as these point the way to the standardized edition bindings of the nineteenth century and beyond.

Perhaps the earliest publisher's binding style accepted by all scholars is the Newbery firm's "vellum manner," introduced in 1768 (fig. 3.1).[36] Newbery's advertising also refers to many of his publications as available both in the vellum manner and in more expensive leather bindings (figs. 3.10–3.12). Although generic, the style of these standard leather bindings is consistent, and survives in many examples; there is no doubt that it was the product of Newbery's own binders. It is these simply-decorated bindings in calf and sheep that point the way back to the earlier publishers' styles of the preceding century.

## IV. EARLIER PUBLISHERS' BINDINGS

When Newbery, Stockdale, Bell, Cooke, and other booksellers offered their books ready-bound in various materials and styles, some of them quite elegant, they were following a practice established at least as early as the Restoration. Fine bindings attracted customers into shops and were highly profitable when sold. Figure 3.13 shows an example by Richard Royston's binder: while it might be bespoke work, its presence on a later edition of a popular devotional work suggests the kind of ready-binding that booksellers "displayed on their counters to tempt customers who, like Pepys, had a weakness for fine bindings."[37] Samuel Mearne certainly had books ready-bound in decorated goatskin for sale in his shop; figure 1.10 illustrates two editions of the Mearnes' goatskin-bound Latin prayer-books.

Historically, fine bindings have been the subjects of scholarly research far more often than their simpler counterparts. Even so, most pre-1800 fine binders, like Royston's, remain unidentified, as do all but a very few ordinary craftsmen. Apart from John Dunton, booksellers and authors rarely, if ever, discussed their binders. The closest one gets is the occasional tantalizing hint, as when Robert Dodsley, writing to the poet William Shenstone in 1759, refers to two of the best binders of his era: "Roubique[t] is dead or dying, & Montagu I believe is near fourscore."[38]

Any binding that Robert Dodsley commissioned from Richard Montagu or John Roubiquet may have been for presentation, just as Thomas Knowles's special bindings were produced for copies of books "dedicated and presented" by John Dunton.[39] But Dodsley, the former footman who became a grand bookseller, would certainly have sold fine bindings in his shop for reasons of status as well as profit, just as Richard Royston and Samuel Mearne did and, later, John Stockdale and John Bell.

Finely decorated publishers' bindings can provide important links to binders' simpler work on

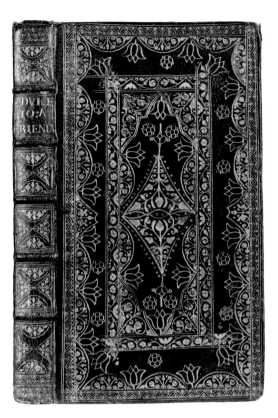

Fig. 3.13.
Simon Patrick, *Advice to a Friend*. London, Printed for R. Royston, 1677, 12mo, third edition. This elegant red goatskin is by a binder who appears to have been "closely associated with Richard Royston." Maggs Bros. Ltd., *Bookbinding in the British Isles*, Catalogue 1212 (1996), item 59. A number of the same tools on this binding appear on two other goatskin bindings on Royston publications. Courtesy of Maggs Bros. Ltd.

calf and sheep. Howard Nixon has identified the same tools on various bindings for John Brindley. Brindley was established as a bookbinder in London in 1723, and in 1728 he moved to Bond Street and set himself up as a bookseller as well. His bindings were sufficiently distinguished to earn him a royal appointment; he also bound for Sir Isaac Newton. According to Nixon, comparison of presentation bindings on Brindley publications in King George III's library "with other presentation bindings at Windsor, with Brindley books from the library of Mr George Smith sold at Sotheby's on 22 July 1959, and with sets of the duodecimo classics published by Brindley between 1744 and 1754 (fig. 3.14), enables us to identify many of the tools used in his shop and some of its specialities."[40]

Less consistently fine, but competent and often interesting bindings were produced by Robert and Andrew Foulis of Glasgow, whose bindery is recorded in 1770 as occupying "two College rooms, which suggests a considerable volume of work."[41] The Foulises began publishing small volumes of classical texts in the early 1740s, contemporaneously with Brindley, and they occasionally produced some virtuoso printings. The Anacreon edition (fig. 3.15) is a copy on paper bound for the Foulises, but they also produced a few copies on silk, also in miniature format.

Links between fine and ordinary publishers' bindings are helpful when they can be found, but do little to identify the vast majority of earlier publishers' bindings, which were executed by journeymen binders in calf and sheep, and with only the simplest of tools. Without supporting evidence, such bindings are difficult to distinguish from trade work for retailers. When Pepys went to John Martin's shop and bought a literary work with Martin's name in the imprint, he was buying it in a publisher's binding. But if he bought a Martin imprint at Samuel Mearne's shop, Pepys was almost certain to get a copy which had been delivered to Mearne in sheets, and then bound by him: a retail binding (fig. 3.16). The more we learn to distinguish earlier publishers' and retail bindings, the more knowledge we will

Fig. 3.14.
Virgil, *Opera*. London, typis J. Brindley, 1744, one of Brindley's duodecimo classics, here in the publisher's handsome mottled calf gilt. Brindley also advertised this series, more expensively, as "ready bound in Morocco, Blue Turkey, white Cambridge Bindings &c. marbled on the leaves." And because Brindley anticipated printing "many volumes of the Classics," he offered to keep "printed Patterns" of the "different Sorts of Bindings that Gentlemen may have them all bound uniform. . . ."

The advertisement appears at the end of Brindley's 1744 edition of Cornelius Nepos, and is quoted by Esther Potter, "To Paul's Churchyard to Treat with a Bookbinder," in *Property of a Gentleman*, ed. Robin Myers and Michael Harris (1991), p. 32. Courtesy of Department of Special Collections, Stanford University Libraries.

Fig. 3.15.
Anacreon, Sappho, and Alcaeus, *Odes* [etc., in Greek]. Glasgow, Excudebant R. & A. Foulis, 1751, 32mo, goatskin with the Foulis bindery's characteristic crosses in the spine compartments. Courtesy of Department of Special Collections, Stanford University Libraries.

Fig. 3.16.
*The Life and Philosophy of Epictetus*, translated by John Davies. London, for John Martyn, 1670, pot 8vo, goatskin by Samuel Mearne's bindery, with his gilt royal cypher in the spine compartments. Although possibly bespoke, this binding's simplicity suggests that multiples were produced for sale in Mearne's shop, on sheets he acquired from Martin either through syndication, purchase, or exchange. Courtesy of the William Andrews Clark Memorial Library, University of California, Los Angeles.

Fig. 3.17.
John Milton, *Paradise Lost.*
London, Printed, and are to
be sold by Peter Parker . . .
Robert Boulter . . . and
Mathias Walker, 1667, pot
4to, one of at least four
copies in strikingly similar,
albeit generic, sheep bindings, and all with the same
variant of the title-page
imprint. An illustration of
one of these other copies
appears in the Sotheby's New
York catalogue *The Library of
Richard Manney,* October 11,
1991, lot 233; the other two
are described in *The Carl H.
Pforzheimer Library, English
Literature* (1940, reprint
1997), item 716, and the
Christie's catalogue, *Books
and Manuscripts from the
Library of Arthur A. Houghton,
Jnr.,* June 11, 1980, lot 313.
Courtesy of the Lilly Library,
Indiana University,
Bloomington, Indiana.

gain, not only about those booksellers' wholesale and retail trade, but also about the way individual buyers, such as Pepys, patronized specific shops.

Occasionally copies of the same edition of a book survive in identical or closely similar bindings.
If we accept that such bindings were executed at the same workshop (though with generic tools such
as simple fillets it is not always easy to be sure) and if the number of surviving copies exceeds a dozen,
that is surely satisfactory evidence of a publisher's binding. But what if the surviving copies number only
three or four? A tantalizing example from Pepys's time is the 1667 issue of the first edition of John
Milton's *Paradise Lost* (fig. 3.17). The binding shown here closely resembles at least three other copies.
Were they retail bindings, or publishers' bindings commissioned by the syndicate and sold wholesale?
Is identifying the uniformity of a few copies within an edition sufficient to support an identification of a
publisher's binding, given the low survival rate of popular seventeenth- and eighteenth-century books
in original condition? These are questions not easily answered.[42]

The guidelines set forth earlier in this chapter suggest that publishers' bindings may be more
readily found on books printed for a single bookseller, especially one with a link to the bindings in catalogues and advertisements. Ideally such a bookseller would have commissioned bindings himself rather
than sold sheets to individual retailers, and controlled as many other aspects of production and distribution as possible. One nearly-ideal candidate is the firm of Francis and John Noble, who published novels and other popular literature from the 1740s through the 1780s. The Nobles commissioned, printed,
bound, sold, and lent to the London and provincial reading public. They so effectively managed all

aspects of their business that they were able consistently to advertise and sell virtually all their books ready-bound at stated prices. They also had excellent sources of supply: in 1769 they boasted that many of their novels were "written by persons of rank, property, and fortune, above accepting any other return for their labours than a few printed copies for themselves and friends."[43]

In his study of eighteenth-century circulating libraries, James Raven notes that just before mid-century, "shifting consumer tastes and innovations in book trades business techniques combined to promote book-reading on an unprecedented scale."[44] Commercial circulating libraries, which received a strong push from the growing popularity of novels beginning with Samuel Richardson's *Pamela* in 1741, were among the most successful of these techniques. The Nobles' large and successful circulating libraries gave them good reason to keep quantities of their publications available ready-bound. Such copies could be sold as gifts, and also to customers who either preferred to own, or who were unwilling to wait for the return of copies already lent. In addition to advertising their novels as sold bound, the Nobles published statements (some of which cite disputes with other traders) to the effect that they were directly distributing ready-bound copies of their publications to London and country booksellers.

Two such statements appear in the 1774 novel *The Assignation*. The first is at the beginning of a 104-item catalogue: "Every Article in the following Catalogue is marked as it is sold *bound*, unless otherwise expressed." No more than three items in the catalogue are "otherwise expressed." The second is an "Advertisement" by the Nobles explaining their refusal to let "Mr. Baldwin, the Publisher of the *London Magazine*," have any more of their books until he retracts an "impudent Falshood asserted in his Magazine for December, 1772." They go on:

> We have sufficient reason to believe, that Orders coming from the Country to him, and perhaps others his Colleagues, will not be complied with, and various malicious and false Pretences assigned for so doing; we hereby acquaint all Country Dealers and Others, that, by sending a Stage-Coachman, or other Person, to our Shops, they will be immediately supplied at the *London Prices* with *any Books of our own Printing*, on paying ready Money for the same.
>
> F. Noble,
>
> J. Noble.
>
> P. S. As we sell for ready Money only, letters directed to us for Credit will be needless.

The next year, in an "Advertisement" at the end of Vol. I of their novel *He is Found at Last: or, Memoirs of the Beverley Family*, the Nobles offer a further enticement to "Country Dealers and others," repeating the offer of London prices for ready money, but offering a discount:

> That those who take 25 Volumes or more of *different Sorts*, will have the same Allowance as is usually made for the same Number, when only one Sort is taken; by which there will be a Saving to the Buyer of more than *fourteen per Cent*.

What did the Nobles mean by this, and why the "fourteen per Cent"? This is carefully chosen language, and because it appears in a novel and would have been read by not only booksellers but also the general reading public, it is likely to have two meanings. In the context of a country bookseller's order, it means that the Nobles will give the bookseller not only the retailer's discount of 3s. in the pound, but also the distributor's discount and the quarterly book. In other words, for every pound of retail value purchased, the bookseller will get an additional 2s. cash discount (ten percent), plus the quarterly book, *i.e.* 26 for the price of 25, an additional saving of four percent: exactly the fourteen percent suggested by the Nobles.[45] The discount also applied to private orders. If an individual sent a coachman to town with ready cash to purchase the same quantity, he would get the quarterly book plus a ten percent cash discount, but not the extra fifteen percent given to retailers. If the Nobles were not selling their books ready-bound as advertised, none of these discounts would make sense to readers, nor would there be much appeal in sending a coachman with ready money to buy a collection of unbound sheets.

All of this advertising does not suggest that the Nobles were unusual in selling their books ready-bound. It rather suggests—just as the "price bound" advertising in the aftermath of the Great Fire of 1666 did—that the Nobles were trying a new way of *marketing* their books. Their catalogue descriptions and other statements make the strategy clear: cut out the middlemen, in this case the wholesale distributors, by selling directly to country retailers and, when possible, to consumers. It is our good fortune that this advertising also throws light on a standard trade practice, ready-binding.

The Nobles' advertising provides as strong a link between a mid-eighteenth-century publishing house and its bindings as one could wish. It therefore seems logical that a representative selection of books published by the Nobles in their original bindings would present some consistent and distinctive features. Finding such a selection proved no easy task, however. The Nobles' books were aimed at a popular audience and were so widely read that most of them survive in no more than two or three copies and—to make the odds even worse—many of these have been rebound. The Nobles published over a hundred different titles, in editions probably averaging five hundred or so copies. This meant a total output of some 50,000 copies, of which perhaps 250 have survived, a rate (disregarding the problem of rebound copies) of about one in two hundred.

Nevertheless, a pattern of identifiable publishers' bindings has emerged. The Nobles published mostly novels, mostly in duodecimo, usually two volumes, never more than four. Throughout the 1750s and '60s they were sold in common calf bindings at 3s. per volume—the most basic kind of trade work.[46] Three well-preserved examples of these common bindings show the work of three different binders. Each one is offered as a prototype, and compared with bindings on other Noble publications. The three are: figure 3.18 *True Merit, True Happiness*; figure 3.19 *Memoirs of the Shakespear's-Head*; and figure 3.20 *The Muse in Good Humour*.

It may be argued that these three bindings are too generic to allow productive comparison. Taken one at a time, such things as the presence or absence of gilt fillets, the pattern of an edge roll, the nature of the sprinkle on a calfskin, or the look of lettering and volume numbering, are unremarkable. But a combination of some or all of these elements can go a long way towards identifying a particular binder's work, and is sometimes the only available approach. Other binders' work can be associated through the appearance of one or more distinctive tools. Both these approaches are taken in the comparisons below.

The binder of the illustrated copy of *True Merit, True Happiness* (fig. 3.18), for example, also bound the British Library's copy of *The Muse in Moral Humour*, 2 vols. (1758).[47] The calf on the latter is darker, but the sprinkle, gilt double-line fillet, and edge-roll are the same. The same binder also bound

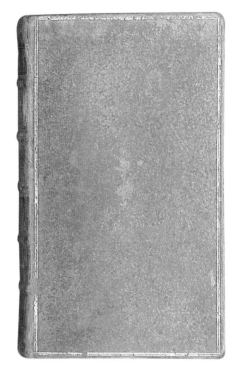

Fig. 3.18.
*True Merit, True Happiness,*
*Exemplified in the Entertaining*
*and Instructive Memoirs of*
*Mr. S —.* London, for Francis
Noble, and John Noble, [undated,
but 1757], 2 vols., 12mo.
Sprinkled calf gilt. Courtesy
of Department of Special
Collections, Charles E. Young
Research Library, University of
California, Los Angeles.

Fig. 3.19.
*Memoirs of the Shakespear's-*
*Head in Covent-Garden: in*
*which are introduced Many enter-*
*taining Adventures. By the Ghost*
*of Shakespear.* London, for
F. Noble, and J. Noble, 1755,
2 vols., 12mo. Sprinkled calf
gilt. Courtesy of Department
of Special Collections, Charles
E. Young Research Library,
University of California, Los
Angeles.

Fig. 3.20.
*The Muse in Good Humour.*
London, for F. Noble, and
J. Noble, 1751–57, 2 vols.,
12mo, sixth edition of Volume I
(which was first published sepa-
rately), first edition of Volume
II. Uniform sprinkled calf gilt.
The set is advertised in the
publisher's catalogue at the end
of this second volume, and else-
where, as "The Muse in Good
Humour. A Collection of Comic
Tales, 2 vols. 6s. bound."

the Beinecke Library's copies of *The Voyages, Travels, and Wonderful Adventures of Capt. John Holmesby* [1757], and *Memoirs of the Shakespear's-Head*, 2 vols. (1755), this last indicating that, as one would expect, copies of any given edition were sent to multiple binders to insure that as many as possible were ready for sale on publication date.[48]

A second binder, identifiable from his distinctive gilt edge-roll, bound the illustrated copy of *Memoirs of the Shakespear's-Head* (fig. 3.19). He also bound, and his edge-roll recurs on, the British Library copies of *The History of Miss Clarinda Cathcart, and Miss Fanny Renton*, 2 vols. (1766) and *Northern Memoirs: or, the History of a Scotch Family. Written by a Lady* [Mrs. Woodfin], 2 vols., [undated, but 1756]. The former has a gilt double-line fillet and volume numbers on the spines, and a similar light sprinkle on the boards; the latter has been rebacked, but the recurrence of the edge-roll is evidence that the rebacking was done with the book's original covers.

Finally, a third binder, responsible for the illustrated copy of *The Muse in Good Humour* (fig. 3.20), also bound the Bodleian Library's single volume (Vol. II is missing) of *The Muse in a Moral Humour* (1757); both the distinctive gilt edge-roll, and the slightly curved volume number "1" are identical. He also bound the Beinecke Library copy of *The Muse in Good Humour* (1751), the same sixth edition as that in figure 3.20, but issued before the second volume was published, and so without any number on the spine.

These recurring features, even on this small sample of bindings, are sufficient to show that cer-tain binders were consistently employed by the Nobles. The varying decorations described above would not have been commissioned by a single customer, and the fact that the same craftsmen produced both ordinary and extra gilt bindings shows that the Nobles, like booksellers before and after, had their nov-els bound in different styles. If the retail prices were the same 3s. per volume, it seems most likely that the Nobles sold the decorated copies in their own shops, and sent plain copies to other town and coun-try booksellers to whom they had to offer trade discounts.

Other copies of Noble novels are puzzling, and act as reminders that the enormous variety of surviving bindings will never allow themselves to be thoroughly categorized. *The Jilts: or, Female Fortune-Hunters*, 3 vols. [undated, but also 1756] was published with "Price 9s. Bound" on the title-page, and the British Library copy is bound in polished calf gilt, with red and green spine labels and marbled endpapers. It has a gilt edge-roll very similar, but not identical to that shown in figure 3.19, *Memoirs of the Shakespear's-Head*; these rolls, like most bookbinding tools, are found in a number of standard patterns which were copied and circulated around the trade. This copy originally belonged to Francis Longe; it has his engraved bookplate on the front pastedown, and the gilt lion crest he had stamped on the covers of all his bindings, old and new.[49] The binding is more a 1770s style than 1750s, but the Nobles continued to advertise *The Jilts* and other 1750s novels in their catalogues, at the same 3s. per volume bound, well into the 1780s. Longe may have taken a publisher's binding and added not only the gilt lion, but labels uniform with those on other books in his library; these were standard embellishments for which many traveling bookbinders advertised their services. But Longe may also have bespoke the binding, as he apparently did for some other novels in his library. A census and comparison of bindings from his now widely-dispersed library may lead to some resolution of this problem.

Two other Noble novels present another mystery: the British Library copies of *The Adopted Daughter*, 2 vols. (1767), and *The Assignation. A Sentimental Novel. In a Series of Letters*, 2 vols. (1774). The two were bound by the same binder in tree calf, with one spine tool repeated on both sets, and the two sets of labels matching. Both have two bookplates, an early one "William Bellingham, Esq.," and a Victorian one "Bellingham Castle Library." The two novels were almost certainly bound at the same time, in 1774 or later, and they could have been part of a single purchase from the Nobles, either directly or through another bookseller. Were these an example of the "calf, lettered and gilt" advertised by the Nobles or of bindings bespoke by William Bellingham? As with Francis Longe's library, the first step to a solution of this problem is a census and comparison of Bellingham's surviving books.

Two booksellers from the earlier eighteenth century also seem certain to have been engaged in publisher's binding, though dozens more deserve fuller investigation. James Woodward, the folio binder who desired John Dunton's custom, was also a bookseller, and in the first years of the eighteenth century Woodward normally published in syndicates. According to Ellic Howe, Woodward signed one of his bindings "Iames Woodward Booke-binder in Threadnedel Street in Christophers Churchyard bound this Booke." This was an unusual action for a bookbinder at that time.[50] Conceivably Woodward also used a floral corner tool with the initials "I.W.," which has been seen on a number of calf bindings of the same period (*e.g.*, fig. 2.16). As David Pearson's research shows, however, "I.W." has strong connections to Cambridge, and a substantial number of surviving bindings on Latin and English books, some of them with Cambridge imprints, suggest that "I.W." was an independent binder working for booksellers and private customers with academic leanings. Nevertheless, Woodward seems to be the only recorded bookseller/bookbinder with sufficient stature to have commissioned such a tool, assuming the initials stand for a name, and not a phrase or motto.[51]

Later, Woodward's name appears as the sole imprint on several books, and figure 3.21 shows the binding of one of these, with a floral corner tool significantly without the "I.W." initials. The "price bound" statement is an unusually early example, and is also interesting because the title leaf itself is a

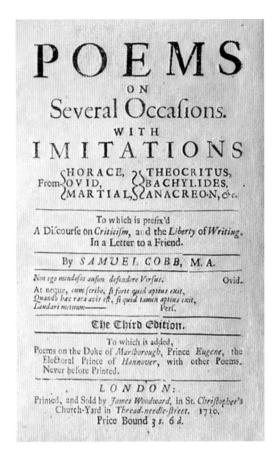

# POEMS

ON

Several Occasions.

WITH

# IMITATIONS

From ⟨ HORACE, ⟩ ⟨ THEOCRITUS,
OVID, ⟩ ⟨ BACHYLIDES,
MARTIAL, ⟩ ⟨ ANACREON, &c.

To which is prefix'd
A Discourse on *Criticism*, and the *Liberty of Writing*.
In a Letter to a Friend.

By *SAMUEL COBB*, M.A.

*Non ego mendosos ausim defendere Versus.*     Ovid.

*At neque, cum scribo, si forte quid aptius exit,
Quando hæc rara avis est, si quid tamen aptius exit,
Laudari metuam———*     Pers.

## The Third Edition.

To which is added,
Poems on the Duke of *Marlborough*, Prince *Eugene*, the
Electoral Prince of *Hannover*, with other Poems.
Never before Printed.

*LONDON:*
Printed, and Sold by *James Woodward*, in St. *Christopher's*
Church-Yard in *Thread-needle-street*. 1710.
Price Bound 3 s. 6 d.

Fig. 3.21.
Samuel Cobb, *Poems on
Several Occasions*, 1710, 8vo,
calf, the third issue of the
first edition, first published
in 1707 by Rebecca and
James Bonwick. Edmund
Curll reissued these sheets in
1709 with a cancel title and
some additions at the end,
and Woodward must have
acquired his remainder from
Curll, as it contains the
additions not present in the
Bonwick publication.

Fig. 3.22.
Sir Francis Bacon, *The Essays
or Counsels, Civil and Moral*.
London, for Samuel Mearne,
1680, 8vo, calf. This gilt spine
is typical of the period; the
covers have only a simple
blind fillet. If executed by
Mearne—calf bindings on
his publications deserve much
fuller investigation—it is
another example of an early
publisher's binding. Courtesy
of the William Andrews
Clark Memorial Library,
University of California, Los
Angeles.

cancellans. Woodward bought the sheets and had his own title printed, which with its "price bound" suggests that he also bound the sheets himself. The binding is definitely not the work of an innovator; it is stylistically similar to the binding on Samuel Mearne's 1680 edition of Bacon's *Essays* (fig. 3.22), and also to the Pepys bindings in Nixon's style F (fig. 1.14). All have red goatskin spine labels, and the other spine compartments are tooled with French corners and a central cross. Although other books were published under Woodward's sole imprint (see, *e.g.*, fig. 4.13), this appears to be the only one with a "price bound" statement on the title. Unfortunately, figure 3.21 depicts one of only four surviving copies. Of the other three, one is in contemporary blind-paneled sheep, another in what appears to be circa 1720–1730 undecorated calf, and the third in marbled boards with a new spine.[52] One would like to see at least one other identical binding to support the thesis that Woodward acted as his own binder, yet the essentially random survival of old books means that only with a great deal of luck can one expect to find a pattern in such a small sample. It is possible that the calf extra binding in figure 3.21 was produced for sale in Woodward's own shop, and that the sheep was for the wholesale trade. Conceivably Woodward might also have bound the copy in later calf; he was still in business in the 1720s. But of course he may also have sold copies in sheets to other retailers, both in 1710 and later, and there may well have been unbound copies in his stock at the time of his death, which would have been dispersed in the trade by auction. With only four, quite different, copies to compare, all one can do is speculate.

Jacob Tonson, the most important literary publisher of England's Augustan age, is also known to have had a bindery. It is not clear from surviving records exactly at what point the bindery became part of Tonson's business, but it seems likely it was no later than the time he acquired his brother's bookselling business in 1698.[53] By this time Tonson was regarded as a literary lion, a status achieved by his printing "the pompous Folio Edition with Cuts" of Milton's *Paradise Lost* in 1688, and by becoming John Dryden's primary bookseller. He was also a major player, if not the leader, in the most important of the booksellers' publishing syndicates.[54]

The workings of syndicates, discussed earlier in this chapter, help to identify Tonson's bindery. Figure 3.23 shows three bindings with tool impressions suggesting that all may have come from the same bindery. But the booksellers' names on each title-page are different. The three are doubtless trade bindings. So how would such different imprints come to be bound by the same bookbindery?

The answer is to be found in Tonson's links both to Dryden and to other booksellers with shares in Dryden's works, some of whom are named in the imprints of the three works illustrated here. Because copyrights were normally owned by booksellers in shares, and sold and traded among them, Tonson was able to acquire shares in Dryden copyrights both by private treaty and at booksellers' private auctions.

Once Tonson became a member of the booksellers' syndicate, there were settled arrangements for distributing books he and his partners had printed. I have described how copies were delivered by the printer in sheets to warehouses operated by bookbinders, from which either unbound or bound copies could be distributed to partners and to other booksellers. Tonson no doubt used his considerable clout as a leader of the syndicate to control the distribution of Dryden's works, probably keeping the syndicate's sheets in his own warehouse. His bookbinder/warehousemen could have ready-bound copies always on hand for delivery both to Tonson's retail shop and to those members of the trade willing to accept ready-bound copies.[55]

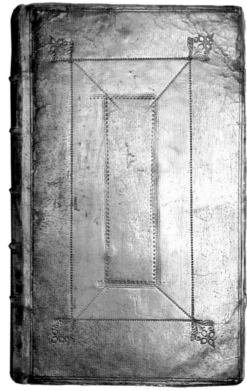

Fig. 3.23.
Charles du Fresnoy, *De Arte Graphica. The Art of Painting*, translated by John Dryden. London, J. Heptinstall for W. Rogers, 1695, foolscap 4to. The paneled calf cover shown here has a floral corner tool and gilt edge-roll. The same edge-roll is on the two other bindings shown here. To the right is Dryden's translation of Juvenal's *Satires*. London, for Jacob Tonson, 1697, 8vo, second edition, with a slightly different corner tool. At the bottom is John Dryden, *Comedies, Tragedies, and Operas*. London, for Daniel Brown, Benjamin Tooke, and George Strahan, 1701, folio, with the same corner tool as the du Fresnoy, but rather more worn, as one would expect after another six years of use. These tools were also used on a set of collective volumes of Dryden's plays in quarto, issued by Tonson in the 1690s, for which see figure 4.9. All three photographs courtesy of the William Andrews Clark Memorial Library, University of California, Los Angeles.

# V. PAPER BINDINGS

## 1. BOARDS

Boards, whether drab, blue, gray, or marbled, are almost invariably considered publishers' bindings as long as they retain their original features, especially the untrimmed leaf edges of the books they contain (fig. 3.24). One scholar, however, sounds a cautionary note. Were board bindings "produced by publishers, booksellers, or a combination of both. . . ? Were all boarded copies of the work produced in a uniform edition at the direction of the same person, whether publisher or bookseller, or were there variations depending on who ordered the binding and when?"[56]

This section considers these questions, and concludes that the vast majority of late-eighteenth-century boarded copies are true publishers' bindings, which is to say produced for commissioning booksellers or syndicates, or for wholesale distributors, rather than for retail traders or private customers. Although variations in board styles on copies of the same edition are regularly seen, there are two reasons for this. First, there was no need to produce an exact match of materials for every copy, and so drab, blue, or gray paper could be used interchangeably on the sides, according to stocks on hand. Some publishers also used a slightly heavier-grade cream paper for the spines, but not always. Second, as with all publishing at this time, entire editions were rarely bound at once, so copies later bound and issued from the warehouse could have a somewhat different appearance.

Board bindings were only one of many available options for book buyers in the middle of the eighteenth century. From about 1750 into the 1760s untrimmed copies in boards usually had a sheep or calf spine. During the 1760s this style began to shift towards cheaper paper spines, although calf or sheep remained in use for circulating libraries where a more durable binding was required.[57] The increase in the use of paper got a boost from the leather shortages of the late 1760s. An advertisement in the *London Chronicle* in May 1768 encouraged "Gentlemen to have their Books done up in Boards, or sewed in blue Paper" as a means of restraining the "exorbitant and repeated rise" in the price of leather.[58] The same problem arose in Dublin, driven both by leather shortages and by rises in the cost of labor. In 1766, the Dublin bookbinders introduced a new scale of binding prices (of which no copy survives), but it was apparently the first revision since the price list of 1743. This created a conflict between bookbinders and booksellers. By May 1768, the Dublin booksellers were sufficiently frustrated that they repeated the advice of the *London Chronicle* advertisement: customers should have their books bound in boards.[59] The year 1768 was also when the Newbery firm introduced its well-known bindings "in the vellum manner."

While the 1770s saw the increasing use of boards, some with printed paper spine labels, the common bindings of calf and sheep were still sufficiently prevalent that the 1779 *General Catalogue of Books . . . with their Sizes and Prices* could assume that readers knew the prices referred to such bound copies; only the occasional exception was cited, where necessary, as "sewed."[60] Figure 3.25 shows the ordinary per-volume price for novels at this time, which corresponds to the prices in the *General Catalogue*, and to the "price bound" charged by the Nobles.

In the 1780s boards became increasingly popular, and by the 1790s they began to supplant other forms of binding and became a standard form of issue. This transition is made clear from the inclusion of an entry for "boarding" one thousand sets of the two-volume Gay's *Fables* (1793), at 2s. 6d. the set, in John Stockdale's accounting to his fellow syndicate members for the expenses of that edition.[61]

THE

SURRY COTTAGE.

❖❖❖❖❖❖❖❖❖❖❖❖❖

By JAMES PENN,

Vicar of Clavering cum Langley, Eſſex;
Chaplain to the Right Hon. Earl Gower,
and Lecturer of St. Ann's, Alderſgate.

❖❖❖❖❖❖❖❖❖❖

LONDON:

Printed for, and ſold by the Author in Wildernefs
Row, Goſwell Street, and Mr. Bladon in
Paternoſter-Row.

❖❖❖❖❖❖❖

MDCCLXXIX.

Price 2s. 6d. unbound, and 3s. bound.

ℐ

Fig. 3.24.
*The Child of Nature, improved
by Chance. A Philosophical Novel.
By Mr. Helvetius.* London, for
T. Becket, 1774, 2 vols., 12mo,
untrimmed in blue boards, advertised at "5s. sewed" and "6s.
bound." This is an original
English novel; "Mr. Helvetius,"
intended to remind the reader of
the philosopher Claude-Adrien
Helvétius, is a fiction. Collection
of William Zachs.

Fig. 3.25.
Not many title-pages provide
such a helpful guide to binding
practice and prices. Presumably
the author, who published this
single-volume novel himself,
wanted to make matters entirely
clear. His prices are standard for
duodecimo novels of the period.

The transition to boards as standard issue was virtually complete by the beginning of the nineteenth century. The bookseller William Bent, in his *Modern Catalogue of Books, 1792–1802* (1803), wrote that the prices in his previous catalogue of 1800 were for copies "*bound*, in the common manner," that is to say in sheep or calf. But in this catalogue the books "are to be understood (unless otherwise mentioned) as *sewed* or *in boards*, which is now the most usual way that new publications are sold."[62] Bent went on to note that other bindings in sheep and calf remained available, and he gave their prices,[63] but when Bent was writing in December 1803, it was clear that the changeover to boards was so widespread as to be settled practice.[64]

From 1750 or so onwards, "sewed" or "in boards" were often used interchangeably. "Boards" of course did not mean "wrappers," but "sewed" could mean either wrappers or boards. This is made clear in a letter by Samuel Johnson's friend James Fordyce. Writing to his bookseller Thomas Cadell, Fordyce enclosed a list of people to whom presentation copies should be sent, discussed the special binding for those copies, and went on to declare his preference that "the *Sewed* copies should be in *Pasteboard* covered with a *light Grey*" (fig. 3.26).[65] "Sewed" and "boards" consistently appear at the same price in advertisements from 1750–1800. Copies in wrappers may have been distributed wholesale to booksellers intending to put them in leather bindings (fig. 3.27), and when wrapped copies were sold retail many certainly went directly to bespoke binders. Boarded copies were for booksellers intending to sell them just as they were.

Stockdale's accounts and Bent's catalogue demonstrate that, by the 1790s at least, boards were well established as publishers' bindings, even if the transition from the leather standard was not complete. What prompted the changeover? The last half of the eighteenth century saw not only an increasing number of new publications, but also many large editions requiring more and more uniform bindings to be commissioned at one time. As the number of books being bound at one time grew larger, the booksellers and distributors footing the substantial bills for these bindings looked for more ways both to economize and to improve their profit margins. One answer was boards.

James Raven also notes "the new vulnerability and rivalry" of the trade in the aftermath of the 1774 abolition of perpetual copyright, another reason for booksellers to try to cut their binding costs.[66] The American Revolution and Napoleonic Wars continually drained supplies of leather, already in short supply as the booksellers' advertisements of the 1760s testified. One result was an ever-increasing number of half leather bindings supplied as "bound" copies. Another, later, result was the public recognition by booksellers that leather bindings were no longer the standard form of issue. Surely it is no accident that Bent's December 1803 catalogue preface describing the shift to "sewed" and "boards" came at the exact time the British most feared a French invasion.

Taking novels, once again, as a microcosm of the book trade, we can trace both the shift to board bindings and the booksellers' determination to protect their profits through the progression of their advertisements in London periodicals. From the first flowering of the English novel in Samuel Richardson's *Pamela* (1741), the settled price for a duodecimo novel was 2s. 6d. per volume sewed or in boards, and 3s. per volume bound.[67] As novels became increasingly popular—around twenty new titles were published per year in the early 1750s, rising to around forty in 1770, and nearly 100 in 1799[68]—and as their formulaic nature became clear, addicted readers may have come to see the permanence of a

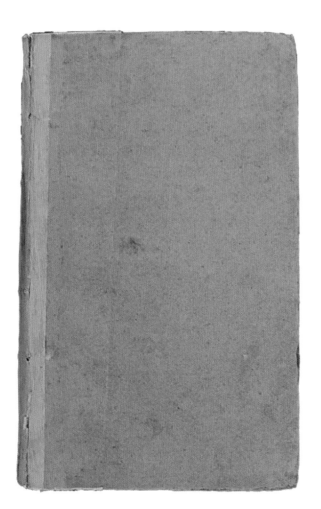

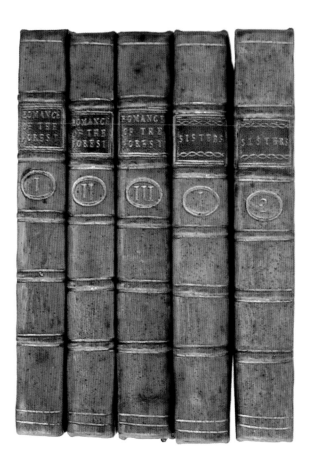

Fig. 3.26.
Hester Lynch Piozzi, *Observations through France, Italy, and Germany*. London, for A. Strahan, and T. Cadell, 1789, 2 vols., 8vo, "in *Pasteboard* covered with a *light Grey*." The cream paper on the backstrips is heavier than the paper covering the boards, to give the spines a little more durability. Courtesy of Department of Special Collections, Stanford University Libraries.

Fig. 3.27.
Left to right: Ann Radcliffe, *The Romance of the Forest*. London, for Hookham and Carpenter, 1791, 3 vols., 12mo; and Elizabeth Hervey, *Melissa and Marcia; or, the Sisters*. London, for W. Lane, 1788, 2 vols., 12mo. Both novels were advertised at 3s. per volume, "sewed." This could be the retail bookshop's standard look, half calf with marbled paper covers and simply gilt spines, or perhaps a purchaser bought them in boards or wrappers, and later sent them along with other novels for uniform binding. If they were a private commission one might not expect to see the discrepancy in the volume numbering (roman on one set, arabic on the other), but consistency is not necessarily a hallmark either of trade or bespoke binding. Collection of William Zachs.

leather binding as unnecessary. Wealthy readers, for whom 2s. 6d. per volume was pocket change, probably treated their novels much the same way modern readers treat their beach paperbacks; the lower reading classes, for whom the purchase of a novel was a major expense, were probably glad to save the extra sixpence.[69] By the end of the eighteenth century, the earlier ready-bound percentages for popular literature were largely turned on their head: probably eighty percent of such books were sold in wrappers and boards, and the remaining twenty percent in the old-style leather bindings, both plain and ornamental.[70]

Before 1780, books were normally advertised in newspapers and journals with no mention of binding style unless they were offered sewed or in boards. As early as 1753 and 1754 the various volumes of the duodecimo edition of *Sir Charles Grandison* were advertised at 2s. 6d. whether sewed or in boards, at a time when almost all duodecimo novels were advertised at 3s. per volume with no binding specified. Clearly these unspecified advertisements referred to bound copies, just as did the prices in general catalogues. When bookseller/library proprietors like Thomas Lownds and Francis and John Noble began to offer alternative bindings in the 1760s, their advertisements were careful to specify "sewed" for the lower priced volumes, as can be seen in Lownds's notice for Mrs. Woodfin's *The Discovery*, 2 vols. (1764), advertised at 5s. "sewed" in the *Critical Review*, and at 6s. with no binding stated in the *Monthly Review*. The Nobles, in keeping with their usual practice, specified both styles, advertising *The History of Mrs. Drayton and her Two Daughters*, 3 vols. (1767), in the same journals at 7s. 6d. sewed and 9s. bound. As the demand for bound copies dwindled, booksellers gradually eliminated "bound" prices from advertising notices, and the identical pricing for sewed and boarded copies of duodecimo novels became even more apparent. To cite one of countless examples, Susanna Rowson's *Victoria, a Novel*, 2 vols. (1786), was advertised in the *Critical Review* at 5s. in boards, and in the *Monthly Review* and the *London Evening Post* at 5s. sewed. Similar advertisements by many different booksellers became standard in the 1790s.

The booksellers' moves to protect their profits can also be seen in these same advertisements, beginning in the late 1780s and continuing through the 1790s. The upward trend in prices, as well as the larger-scale shift to boards, began in 1786. One contributing factor must have been the bookbinders' strike of that year. In the spring, more than eighty journeymen binders were dismissed when they went on strike to seek a reduction in their daily hours from fourteen to thirteen. One of the strikers reported that the booksellers had consented to take books in boards instead of bindings, and that the women and apprentices were "doing books in boards."[71] The journeymen therefore did their best to bring the women out too. Once the strike was settled, the booksellers must have realized they could sell larger quantities of books in boards, and that if they had to pay the bookbinders higher rates, at least they could save money by getting cheaper boarded copies.

The next logical step for the booksellers was to ease the prices of boarded copies up to the prices previously charged for bound ones. The larger publishing houses began the process by raising prices to 3s. per volume sewed and in boards.[72] The first nudge seems to have been given by George Robinson, described by John Nichols as "one of the most eminent booksellers of his time."[73] In 1786 Robinson's firm, G. G. J. and J. Robinson, published Harriet Lee's *The Errors of Innocence*, 5 vols., at 15s. sewed, and Thomas Holcroft's translation of Mme. De Montolieu's *Caroline of Lichtfield*, 3 vols., at 9s. sewed. The firm continued its pioneering price hikes, although more tentatively, in 1787, advertising *The Disinterested*

Fig. 3.28. Robert Jephson, *The Confessions of James Baptiste Couteau, Citizen of France, Written by Himself. And Translated from the Original French.* London, for J. Debrett, 1794, 2 vols., 12mo, untrimmed in wrappers. Although in fact an original English novel, Debrett advertised the two volumes at 8s. in boards—2s. above the normal price for a two-volume novel. Perhaps this was due to its containing some illustrations, and also its pretense of being an original French Revolution memoir. Collection of William Zachs.

*Nabob*, 3 vols., in one periodical at 9s. and in another at 7s. 6d. for the three volumes, sewed; similarly Charles Dodd's *The Curse of Sentiment*, 2 vols., at 6s. and at 5s. for the two volumes, sewed; and Anne Burke's *Ela: or, the Delusions of the Heart*, at 3s. and also at 2s. 6d.

Not surprisingly, other booksellers followed the trend. In the autumn of 1787, George Kearsley advertised James Rutlidge's *The Adventures of Monsieur Provence*, 2 vols., at 6s. sewed, also stating the same price upon the book's half-titles; the next year Kearsley published the single-volume *Adventures of a Watch*, at 3s. sewed. William Lane, a dedicated fiction publisher, tried out the higher price on a few titles from 1788 through 1790 and, having added "Minerva Press" to his business at the end of 1790, he made 3s. per volume his standard price, beginning in 1791.[74] The rest of the fiction publishers followed suit,[75] selling boarded and wrappered copies interchangeably (fig. 3.28) at 3s. per duodecimo volume for the remainder of the decade.

## 2. PAPER LABELS

Extrinsic evidence linking bindings and their publishers includes such things as advertisements, catalogues, and business ledgers like John Stockdale's. Intrinsic evidence includes distinctive binding materials and features, and in some cases the mere survival of a number of identical copies. Another intrinsic link between board bindings and their publishers is supplied by printed paper spine labels. Between 1765 and 1800 paper spine labels were printed in substantial numbers, and were clearly intended for a large volume of books. Such quantities would have been ordered only by the commissioning bookseller or syndicate, or by a wholesale distributor.

Fig. 3.29.
Inayat-Allah, *Bahar-Danush; or, Garden of Knowledge,* translated by Jonathan Scott. Shrewsbury, Printed by J. and W. Eddowes: for T. Cadell, jun. and W. Davies, 1799, 3 vols., 8vo, untrimmed in boards with printed paper labels. The slightly different color of the paper backstrip of Vol. I is not unusual. Binders were rarely meticulous about the papers they used with board bindings. Collection of William Zachs.

Graham Pollard discusses what he describes as one of the earliest "printed horizontal labels . . . on Baskerville's edition of Barclay's *Apology* (1765)," suggesting it was printed, not by Baskerville, but for a "wholesale agent handling the book in bulk."[76] Possibly the labels were for a remainder issue, as the book was originally advertised "bound" at 15s.[77] One additional point can be added in support of Pollard's argument. There is a likely link between this label and a specific distributor, one who commissioned the London printers Phillips and Fardon to reprint an errata leaf.[78] This errata leaf is partly printed in Caslon type, and the same printers may also have been responsible for the label.

Another of the earliest surviving printed paper labels is on an Oxford edition, the four quarto volumes of William Blackstone's *Commentaries on the Laws of England* (1765–69), printed at the Clarendon Press. As Graham Pollard notes, these labels are virtually certain to come from a distributor, because the Clarendon Press, unlike most publishers, issued all of its books at this time exclusively in sheets.[79] What is interesting about this label is that it must be contemporary with the printing of the text. The first edition of Blackstone's classic was so successful that new editions of the various volumes appeared almost immediately; there is, therefore, no possibility that sets with paper labels were a remainder issue.[80]

It is significant that these early examples of printed paper labels involve editions printed outside London and distributors in London. It is also significant that the labels date from 1765–69, a period when, as previously discussed, the bookbinding trade in London was under pressure from shortages of leather. In 1768 the Newbery firm introduced printed paper labels on bindings of vellum-backed boards; at the same time the *London Chronicle* was encouraging book buyers to accept wrappers and boards as alternatives to leather bindings.

From the 1770s onwards, printed paper labels were well established as features of publishers' bindings (fig. 3.29). A few books survive where printed labels are actually included on a leaf integral to the book itself, and Gra[ham] Pollard states that "although the publisher had, in those cases, assumed the responsibility for [...]els for the bookseller's retail stock, the bookseller still had to have the sheets pu[...] not so sure. The earliest example Pollard cites is Samuel Johnson's *Lives of [...]* have seen a copy of the 1783 edition of that work, also four volumes, w[...]els present as part of the collation, but another set of paper labels appea[...] [t]he original boards. This suggests that at least some copies were bound up [...] access to separate sets of labels. It is also possible that the printer included [...] [si]mple reasons of thrift, when there was a spare leaf in the collation, leaving [...] [o]wn binder to excise the leaf when required.[82]

Printed paper lab[...] [...]y, even an aberration, but labels on boards, and even wrappers, became incre[...] [...] the eighteenth century. Clearly Stockdale's "boarding" large numbers of co[...] [...] issue was a standard practice during the 1790s, and in the uncertain world [...] [...]lling the normal untrimmed copy in boards with a printed paper label a pu[...] [...] sure thing as we are likely to get.

Wrappers were used as bindings for books fr[...] [...]. Vellum wrappers were common before the Restoration and paper wrappe[...] [...]nd marbled, were regularly used afterwards (fig. 3.30). Most wrappers wer[...] [...]rs before wholesale distribution (fig. 3.31). Michael Sadleir noted "a curious [...] [...] "at the foot of the half-title the legend: 'price two shillings and sixpence [...] is, as Sadleir notes, "a very early date for conscious wrappering."[83]

Until the 1790s printed wrappers—separately printed as [...] [ap]peared in England except on periodicals, including books published in p[...] [...]her William A. Jackson defines such wrappers:

> If the printed matter on the wrapper is applicable only to one book, [...] [ev]en book in original condition are covered by the same printed wrapper w[...] [...]d on any copy of another book, it may be called a publisher's wrapper. But if the de[...] [...] applicable to any book of the same size, or if it occurs on books of different publishers or even different books of the same publisher, then it is properly termed a binder's wrapper.[84]

This is fine for lettered wrappers, and the apparently unique surviving copy of the 1733 satirical pamphlet *Rome Excis'd. A New Tragi-Comi Ballad-Opera* (fig. 3.32) is a splendid example of an early English printed publisher's wrapper, in this case parodying the convention of the black mourning wrapper.[85] More typical is this 1787 printed wrapper on one part of *The Cabinet of Genius* (fig. 3.33).[86] Not only is it a publisher's wrapper, it even says so: "Published by C. Taylor, London." Similar lettered wrappers began to appear on English magazines at least as early as the 1720s, usually blue, but occasionally gray paper.[87] The bookseller Robert Dodsley used printed blue wrappers on a number of different pamphlets

Fig. 3.30.
Samuel Richardson, *Pamela.*
Dublin, for George Ewing . . .
and George Faulkner, 1742,
4 vols.,12mo, sixth edition,
untrimmed in blue-grey
wrappers. The volume num-
bers were probably written by
a bookseller's employee; the
titles are in the same hand as
the inscription "Jane Wood"
on each title-page. Courtesy
of Department of Special
Collections, Stanford
University Libraries.

Fig. 3.31.
*The Rules and Constitutions for
Governing and Managing the
Maiden-Hospital.* Edinburgh,
Robert Fleming and Company,
1731, 12mo, one copy in standard Dutch marbled wrappers,
and another in more elaborate
embossed German wrappers.
A large remainder of this
pamphlet surfaced in Scotland
around 1990. Most were in
the Dutch wrappers; the
embossed wrappers appeared
in several different colors.
This pamphlet may not have
been commercially sold, but
the remainder's survival confirms that large numbers of
copies were identically bound
before distribution.

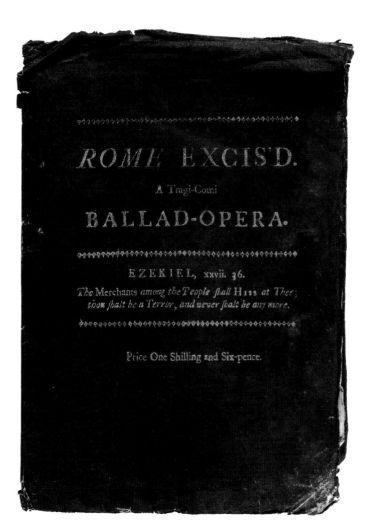

Fig. 3.32
*Rome Excis'd. A New Tragi-Comi Ballad-Opera. Of Three Acts. As it is now Acting with General Applause. By a Polite Company of Courtiers.* London, for T. Jones, 1733, 4to. The "excis'd" in the title gives its subject away: it is a satire on Robert Walpole and his excise taxes, with the mock mourning wrappers, printed in white against a black background, adding to the effect. By permission of the Houghton Library, Harvard University.

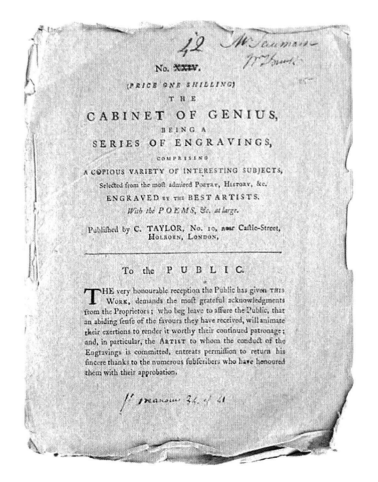

Fig. 3.33.
*The Cabinet of Genius.* London, C. Taylor, [1787], 4to, untrimmed in printed blue wrappers, one of the 47 original parts, each of which had two engraved plates. When completed, it was normally bound into two volumes.

Fig. 3.34.
Francis Segar, *The School of Vertue, and Book of Good Nurture; Teaching Children and Youth their Duties*. Dublin, reprinted by J.B. and S.P., 1698, 12mo. This woodcut, on a leaf comprising an integrated wrapper both at beginning and end, must have been rather worrying for any small child given a copy of the book. It is unique to this Dublin edition; earlier English editions also had illustrated integrated wrappers, but with a gentler domestic scene.

at least as early as the 1740s, but these are properly "binder's" rather than publisher's wrappers, as they contain only advertisements for other Dodsley publications, and nothing specific to the work at hand.[88]

Another kind of wrapper, occasionally seen in the British Isles, is unquestionably publisher's—but it is not a binding. These wrappers are integral to the collation of the book—Jackson calls them "integrated wrappers"[89]—with the upper wrapper printed on the recto of the first leaf, and the lower wrapper on the verso of the last. These two leaves contain no other printing, and if they were removed, the pamphlet would appear to be lacking no more than two leaves which might well have been blank. The illustration here, on an early Irish children's book (fig. 3.34), leads nicely into a discussion of the special bindings that evolved for children's books during the eighteenth century.

## VI. CHILDREN'S BOOKS

Jackson's definition of a publisher's wrapper is too strict when it comes to decorated, but unlettered, wrappers and boards. Beginning around 1740, many children's books were bound by their publishers in floral paper and paper-covered boards, commonly called "Dutch."[90] These charming little bindings were advertised and sold by the Newbery firm, but they seem to have been introduced by Thomas Boreman, on his *Gigantick Histories* and other miniature books for children (fig. 3.35). Dutch boards were also used by Mary Cooper on the earliest known book of nursery rhymes, *Tommy Thumb's Pretty Song Book* (1744).[91] Rare as Boreman's little books are, the survivals are both distinctive and consistent enough to be clearly identifiable as publisher's bindings. John Newbery, his successors, and other publishers continued to use Dutch floral paper bindings until the end of the eighteenth century (fig. 3.36).

Jackson would describe these floral boards and wrappers as "binder's" by virtue of their interchangeability: Dutch floral boards and wrappers on one book look much the same as those on another.

Fig. 3.36.
*The Interesting and Affecting History of Prince Lee Boo, a Native of the Pelew Islands.* Dublin, for J. Rice . . . and R. White, 1791, 18mo. Embossed floral paper over boards. "Dutch" floral paper was consistently used on Irish as well as English editions of entertaining children's titles. Courtesy of Department of Special Collections, Charles E. Young Research Library, University of California, Los Angeles.

Fig. 3.35.
Thomas Boreman, *Westminster Abbey. By the Author of the Gigantick Histories.* London, for Tho. Boreman, Bookseller, near the two Giants in Guildhall, 1742–43, 3 vols., 64mo. Boreman seems to have pioneered this more colorful look for children's books. His *Gigantick Histories* were miniature books of London sights for children. The illustrations here are the floral boards of Vols. II and III, with the imprint taken from the title-page of Vol. II; that of Vol. III includes a second bookseller. Courtesy of Department of Special Collections, Charles E. Young Research Library, University of California, Los Angeles.

But their use on children's books is so distinctive, and so limited, that I have no hesitation in extending the term "publisher's" to them. That they were the binding of choice for "those books designed primarily for pleasure, not for instruction and education"[92] is made clear by an aberration in Newbery's bindings in 1782 and 1783. There must have been a shortage in the supply of Dutch floral paper at that time, probably because of naval actions in the European theatre of the American Revolution. For a short time the Newbery firm's books appeared in pictorial boards, as can be seen in figures 3.37–3.38.[93] But when the supply of Dutch floral paper was restored, Newbery and the other children's publishers went straight back to the old style. But not for long: by the 1790s printed pictorial boards and wrappers began to reappear (figs. 3.39–3.40), and by the early years of the nineteenth century Dutch floral bindings had all but vanished (figs. 3.41–3.42).

Educational books during the period 1660–1800 were bound in the styles of those used for adult books of the period (fig. 3.43), with the bookbinders' price-lists occasionally indicating specific titles to be bound in the cheapest style, that is, sheep (figs. 2.35–2.36). Cloth became a substitute binding, probably

Fig. 3.37.
*The Valentine's Gift: or, a Plan to enable Children of all Sizes and Denominations, to behave with Honour, Integrity, and Humanity*. London, T. Carnan, (Successor to Mr. J. Newbery), 1782, 32mo, in unusually fine pictorial boards. The title-page declares the price "Six-pence bound." Courtesy of Department of Special Collections, Charles E. Young Research Library, University of California, Los Angeles.

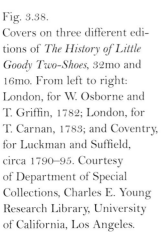

Fig. 3.38.
Covers on three different editions of *The History of Little Goody Two-Shoes*, 32mo and 16mo. From left to right: London, for W. Osborne and T. Griffin, 1782; London, for T. Carnan, 1783; and Coventry, for Luckman and Suffield, circa 1790–95. Courtesy of Department of Special Collections, Charles E. Young Research Library, University of California, Los Angeles.

Fig. 3.39.
Printed boards on two differ-
ent publishers' editions of the
*Hieroglyphical Bible*, 18mo.
From left to right: London,
G. Thompson, 1794; and
London, Robert Bassam, 1796.
Courtesy of Department of
Special Collections, Charles E.
Young Research Library,
University of California, Los
Angeles.

Fig. 3.40.
*The Children's Cabinet: or, a Key
to Natural History.* London,
Laurie and Whittle, 1798,
oblong 12mo, printed wrap-
pers. Courtesy of Department
of Special Collections, Charles
E. Young Research Library,
University of California, Los
Angeles.

in the late 1760s as a result of the same scarcity of leather which prompted Newbery's introduction of
his vellum bindings, although the illustration here (fig. 3.44) suggests it may have been used even earlier.[94] Bookbinders of the period called this cloth "linen," but it is more properly canvas, "coarse, very
similar to that now used by tailors, and buff or yellowy-brown in colour."[95] It remained in fairly wide use
through the early nineteenth century, and in Ireland up to about 1850, although these books had a low
survival rate. Until the middle of the eighteenth century most children's books were probably bought
by grown-ups, who were more concerned with texts than appearances. The majority are unlettered,
were probably bulk-bound, and sold by booksellers out of cupboards or bins. But the Newberys decided
to make their shop attractive to children, and if a child was to have the pleasure of choosing his or her
own books, they needed to be displayed. Hence colored bindings, and lettering.

  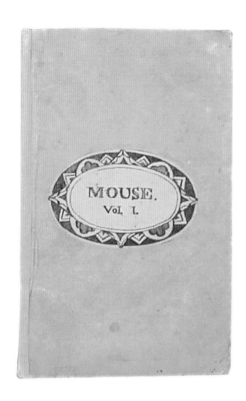

Fig. 3.41.
Covers on three different
editions of Dorothy Kilner,
*The Life and Perambulation
of a Mouse.* London, John
Marshall, [all undated, but
the two on the left from
the mid-1780s, and the one
on the right circa 1800],
24mo and 18mo. Courtesy
of Department of Special
Collections, Charles E.
Young Research Library,
University of California,
Los Angeles.

Fig. 3.42.
*The Foundation of all Learning,
or Child's First Book. By which
a Child will learn more in one
Month than by many others in
Twelve.* London, Watts and
Bridgewater, [no date, but
circa 1800], 18mo, eighth edition, printed wrappers. The

British Library has the only
other recorded copy of any
edition of this charming little
book. ESTC suggests the date
1800 for their copy (the fifth
edition), so this edition may
have been printed just after the
turn of the century.

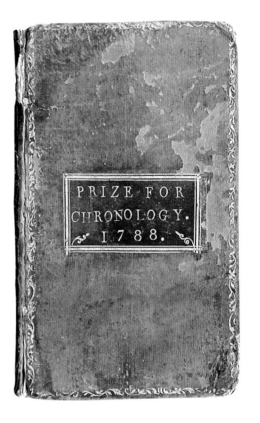

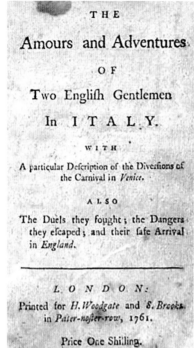

THE
Amours and Adventures
OF
Two Englifh Gentlemen
In ITALY.
WITH
A particular Defcription of the Diverfions of the Carnival in *Venice*.
ALSO
The Duels they fought; the Dangers they efcaped; and their fafe Arrival in *England*.
——————
LONDON:
Printed for *H. Woodgate* and *S. Brooks*, in *Pater-nofter-row*, 1761.
Price One Shilling.

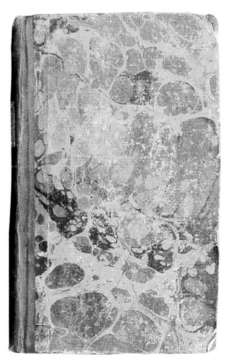

Fig. 3.43.
Richard Grey, *Select Parts of Grey's Memoria Technica: to which are added . . . the General Divisions of Ancient and Modern Geography . . . For the Use of the Grammar-School at Wolverhampton.* Wolverhampton, by J. Smart, 1786, 12mo, calf gilt, certainly bound locally, where the appropriate prize labels could be added as needed.

Fig. 3.44.
*The Amours and Adventures of Two English Gentlemen in Italy.* London, for H. Woodgate and S. Brooks, 1761, 12mo, canvas or "linen," on an apparently unique copy of this little novel. The price "One Shilling" on the title-page would certainly have been for bound copies. Courtesy of the William Andrews Clark Memorial Library, University of California, Los Angeles.

Fig. 3.45.
"The Rev. Mr. Cooper,"
*The History of South America.*
London, for E. Newbery, 1789, 18mo, in standard Newbery "vellum manner." Courtesy of Department of Special Collections, Charles E. Young Research Library, University of California, Los Angeles.

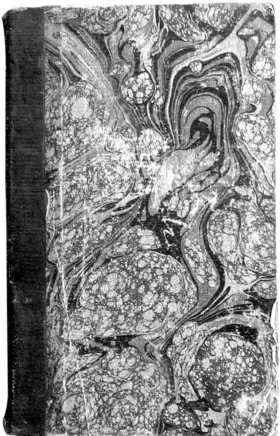

Fig. 3.46.
"Tom Telescope," *The Newtonian System of Philosophy explained by Familiar Objects*. London, Ogilvy and Son, Vernor and Hood, J. Walker, Lackington, Allen, and Co., and Darton and Harvey, 1798, 12mo, new edition, the earliest example of colored roan-backed boards on a children's book I have seen. The title states "Price One Shilling and Sixpence bound." The printing for such a large syndicate of this popular children's book (first published in 1761; this is apparently the ninth edition) suggests that a large number of copies was probably produced—just the kind of circumstances that would prompt considerations of economy. This is clearly the publisher's binding, and it gives every appearance of being strictly contemporary with the publication date, including the 1790s style of the "spot pattern" marbled paper sides, and the laid endpapers and binder's waste. The spine originally had a printed paper label, as can be seen from the gap between the two topmost fillets. Courtesy of Robin de Beaumont.

Newbery's vellum manner was widely imitated and used until around 1800, with occasional examples appearing a dozen or more years later.[96] Spines were usually green, but occasionally blue, with printed paper spine labels, and the covers either a single glazed color or marbled (fig. 3.45). In the earlier eighteenth century, vellum and parchment were occasionally used for trade bindings, and the classical revival made certain styles of decorative vellum popular as well. As a bookbinding material, it was probably comparable in price to sheep, and perhaps sometimes even cheaper, especially when bought in small pieces.

In the last decade of the eighteenth century, new styles of children's bookbinding appeared. As mentioned above, Dutch floral paper gradually gave way to less expensive printed styles, both on wrappers and boards. Then in the late 1790s, roan began to be substituted for colored vellum spines.[97] Made from split sheepskin and tanned with sumach, roan could hold color almost as uniformly as goatskin, and was vastly cheaper. It must have been cheaper than vellum as well, because it became immediately popular (fig. 3.46). By the first few years of the nineteenth century, colored roan spines were the standard for children's books, and paper labels gave way to gilt lettering. By 1820 multi-colored roan spines were so standardized that the poet Mary Belson Elliott accused girls of caring too much for the outsides of their books, and too little for the insides. Her poem, "The Bookcase" begins:

Julia's book-case makes a show,

Tempting to youthful scholars' sight,

And offers in each well-bound row,

A store of pleasure and delight. . . .[98]

## CHAPTER FOUR

# COMMON TRADE BINDINGS: A SAMPLER

The previous two chapters showed, respectively, bindings from the bookbinders' price lists, and various styles produced for publishers. Without repeating those illustrations, this chapter further addresses the evolution of common trade bindings, showing how old and new patterns co-existed, and suggesting how individual binders can sometimes be identified.

During the course of the seventeenth century, the mode of shelving books gradually changed from fore-edges to spines outwards. Many owners preferred these rows of spines to be decorated and, as they acquired more and more books, they needed the titles to be recognizable. The result was gilt-tooled and lettered spines, increasingly common after the Restoration. The cheapest bindings remained unlettered, however, and continued so throughout the eighteenth century. Figures 4.1–4.7 show unlettered bindings, grouped together to allow comparison of their features.

Undecorated bindings in multi-volume sets normally had gilt volume numbers in either the second or third compartment of their spines (figs. 4.4–4.7, but see fig. 2.15 for an unnumbered set). There does not seem to have been a settled rule, although sheep bindings were somewhat less likely than calf to be numbered in the second compartment (figs. 4.6–4.7). More expensive calf bindings may have been more likely to be labeled or decorated later; a label would cover a publisher's volume number in the second compartment, and allow all the spines of that and other sets to be uniformly decorated.

Panels, including the distinctively English "cottage-roof" variation, were established on fine bindings before the Restoration,[1] yet well into the 1660s standard trade bindings normally had little more than a basic double blind fillet framing the covers, with the same double fillet run vertically about a third of the way in from the spine (fig. 4.8). Decorative panels became increasingly prominent on trade work in the 1670s, and this style characterized the next fifty years of English trade bookbinding. As the illustrations in Chapter 2 show, panels co-existed with simpler blind rules and frames during the 1680s. By the 1690s, as Baker's broadside *The Bookbinder's Case Unfolded* confirms, panels with floral corners were fully ascendant (figs. 4.9–4.11). They remained so through the 1720s (figs. 4.12–4.19), when trade binders began to revert to simpler patterns which they could produce more rapidly (figs. 4.20–4.21).

Lettering styles even on otherwise undecorated books can provide important clues to a binding's date. Figure 4.22 shows original lettering on a group of London trade calf bindings from 1675 to 1730, of which only Rochester's *Letters* (1698) and Shakespeare's *Works* (1714) are lettered directly onto the spines; all the others are on red goatskin labels. The Shakespeare (in the center of fig. 4.22) has gilt fillets and lettering on the spines, features that could appear at any time before 1800. But the typeface and the presentation of the lettering, with the break in the author's name and the irregular spacing of the letters, is typical of the late seventeenth and early eighteenth century. It is safe to say that lettering

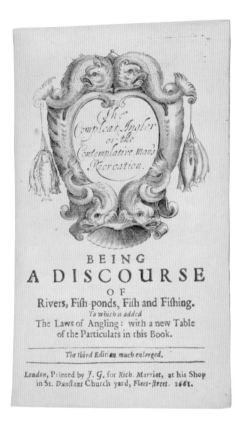

Fig. 4.1.
Izaac Walton and Charles Cotton, *The Compleat Angler*. London, J.G. for Rich. Marriot, 1661, pot 8vo, unlettered, probably publisher's sheep, a remarkable survival of a book usually found in later bindings. Courtesy of the Lilly Library, Indiana University, Bloomington, Indiana.

Fig. 4.2.
John Wilmot, Earl of Rochester, *Poems*. London, Printed for A.B. and are to be Sold by most Booksellers, 1731, 12mo, calf. Unlettered bindings on such clandestine literature normally took the simplest form. The manuscript label is on a slip of paper pasted to the lower edge of a text page, suggesting that the volume was kept flat, perhaps in a cupboard, rather than on a shelf.

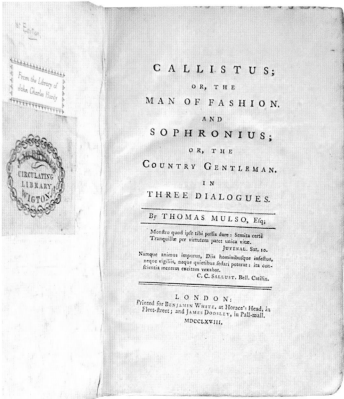

Fig. 4.3.
Thomas Mulso, *Callistus; or, the Man of Fashion*. London, for Benjamin White, 1768, 8vo, a circulating library binding of half parchment. The coarse grain of the membrane shows this to be parchment made from sheepskin, also called forel, rather than finer-quality vellum made from calfskin (the two are not always easily distinguished, however). The provincial circulating library label can be seen to the left of the title-page; the leaves were left untrimmed to allow for later rebinding. Circulating library books were more likely to be half- or quarter-bound in sheep or calf (see fig. 4.38) than parchment or vellum. Collection of William Zachs.

Fig. 4.4.
Two pairs of eighteenth-century unlettered spines, left to right: Montesquieu, *Persian Letters*, translated by Mr. Ozell. London, for J. Tonson, 1722; and Christopher Smart, *The Poems*. Reading, Smart and Cowslade, 1791, both 2 vols., 12mo, respectively in calf and sheep. Stylistically there is no difference, yet the two are seventy years apart. The Smart may be a some-what anachronistic provin-cial publishers' binding, but this elementary trade style changed little throughout most of the century. The first, collection of William Zachs; the second, courtesy of the William Andrews Clark Memorial Library, University of California, Los Angeles.

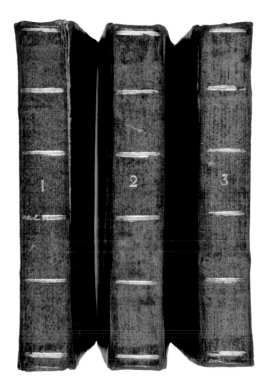

Fig. 4.5.
*The History of Miss Indiana Danby.* London, for J. Dodsley, 1765–67, 4 vols., 12mo. The first two volumes of this novel were printed in 1765, and here are in simple calf with gilt spine labels; the second two, dated 1767, are in a cheaper binding of sheep-backed plain boards, edges untrimmed. Courtesy of the Lilly Library, Indiana University, Bloomington, Indiana.

Fig. 4.6.
Dorothy Kilner, *Dialogues and Letters on Morality, Economy, and Politeness, for the Improvement and Entertainment of Young Female Minds.* London, John Marshall, 1787, second edition, 3 vols., 12mo, quarter sheep, probably publisher's. This copy was sewn on four cords, but the binder did not nip the bands to create a more decorative look or provide any finishing other than the gilt volume numbers. The marbled paper on the covers is a spot pattern used in England from the 1770s to the 1790s.

Fig. 4.7.
Thomas Day, *The History of Sandford and Merton. A Work intended for the Use of Children.* Belfast, William Magee, 1797, 3 vols., 12mo, sprinkled sheep. There is no decoration at all on the covers. Courtesy of the Lilly Library, Indiana University, Bloomington, Indiana.

Fig. 4.8.
Thomas Sprat, *Observations on Monsieur de Sorbier's Voyage into England*. London, for John Martyn, 1665, pot 8vo. The spine of this calf binding has similar conventional blind fillets to those seen on the 1661 *Compleat Angler* (fig. 4.1), but the covers are attempting something a little different, with a blind ornament repeated not just in the corners, but also inside the second double fillet—the beginning of a panel. Courtesy of the William Andrews Clark Memorial Library, University of California, Los Angeles.

Fig. 4.9.
John Dryden, a collective volume of quarto plays, from the four-volume set sold by Jacob Tonson with and (as here) without general titles in the 1690s. This copy is bound in paneled calf, perhaps by Tonson's own workshop (see fig. 3.23). The alternating light and dark panels were a feature of many bindings from the 1690s to about 1730. Courtesy of the William Andrews Clark Memorial Library, University of California, Los Angeles.

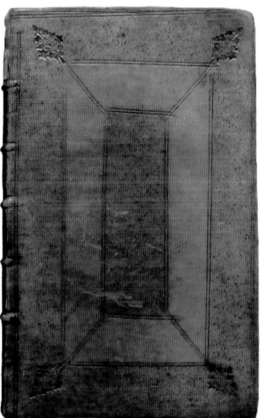

Fig. 4.10.
Left to right: Edmund Waller, *Poems.* London, for H. Herringman, and sold by Jacob Tonson, 1694; and Sir John Denham, *Poems and Translations.* London, for Jacob Tonson, 1709, both 8vo, paneled calf with blind-ruled but unlettered spines, standard trade bindings with no gilt extras in near-identical style. Courtesy of the William Andrews Clark Memorial Library, University of California, Los Angeles.

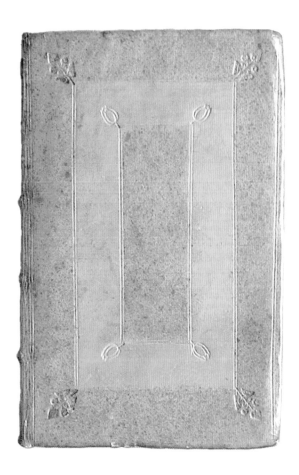

Fig. 4.11.
Sir William Temple, *Introduction to the History of England.* London, for Richard Simpson and Ralph Simpson, 1695, 8vo, paneled calf. Occasionally binders played with the standard forms: here an extra tulip has been added, not especially harmoniously, to the central cover panels. Richard Simpson was John Dunton's "grave and antient binder," and apparently his brother Ralph also had a bookbindery. One or the other might have bound this copy, and perhaps they even acted as their own warehousemen, supplying bound copies to the trade. Courtesy of the William Andrews Clark Memorial Library, University of California, Los Angeles.

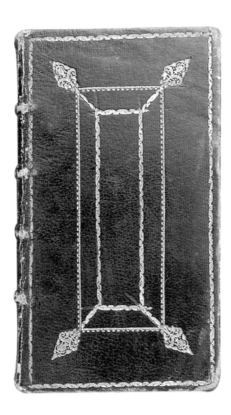

Fig. 4.12.
Peter Berault, *The Narrow Way which leads to Heaven; and the Broad Way which leads to Hell*. London, William Redmayne for the Author, 1703, 12mo, paneled stained sheep. The author was a sea-chaplain, "who preached this Doctrine . . . in going to, and returning from Jamaica." This is a deluxe binding, perhaps for presentation to a ship's captain, or for retail sale, but done on the cheap. Courtesy of Department of Special Collections, Stanford University Libraries.

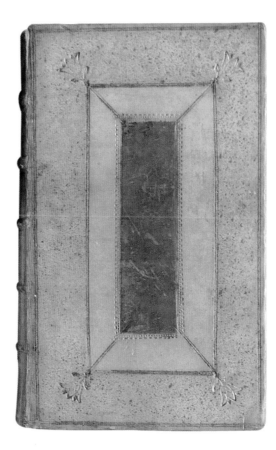

Fig. 4.13.
Francois Rabelais, *The Whole Works . . . done out of the French, by Sir Thomas Urchard, Knight, Mr. Motteux, and Others*. London, for James Woodward, 1708, 2 vols., 8vo, in two very different trade calf bindings, one sprinkled and paneled, the other dark with a blind double fillet border and single roll on the covers, a more old-fashioned style (the spines are in reverse order in the photograph of this latter set). The paneled binding is exactly what one would expect of the period. The dark binding poses a problem with its spine lettering. In the absence of any other volume numbers on the two spines, one would assume this lettering is original, gilt over "blacked" compartments (as described in the 1743 Dublin bookbinders' price list). But lettering on black is unusual on a London binding this early, and both the gilt frame with its short dashes and the lettering itself look later than 1708. The paneled calf binding appears courtesy of the William Andrews Clark Memorial Library, University of California, Los Angeles.

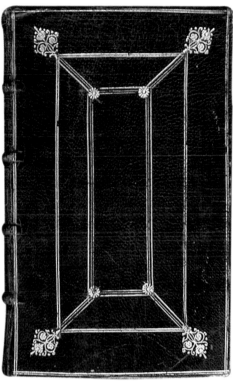

Fig. 4.14.
George Herbert, *The Temple.*
*Sacred Poems, and Private*
*Ejaculations.* London, for John
Wyat . . . and Eben. Tracy, 1709,
12mo. Black goatskin, gilt-paneled in standard style, with the
title lettered directly into the
second spine compartment.

Fig. 4.15.
William Shakespeare, *A*
*Collection of Poems, in Two*
*Volumes.* London, for Bernard
Lintott, [undated but
1709–10], 2 vols. in one,
pot 8vo. This original sheep
binding has been finished in
every way one would expect
to see on trade calf, with the
exception of a gilt edge-roll.

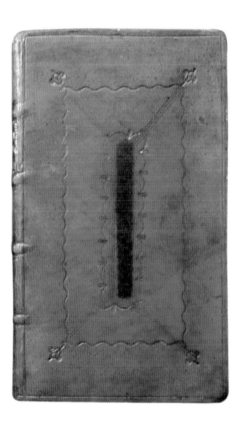

Fig. 4.16.
Gilbert Burnet, *An*
*Abridgment of the History of*
*the Reformation.* London,
for J. Walthoe and B. Tooke
[Vol. 3 for W. Churchill],
1719, 12mo, calf. The paneled style appears somewhat
shrunken on this binding,
with its very narrow dark
center rectangle. Both titles
and volume numbers are
placed in a single, blacked,
spine compartment.
Courtesy of the William
Andrews Clark Memorial
Library, University of
California, Los Angeles.

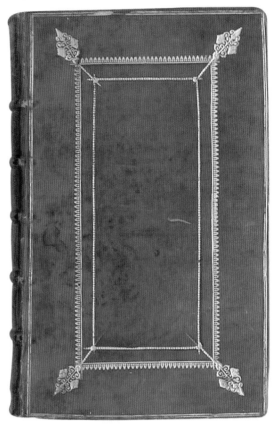

Fig. 4.17.
Joseph Addison and Richard Steele, *The Lucubrations of Isaac Bickerstaff*. London, Printed: And to be deliver'd to Subscribers, by Charles Lillie, Perfumer, 1710–11, 4 vols., royal 8vo, a large-paper copy, in honey-colored calf anticipating russia. Several copies are known in similar bindings, although this one is unusual in its variety of spine ornaments (only those on Vols. 3 and 4 are uniform). This may be a deluxe subscriber's copy, and probably Lillie also had some for sale in his shop with those other "baubles," for which Steele said he had "a genius." Courtesy of the William Andrews Clark Memorial Library, University of California, Los Angeles.

Fig. 4.18.
*Glossographia Anglicana Nova: or, a Dictionary.* London, for D. Brown [et al.], 1719, 8vo, second edition, calf. This was published by a syndicate, and the binding may be by one of its warehousemen. On the other hand, given the irregularities of the finishing, and the somewhat uneven tone of the calfskin, it could be provincial. There is a contemporary ownership inscription "Willm. Ross, Peterborough." Courtesy of Department of Special Collections, Stanford University Libraries.

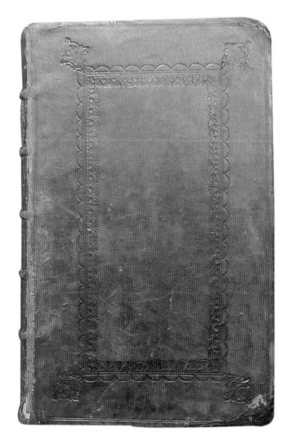

Fig. 4.19.
*Miscellany Poems . . . Publish'd by Mr. Dryden.* London, for J. Tonson, 1727, 6vols.,12mo, fifth edition, paneled calf. If it were not for the rather advanced sawtooth edge to the spine labels, the bindings might easily be dated twenty years earlier than the books.

Fig. 4.20.
Sir Isaac Newton, *The Chronology of Ancient Kingdoms Amended.* London, for J. Tonson . . . J. Osborn and T. Longman, 1728, 4to, a large paper copy in calf gilt. The gilt spine is typical of earlier decades, but the frame on the covers foreshadows the increasingly simple trade bindings of the next half century. Courtesy of Department of Special Collections, Stanford University Libraries.

Fig. 4.21.
Andrew Mahon, *The Art of Fencing . . . Translated from the French of the late celebrated Monsieur L'Abbat.* London, for Richard Wellington, 1735, 8vo, sheep, spine gilt with goatskin label, the covers decorated in what can fairly be described as paneled calf's last gasp.

Fig. 4.22.
Lettering styles and spine decoration on London trade calf, 1675–1730, from left to right: Christopher Harvey, *The School of the Heart.* London, for Lodowick Lloyd, 1675, 12mo, third edition, covers mottled, with a blind edge-roll; Thomas Flatman, *Poems and Songs.* London, for Benjamin Tooke, 1686, crown 8vo, fourth edition, covers mottled, with a gilt edge-roll; John Wilmot, Earl of Rochester, *Familiar Letters.* London, for S. Briscoe, 1697, 2 vols. in one, foolscap 8vo, covers blind-paneled, with a blind edge-roll; William Shakespeare, *The Works.* London, for J. Tonson [and ten others], 1714, 2 vols. [of nine], 12mo, covers sprinkled with a gilt frame and small corner fleurons, and a gilt edge-roll; *Familiar Letters of Love, Gallantry, and several Occasions.* London, for Sam. Briscoe [and 14 others], 1718, 2 vols., 12mo, covers blind-paneled, with a gilt edge-roll, and a contemporary inscription on the front free endpaper "2 vols. 5. 6."; George Granville, Lord Lansdowne, *Poems upon Several Occasions.* London, for J. Tonson, 1721, 12mo, covers sprinkled, with a gilt frame and a blind edge-roll; Edmund Waller, *The Works.* London, for J. Tonson, 1730, 12mo, covers finely sprinkled but otherwise undecorated, and a gilt edge-roll.

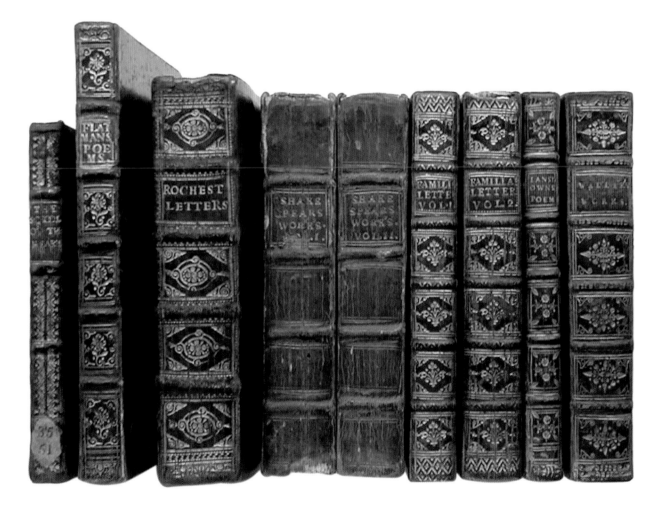

on later bindings (the two on the far right of fig. 4.22 show the trend) is generally more regularized and essentially neater. Lettering did not remain uniformly tidy throughout the eighteenth century, but the random breaks in names and words seen on earlier bindings were gone for good. Precise lettering reached its apogee when John Bell's bindery began to set spine titles in type-holders around 1780; before Bell, finishers in England worked one letter at a time.

Another key element in the dating of bookbindings is the association of tools with particular bookbinders. Very occasionally there are sufficient records of a trade bookbinder's work to allow such links. One such binder, William Bonnor, was employed by Cambridge University in the 1730s, and others working in London, Oxford, and Durham have also been identified.[2] Robert Steel is another example. Steel acquired Samuel Mearne's tools and perhaps even his premises after the death of Charles Mearne in 1686. After Steel's death in 1710, his daughter Jane continued the business.[3] Some of Jane Steel's bindings are identified in orders and bills from the Harleian Library, which means that a significant number of Steel tools can be identified both from the beginning and the end of this bindery's career. Figures 4.23–4.24 show variations of what Maggs Bros. have called the "electric carnation" tool, and which G.D. Hobson describes as having "a distant resemblance to a hedgehog."[4] Another trade calf binding, on a late edition of *The Temple of Death* poetical miscellany (fig. 4.24, left), shows the same distinctive small fan-shaped tool found on other Steel bindings, such as the goatskin on Barville's *Conversion*, 1710 (fig. 4.25). All of these tools are not only characteristic of the period, they are identifiably Steel's. Moreover, there is an exact match of the gilt edge-rolls on Collier's *Miscellanies*, *The Temple of Death*, Barville's *Conversion*, and Quillet's *Callipaedia* illustrated in figure 1.1, with the only difference being that a larger amount of gold leaf has adhered to the calf edges, creating a more smudged effect than on the

Fig. 4.24.
From left to right: *A Collection of Poems: viz., The Temple of Death.* London, for Ralph Smith, 1702; and Thomas Brown, *Select Epistles or Letters out of M. Tullius Cicero.* London, for Sam. Briscoe, and sold by J. Nutt, 1702, both 8vo, calf. The binding on the left is by Robert Steel; its fan-shaped tool and gilt edge-roll (not shown here) also appear on Barville's *Conversion* (fig. 4.25). The binding on the right may be by Steel; the covers show a carnation tool similar to the one on Collier's *Miscellanies*, but this is not in itself determinative. The Brown volume appears courtesy of the William Andrews Clark Memorial Library, University of California, Los Angeles.

edges of the goatskin, as one would expect given the different porosity of the two skins. These identifications seem comparatively straightforward, but not all scholars may agree. Figure 4.26 indicates some of the problems with Steel bindings.

Bindings of the 1730s have much in common with those of earlier decades, but their decoration is increasingly simple (figs. 4.27–4.28). Their features include raised bands, often with blind or gilt rules to either side, and usually a blind or gilt roll or fillet framing the covers (figs. 4.30–4.31). Apart from the label on one of them, the spines of the two bindings in figure 4.29 could easily be from the same decade, but the 1732 binding has blind-paneled covers with a dark central rectangle, decoration almost never seen after the end of that decade.

From the 1740s through the 1760s, trade calf for the most part remained in this rather uninspired state, with less and less decoration on the spines, usually fillets or a single tool in the spine compartments, and little, if any, decoration on the covers (figs. 4.32–4.35; see also figs. 4.3 and 4.5). As leather became increasingly expensive, paper, both marbled and plain (figs. 4.28 and 4.34), found its way onto covers. Half and even quarter leather bindings were often substituted for full bindings, and advertised and sold "bound" at the same price.

From about 1770 to the end of the century, sawn-in sewing cords again became increasingly fashionable on trade leather bindings, with neat gilt fillets repeated across the spines (figs. 4.36–4.37; compare fig. 4.38). Two collective photographs of spines on novels show their development (figs. 4.39–4.40); by the 1790s, raised bands had all but disappeared. Figure 4.41 illustrates one remarkable aberration: 1770s trade calf with a gilt price on the spine.

Pre-1740 English, Irish, and Scottish simple trade styles are essentially impossible to tell apart.

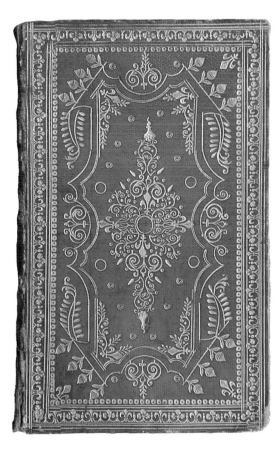

Fig. 4.25.
John Barville, *An Account of the Late Conversion of Mr. John Barville alias Barton, from Popery.* London, for John Phillips, 1710, 8vo, goatskin, cottage-roof style, by Robert Steel. The fan-shaped tool at the top and bottom of the central ornament on the covers is seen on several other Steel bindings, including the 1702 *Temple of Death* (fig. 4.24). Even more distinctive is the gilt edge-roll, which is discussed in more detail in the caption to figure 4.23.

Fig. 4.26.
Jacques Du Bosc, *The Excellent Woman Described.* London, for Joseph Watts, 1692, 8vo, another carnation/hedgehog tool, on a binding that may or may not be by Steel. The outer roll border on the cover is similar, but not identical, to the edge-roll discussed in the previous illustrations. Like many bindings of the period, this one presents problems for scholars attempting to identify the work of individual workshops, and shows the extent to which tools were copied in the trade. Difficulties with Steel bindings are discussed by Howard M. Nixon, *English Restoration Bookbindings* (1974), pp. 23–24 and plates 40–41, and Maggs Bros. Ltd., *Bookbinding in the British Isles*, Catalogue 1075 (1987), item 117, this last with a note on the different carnation tools. Courtesy of Maggs Bros. Ltd.

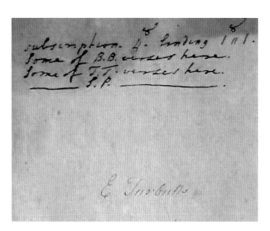

Fig. 4.27.
Henry Travers, *Miscellaneous Poems and Translations.* London, for Benj. Motte, 1731, demy 8vo, calf. The covers are sprinkled but otherwise undecorated, and there is a gilt edge-roll. This was a normal tenpenny binding with an extra gilt spine, typical of the period. The note of costs is written on the front free endpaper, along with identifications of some of the contributors to the volume, of which the subscriber "S.P." may have been one. He paid 4s. for the book and 1s. 1d. for the binding, a trade price which suggests the binding was commissioned at the same time the book subscription was paid. Booksellers appear to have added little or no mark-up onto their binding costs, as discussed in the caption to figure 2.13.

Fig. 4.28.
John Gay, *The Wife of Bath. A Comedy.* London, for Bernard Lintot, 1730, 4to. Large-paper copies of plays are uncommon; the title-page of this one gives an idea of its dimensions. The binding is a highly economical trade form, with an undecorated calf spine, and the boards covered with scraps of Dutch marbled paper. Courtesy of the William Andrews Clark Memorial Library, University of California, Los Angeles.

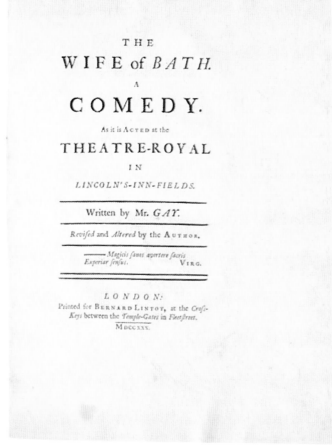

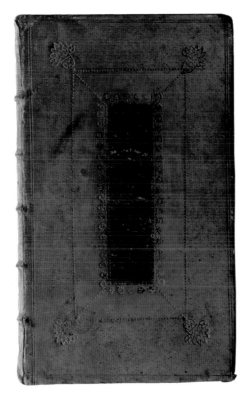

Fig. 4.29. Left to right: John Earle, *Microcosmography: or, a Piece of the World Discover'd.* London, Printed by E. Say, 1732; and *The Works of Christina Queen of Sweden.* London, for D. Wilson and T. Durham, 1753, both 12mo, calf. I have seen three identical copies of the latter book, including the label and lettering.

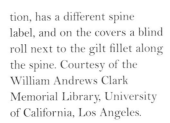

Fig. 4.30.
*The Hive. A Collection of the most Celebrated Songs.* London, for J. Walthoe, 1732, 4 vols., 12mo, calf gilt with double fillets, but the set is not quite uniform. The first three volumes show some wear and rubbing to the gilt; the fourth, in much brighter condition, has a different spine label, and on the covers a blind roll next to the gilt fillet along the spine. Courtesy of the William Andrews Clark Memorial Library, University of California, Los Angeles.

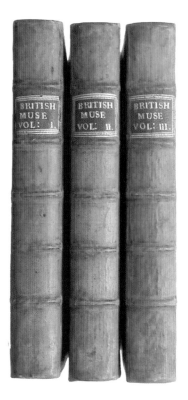

Fig. 4.31.
Thomas Hayward (ed.),
*The British Muse*. London,
for F. Cogan, 1738, 3 vols.,
12mo, lightly sprinkled
smooth calf. By incorporating volume numbers into
the goatskin labels, bindings
like these could be produced
without any other finishing.
Courtesy of the William
Andrews Clark Memorial
Library, University of
California, Los Angeles.

Fig. 4.32.
Samuel Squire, *An Enquiry
into the Foundation of the
English Constitution*. London,
by W. Bowyer for C. Bathurst,
1745, 8vo, sprinkled sheep,
the decoration not quite con-
cealing the fact that the
binder has used more than
one piece of leather on the
binding: they are joined on
the cover just in from the
spine. Courtesy of the Lilly
Library, Indiana University,
Bloomington, Indiana.

Fig. 4.33.
Theophilus Cibber, *The Lives
of the Poets*. London, for R.
Griffiths, 1753, 5 vols., 12mo,
calf, the covers sprinkled
but otherwise undecorated.
Courtesy of the William
Andrews Clark Memorial
Library, University of
California, Los Angeles.

Fig. 4.34.
Ferdinando Warner,
*Bolingbroke. Or, a Dialogue.*
London, for J. Payne, 1755,
8vo, sheep-backed plain
paper-covered boards, all
edges untrimmed. This
was the simplest of 1750s
publishers' bindings; the
sheep spine later gave way
to paper, which of course
was even cheaper.

Fig. 4.35.
Lettering styles and spine
decoration on London-
printed duodecimo novels,
1737–1774, from left to
right: Alain René le Sage,
*The Bachelor of Salamanca,*
for A. Bettesworth [et al.],
1737, 2 vols.; Claudine de
Tencin, *The Siege of Calais,*
for T. Woodward, 1740;
Francois Génard, *The School
of Woman,* for J. Robinson,
1753; Jean de Kerguette,
*True Merit, True Happiness,*
for F. and J. Noble, 2 vols.,
[1757]; Johann Bodmer,
*Noah,* for J. Collyer, 1767,
2 vols.; John Potter, *The
Curate of Coventry,* for
F. Newbery, 1771, 2 vols.;
Henry Brooke, *Juliet
Grenville,* for G. Robinson,
1774, 3 vols. Collection of
William Zachs.

Fig. 4.36.
*The Roundelay or the New Syren,*
*a Collection of Choice Songs.*
London, for W. Lane, [circa
1780], 12mo, "a new edition,"
sprinkled calf with sawn-in
sewing cords, double gilt fillets
and a goatskin label on the
spine, a standard simple binding
of the period, possibly bound for
Lane himself. Lane later trans-
formed his business into the
Minerva Press, but at this stage
in his career many of his publications were remainder sheets
of various types, reissued, as
here, with new title-pages.

Fig. 4.37.
Jane Bowdler, *Poems and Essays*
*by a Lady Lately Deceased.* Bath,
Printed by R. Cruttwell, and
sold by C. Dilly, London, 1786,
2 vols., 8vo, polished calf, the
elegant spines with sawn-in
sewing cords, but the covers
with only a very simple gilt
perimeter roll. The title-page is
inscribed "A gift from Miss H.
Bowdler," the author's sister.
Charles Dilly was Samuel
Johnson's hypothetical "wholesale bookseller." The imprint of
this book shows him to be the
primary distributor, but this
copy may have been bound in
Bath, where the book was printed and where Miss Bowdler
lived. Courtesy of the Lilly
Library, Indiana University,
Bloomington, Indiana.

Fig. 4.38.
George Monck Berkeley, *Maria;*
*or the Generous Rustic.* London,
for T. Cadell . . . and C. Elliot,
Edinburgh, 1784, 8vo, quarter
calf over plain pasteboard,
untrimmed, a typical circulating
library binding of the period,
complete with the label on the
upper cover and two different
shelf numbers on the undecorated spine. The binder has made
no extra effort either to saw in
the sewing cords, or to nip them
into a neater shape. Collection of
William Zachs.

Fig. 4.39.
A cross-section of leather binding styles on late-eighteenth-century two-volume duodecimo novels, from left to right: Christof Wieland, *The History of Agathon.* London, for T. Cadell, 1773; Antoine Prévost d'Exiles, *Manon l'Escaut: or, the Fatal Attachment.* London, for T. Cadell, 1786; Agnes Maria Bennett, *Agnes de Courci.* Bath, for the Author, by S. Hazard, 1789; Richard Hey, *Edington.* London, for Vernor and Hood, 1796; George Walker, *The Vagabond.* London, Sampson Low, for G. Walker, 1800. Collection of William Zachs.

There is no question that Irish and Scottish craftsmen were active throughout this period, but it is not until 1720 or so that their fine bindings took on a distinctive national character, and not until about 1740 that identifiable features emerged on Irish and Scottish trade calf.[5]

Maurice Craig's *Irish Bookbindings 1600–1800* has a few notes of early eighteenth-century Irish bindings, such as "a curious tool of a dog" and the "dismal work of the Irish Sombre Binder,"[6] but these are hardly national characteristics. Many Irish and Scottish books, such as almanacs, were likely bound in the towns where they were printed, but do not reveal distinctive tooling. Around 1740, however, some specific traits begin to emerge. Taken one at a time, these traits are unremarkable, but collectively they show the emergence of some national trade styles.

Figure 4.42 is typical of many bindings on books with George Faulkner's imprint. They appear to have come from a single workshop which, as suggested in the caption to figure 2.18, may be called Faulkner's "smooth calf" bindery because of its consistently highly polished calf. Examples normally have only the simplest of blind frames on the covers, with spine lettering, usually but not always, in a "blacked" compartment.

Similarly distinct Scottish trade styles appear at about the same time. The half-parchment, or forel, binding shown here (fig. 4.43) is probably Scottish, and even from the Foulises' own bindery, but the gilt ornaments are not among those known to be from that workshop (see fig. 3.15). Figure 4.44 depicts Scottish trade calf on the Edinburgh edition of Samuel Johnson's *The Rambler:* the covers are heavily mottled in a style more reminiscent of France than England, and such disproportionately large

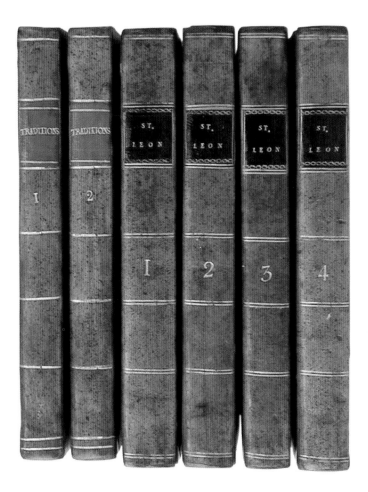

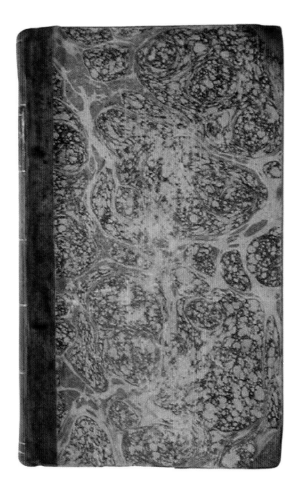

Fig. 4.40.
From left to right: Mary Sherwood, *The Traditions.* London, for William Lane, Minerva, 1795, 2 vols.; William Godwin, *St. Leon.* London, for G.G. and J. Robinson, 1799, 4 vols., all 12mo, half calf. At the far right is an upper cover of one volume of *The Traditions,* with the predominantly blue Stormont paper pattern seen around this time. Collection of William Zachs.

Fig. 4.41.
William Speechly. *A Treatise on the Culture of the Pineapple and the Management of the Hot-House.* York, Printed by A. Ward, for, and Sold by the Author, at Burlington-House, London; and at Welbeck in Nottingham-shire, 1779, royal 8vo, calf. A most *un*common trade binding: the covers are com-pletely undecorated, but the spine is fully gilt and includes the highly unusual "One Guinea" price. This must have been a special binding for copies sold retail by the author at one or the other address in the imprint. Courtesy of the Lilly Library, Indiana University, Bloomington, Indiana.

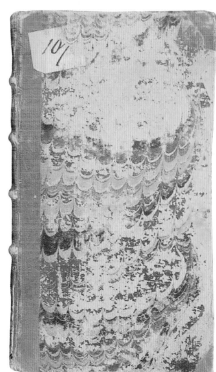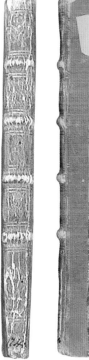

Fig. 4.42.
Jonathan Swift, *A Tale of a Tub*. Dublin, by S. Powell, for W. Smith . . . and G. Faulkner, 1741, 12mo, polished "smooth" calf, gilt-lettered in a blacked spine compartment. Courtesy of the William Andrews Clark Memorial Library, University of California, Los Angeles.

Fig. 4.43.
Theophrastus, *Characters* [in Greek]. Glasgow, Robert Foulis, 1748, 12mo, untrimmed in half parchment over marbled boards, the parchment stained rose, but beginning to rub off the spine. Courtesy of Department of Special Collections, Stanford University Libraries.

Fig. 4.44.
Samuel Johnson, *The Rambler*. Edinburgh, Sold by W. Gordon, C. Wright, and the other Booksellers, 1750, 2 vols., foolscap 8vo, mottled calf, covers with a double gilt fillet frame and gilt edge-roll.

Fig. 4.45.
Two copies of David Hume, *Political Discourses*. Edinburgh, for A. Kincaid and A. Donaldson, 1752, foolscap 8vo, in the same publisher's binding of Scottish sprinkled calf, spine gilt in compartments with a single fillet and crown. The copy on the right has a modern label, as does the similarly-tooled book in the center, which is Robert Wallace, *A Dissertation on the Numbers of Mankind in antient and modern Times . . . With . . . some remarks on Mr Hume's Political Discourse, of the Populousness of antient Nations*. Edinburgh, for G. Hamilton and J. Balfour, 1753, 8vo. Courtesy of Bernard Quaritch Ltd.

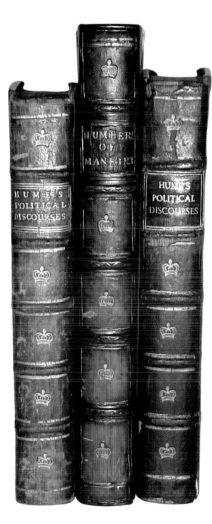

gilt spine numerals are not often seen south of Hadrian's Wall. Another calf binding from this period, on David Hume's *Political Discourses*, is both Scottish and publisher's. Figure 4.45 shows two separate copies, both with a distinctive crown ornament in the spine compartments. This ornament also appears on a number of other books printed for the Edinburgh bookseller Alexander Kincaid. The book by Robert Wallace (between the two copies of the Hume in fig. 4.45) shows how similarly books were treated by different binders. The crown ornament is a close copy, but Kincaid's tool is distinguishable by the greater arch at the outer edges.

Figure 4.46 shows spines of several Irish trade bindings to illustrate their essential similarities. One of these books, Oliver Goldsmith's *Vicar of Wakefield*, is an edition purportedly printed in London, but both typography and binding give the game away. Figure 4.47 depicts another book with a false imprint, a Scottish piracy of Milton's *Paradise Lost*, which (along with many other such piracies) brazenly reproduces the names of prominent London syndicate members on the title-page. Like the Irish *Vicar of Wakefield*, this book's printing and binding show its origin: the cheapest form of sheep was usually the binding material of choice for these bottom-of-the-line editions.

The austere elegance of simple late-eighteenth-century Irish calf and half calf bindings is appealing, and rows of novels bound this way are a handsome sight. The basic style did not change over thirty or forty years, and there is little difference between *The Picture* and *Anastatia* (figs. 4.48–4.49), although the latter, with its double gilt labels and tree-patterned covers, must have been the more upmarket of the two bindings. The Irish binders adopted sawn-in sewing cords at about the same time as the English, and with about the same consistency. In multi-volume sets, Irish binders regularly used pairs of goatskin labels, usually in two colors, with only minimal decoration on the bindings. The labels on *New Picture of Paris* (fig. 4.50) are unusual: the central "Vol." ornament requires only the addition of the appropriate number, and the title label employs both upper and lower case letters.

As one would expect, fully decorated Scottish and Irish calf bindings show other distinctive features. Particularly interesting is this exuberant calf spine on a volume of an Edinburgh-printed set of *British Poets* (fig. 4.51). The style is suggestive of the bindings of James and William Scott, whose work has been well documented, but not one of the tools on this binding can be identified as theirs, although they did other work for these same publishers. An Irish binding as striking as that on the Edinburgh *British Poets* is the polished tree calf on the Cork-printed *Modern Monitor* (fig. 4.52). In light of the title-page, it is easy enough to suggest this may be a Cork binding, but the character of the finishing is unlike Dublin work of the period, and the tools are sufficiently unusual that it ought to be possible to correlate them with other Irish bindings, especially on surviving Cork imprints.

Any survey of trade styles from 1660–1800 would be incomplete if it did not mention some of the problems the field presents to novices and experts alike. Dating bookbindings can be difficult. Title-page dates are helpful but not conclusive; perhaps the best general rule is that most books are unlikely to be bound more than once in the first thirty or so years of their lives. Obvious exceptions include circulating library copies, where leaf edges were left untrimmed so they could be sold and rebound (fig. 4.38), and also books in fragile wrappers and boards, which were rebound either for reasons of taste or because of the disintegration of the original covering. Rebindings within a half-century or so of a book's publication can also be confusing (figs. 4.53–4.54), and *remboîtage*—there is no English

Fig. 4.46.
Irish calf bindings, from left to right: *The Batchelor; or Speculations of Jeoffry Wagstaffe, Esq.* Dublin, J. Hoey, 1769–72, 3 vols., 12mo; James Burgh, *The Art of Speaking.* Dublin, Messrs. Price [et al.], 1779, 12mo; Oliver Goldsmith, *The Vicar of Wakefield.* "London: Printed for John Murray" [but certainly Irish], 1775, 12mo; Charles du Fresnoy, *The Art of Painting.* Dublin, Whitestone [et al.], 1783, 8vo. Courtesy of Department of Special Collections, Stanford University Libraries.

Fig. 4.47.
John Milton, *Paradise Lost.* "London: for R. Bladon" [etc., but printed and bound in Scotland], 1769, 12mo, sheep. Courtesy of Department of Special Collections, Stanford University Libraries.

Fig. 4.48.
Margaret and Susannah Minifie, *The Picture. A Novel.* Dublin, for W. Smith and Son [and eleven others], 1766, 2 vols. in one, 12mo, sprinkled calf. The English edition of this novel was also published in 1766, but in three volumes, price 9s. bound. This more compact two-in-one edition may have been as little as half the price. Courtesy of the Lilly Library, Indiana University, Bloomington, Indiana.

Fig. 4.49.
*Anastatia: or, the Memoirs of the Chevalier Laroux. By a Lady.* Dublin, John Chambers, 1797, 2 vols., 12mo, tree calf gilt. The binder has incorrectly transcribed the title onto the spine label. Courtesy of the Lilly Library, Indiana University, Bloomington, Indiana.

Fig. 4.50.
Louis-Sébastien Mercier, *New Picture of Paris.* Dublin, N. Kelly, 1800, 2 vols., demy 8vo, polished tree calf.

Fig. 4.51.
*The British Poets*, Vol. XII. Edinburgh, for A. Kincaid and W. Creech, and J. Balfour, 1773, 12mo, calf, with a gilt rope border on covers. J. H. Loudon, *James and William Scott* (1980), illustrates a

volume from the same series bound in morocco by James Scott, but none of the tools in Loudon's catalogue match those on the present binding. Collection of William Zachs.

Fig. 4.52.
William Flyn, *The Modern Monitor; or, Flyn's Speculations.* Cork, William Flyn, 1771, 12mo, second edition, polished tree calf. Courtesy of

Department of Special Collections, Stanford University Libraries.

Fig. 4.53.
Richard Crashaw. *Steps to the
Temple*. London, for Henry
Herringman, 1670, pot 8vo,
second edition, rebound
circa 1729, as shown by the
charming ownership inscription. While one can see
that the binding could not
possibly be 1670, ownership
inscriptions like this one
are a guide to more accurate
dating. This gilt spine is
typical of trade work of
1720–1730; the covers have
been left undecorated.

Fig. 4.54.
*Dictionarium Sacrum seu
Religiosum. A Dictionary of
all Religions.* London, James
Knapton, 1723, 8vo, second
edition, quarter calf over
marbled boards, circa 1770,
an unusually elaborate gilt
spine for such a simple
binding.

word for it—where a good book in a poor binding is removed from that binding and inserted in a better one, can be difficult to detect. (Quite a few valuable works of literature have thus been re-housed in devotional bindings, not always of the right period.) There is always some tell-tale sign of *remboîtage*, however: a new lettering-piece, new or repaired endpapers, a hint of mis-alignment around the cover edges, or a combination of all three.

A further difficulty stems from the fact that some binders, particularly those at the lower end of the trade, worked in old styles and with old tools (fig. 4.4). Bookbinding tools were expensive, and were handed down, or sold, from generation to generation. A binding that looks older than the date of its book is simply old-fashioned, but without a dated inscription it can be difficult to tell the difference between an avant-garde binding and one put on twenty or more years after publication.

Other problems researchers regularly encounter are considered under the following four headings:

(1) Foreign bindings. Books were exported, and also bound and rebound, all over the world. Continental bindings are regularly found on books printed in the British Isles (fig. 4.55). The finishing, especially the lettering, usually provides clues: an initial "The" is rarely used on English labels, and of course "Tom." instead of "Vol." is another good hint. British and Continental styles of leather marbling and staining are also different. Dutch work is often closest to that of the British, but even the Dutch used types of marbled endpapers that were common in Continental binding, but less often seen on the other side of the Channel.[7]

English, Irish, and Scottish books also turn up in American bindings, but the majority of books sent to the Americas before 1800 were ready-bound, mostly in sheep. The origin of these simple bind-ings can be difficult to determine, especially after they have dried out, as so many have, in overheated

Fig. 4.55. Continental bindings on English-language books, 1715–1773, from left to right: George Villiers, Duke of Buckingham, *The Works.* London, for Sam. Briscoe, 1715, 2 vols., 8vo, polished calf, spines gilt with red and green goatskin labels. The endpapers (not shown) are marbled, a French persillé pattern unlikely to be seen in an English binding; Alexander Pope, *The Works.* "London" [but The Hague], T.J. for the Company, 1720, pot 8vo, finely sprinkled calf, very likely Dutch or French, spine gilt with a red goatskin label lettered in a font not usually seen in England, and the edges of the leaves sprinkled in brown and red, also typical of Continental work; Jonathan Swift, *The Poetical Works, of J.S.D.D.D.S.P.D.* [Holland], Printed in the Year, 1736, 12mo, marbled calf, spine with sawn-in cords and gilt, with distinctively Continental lettering on the red goatskin label; Horace Walpole, *The Castle of Otranto.* Dublin, for J. Hoey [and nine others], 1765, 12mo, French marbled calf, flat spine gilt with a red goatskin label, and marbled endpapers in a typical French curl pattern; Eliza Haywood, *The Invisible Spy.* London, for H. Gardner, 1773, new edition, 2 vols., 12mo, polished marbled sheep, spines with sawn-in cords and gilt with blue and red labels, probably a Northern European binding.

storage facilities. Some American binders treated deer and other skins instead of sheep to make a kind of roan, and the grain of these skins has a more coarse and irregular appearance than standard sheep bindings from the British Isles.

(2) Original bindings redecorated. Figure 4.56 shows more than one generation at work on the binding of Stapylton's Juvenal (1647). Many bindings were similarly updated, especially in the last half of the eighteenth century. Redecoration was normally limited to spines, which were sometimes just given new labels (fig. 4.57), but which could also be elaborately gilded to make rows of books in libraries more imposing and uniform (in the spirit of Pepys). This must have been quite profitable for binders, and many advertised such services. As one trade card puts it, "Gentlemen may have their Libraries Gilded and Titled on the Backs in a very cheap way, yet very Ornamental . . . this may be performed at their own House."[8] Figure 4.58, John Oldham's *Works* (1695) is a dramatic example of the process. Its binding is clearly original—a simple paneled dark calf—but the spine tooling and label were added seventy or eighty years later, in the same style as the spine on Francis Longe's copy of *The History of Lady Julia Mandeville* (fig. 4.59).

(3) Dated bindings misinterpreted. A date on a book's spine refers to the date of the text, not the binding, but confusion sometimes arises nonetheless. In Chapter 2 (fig. 2.24), there is an illustration of Francis Hutcheson's *An Enquiry into the Original of Our Ideas of Beauty and Virtue* (1753), a binding unusual for its time in showing the date and place of publication on the spine. The binding is contemporary, however, and can usefully be compared with two later examples. The first, Overbury's *Works* (fig. 4.60), is also dated 1753, but of course that refers to the date of the book, which was probably bound for

Fig. 4.56.
Sir Robert Stapylton, *Juvenal's Sixteen Satyrs or, a Survey of the Manners and Actions of Mankind.* London, for Humphrey Moseley, 1647, pot 8vo. The binding is blind-ruled dark calf; the only original gilding is the barely discernable edge-roll.

The fore-edge has been lettered "Staple/ ton's Engl/ Juvenal/ 250" (the number presumably either recording the acquisition, or the order for shelving). Manuscript labeling on fore-edges was old-fashioned in 1647, but not remarkably so. Later, probably in the nineteenth century, the gilt ornament and fillet, and the spine label were added. The label's appearance, with the author's name alone type-set in capitals, has a decidedly Victorian look.

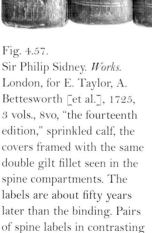

Fig. 4.57.
Sir Philip Sidney. *Works.* London, for E. Taylor, A. Bettesworth [et al.], 1725, 3 vols., 8vo, "the fourteenth edition," sprinkled calf, the covers framed with the same double gilt fillet seen in the spine compartments. The labels are about fifty years later than the binding. Pairs of spine labels in contrasting colors became especially popular in the 1770s and later. Possibly there were title labels in the second spine compartments in 1725, discarded when the new set was added, but the original gilt volume number can be seen on Vol. 3, where the later numeral label has chipped away.

Fig. 4.58.
John Oldham, *The Works.* London, for Nathaniel Rolls, 1695, 8vo, paneled calf, the spine fully gilded and labeled, perhaps for the Henry Corbet whose mid-eighteenth-century bookplate appears on the pastedown endpaper. Courtesy of

Department of Special Collections, Stanford University Libraries.

Fig. 4.59.
Frances Brooke, *The History of Lady Julia Mandeville*. London, for R. and J. Dodsley, 1763, 2 vols. in one, 12mo, calf, covers with Francis Longe's crest but otherwise undecorated. Combining two volumes in a single binding was an obvious way to save on binding costs, both for booksellers and customers. The fully gilt spine seen here could have been ordered by Longe from the same binder who gilt-stamped the crest. Longe's library is discussed in Chapter 3, note 49. Courtesy of the Lilly Library, Indiana University, Bloomington, Indiana.

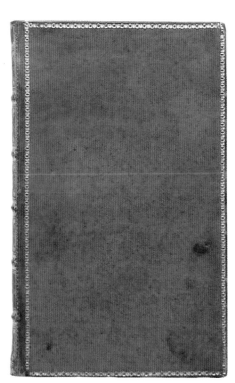

Fig. 4.60.
Thomas Overbury, *The Miscellaneous Works in Verse and Prose*. London, for J. Bouquet, 1753, 12mo, mid-nineteenth-century polished calf gilt. Thomas Westwood's bookplate, dated signature, and a note concerning a reference to Overbury in Walton's *Compleat Angler* appear inside. The marbled endpapers in this binding are glazed "antique spot," identified by Richard J. Wolfe, *Marbled Paper* (1990), plate XXXVI, no. 163, as "British, 1840s–1850s."

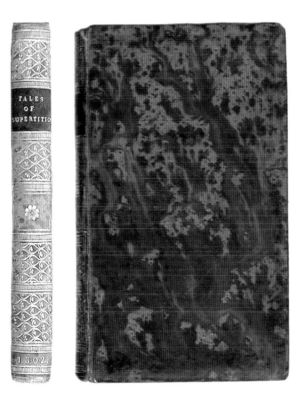

Fig. 4.61.
Anne Bannerman, *Tales of Superstition and Chivalry*.
London, Vernor and Hood, 1802, pot 8vo, polished tree calf, spine gilt and dated at the foot, as often seen on bindings of this period.

Fig. 4.62.
Mary Pilkington, *A Mirror for the Female Sex. Historical Beauties for Young Ladies*.
London, for Vernor and Hood . . . and sold by E. Newbery, 1798, 12mo, roan-backed marbled boards circa 1810–20. Certainly Elizabeth Newbery, who sold her business to John Harris in 1801 or 1802, never had a binding like this in her shop, but it is typical of the later trade style for children's books, and at least a couple of other Mrs. Pilkington books are known in similar bindings. The covers on this one are a Stormont marbled paper that came into use in Britain around 1805 and was common through about 1825.

the collector Thomas Westwood. Dating the foot of spines became popular around 1790, and may have become fashionable because of its use by high-end German immigrant binders like Christian Kalthoeber (see fig. 5.5). Another binding, on Anne Bannerman's *Tales of Superstition* (fig. 4.61), follows this fashion. The date on its spine, like that on the Hutcheson, is accurate both as to book and binding.

(4) Remainder bindings. The concept of remainder binding has been little applied to pre-nineteenth-century bookbindings. From the earliest days of printing, however, booksellers had to decide how many copies were likely to sell within a reasonable time, send those to their binders, and warehouse the remainder until there was call for them. During most of the hand-bookbinding era there was not likely to be a dramatic difference in the look of copies bound during the course of five—or even fifteen—years, especially if booksellers involved with an edition continued to use the same binders. By the end of the eighteenth century, however, certain publishers' styles were in a state of flux, and fifteen years could mean a significant difference in the appearance of bindings. Figure 4.62 illustrates this principle.

## CHAPTER FIVE

# DELUXE BINDINGS

So far this book has mostly illustrated simpler bindings, but trade bookbinding encompasses what David Pearson has called "the spectrum of options from the simple to the elaborate."[1] Book buyers would see the entire spectrum for sale in shops. A descriptive term is thus required to identify those at the more elaborate, expensive end. Anachronistic as it is, I have settled on the word "deluxe," which was first used in English in the phrase "edition de luxe" in 1819, according to *The Shorter Oxford Dictionary*.[2]

The idea that all deluxe bindings were individually bespoke may be dismissed out of hand. One need look no further than miniature Bibles and almanacs (figs. 5.1–5.3), to find multiple surviving copies of fine edition bindings. Some children's books were also given special treatment: the copy shown here of Darton and Harvey's *People of all Nations* (fig. 5.4) is certainly a publisher's issue. These are the precursors of nineteenth-century publishers' gift bindings, so popular for literary annuals, anthologies, and illustrated editions of poetry. In the eighteenth century, John Brindley advertised his editions of the classics "ready bound in Morocco, Blue Turkey, white Cambridge Bindings [*i.e.* vellum] &c. marbled on the leaves."[3] Other advertisements for deluxe bindings by John Stockdale and John Bell have already been quoted, and the Edinburgh bookseller Alexander Donaldson confirmed similar practices in Scotland in 1764 when he advertised his wares "bound in various forms, some in turkey with gilt leaves, and bordered with gold on the edges; others in calf and lettered."[4] Another upscale London bookseller, Benjamin White in Fleet Street (fig. 5.5), went furthest of all by advertising his best bookbinder. In a 1779 catalogue, White offered his own publication, the fourth edition of Thomas Pennant's *British Zoology*, 1776–77, 4 vols., in boards at £4.4s., "bound new and neat" at £4.14s.6d., or "elegantly bound by Baumgarten" at £5.5s.[5] Even earlier, seventeenth-century high-end establishments, like those of Richard Royston and the Mearnes, commissioned fine bindings and probably sold them both wholesale and retail.

If we accept that books in deluxe bindings, including fine and large paper copies, were sold ready-bound in bookshops, the question remains "how many?" Unlike the calf and sheep noted in the bookbinders' price lists and in Starkey and Clavell's catalogues, early deluxe bindings have no comprehensive descriptive or price history, only occasional, tantalizing booksellers' advertisements. We know that the vast majority of books in calf and sheep were ready-bindings sold in bookshops. Ought we assume that the majority of goatskin bindings were as well? It may be likely, but as yet there is no hard evidence to support this assumption.[6]

Another question is whether the most elaborate of deluxe bindings were invariably private commissions. The answer is surely no: deluxe bindings of all kinds were certainly available in bookshops (fig. 5.6). Simpler, less expensive, goatskin bindings survive in the largest quantity, but that is what one would expect whatever the relative percentage of bespoke to ready-bound might be.

Finely-bound books serve a number of purposes. They are desirable and memorable gifts, whether as tokens of affection or requests for patronage. In the case of Bibles and devotional books (figs.

and a central onlay in black or dark green, bearing the sacred monogram." W. Harris first published this miniature Bible in 1771, reprinting it in 1774 and 1775. Another edition appeared in 1778 under the imprint of J. Harris, and this was Elizabeth Newbery's copy-text for her edition of 1780, which remained in print for twenty years. Could this "J. Harris" have been the bookseller John Harris, who worked for, and ultimately took over the Newbery business? Harris was in his mid-twenties in 1780; conceivably he inherited the copyright of the miniature Bible, and sold it to his prospective employer. Courtesy of the Lilly Library, Indiana University, Bloomington, Indiana.

Fig. 5.1.
*The Bible in Miniature.*
London, for W. Harris, 1774, 64mo, in two standard bindings: calf, sold at 1s., and goatskin, sold at 2s. S. Roscoe, *John Newbery and his Successors* (1973), p. 57, describes the bindings of the 1780 and later Newbery editions, which are the same as these earlier, Harris, editions; all were "issued in plain calf [or] crimson morocco with gilt tooling

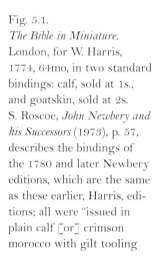

Fig. 5.2.
John Taylor, *Verbum Sempiternum.* London, F. Collins for T. Ilive, 1693, 64mo, goatskin gilt. Several other deluxe bindings on this edition of Taylor's rhyming Bible history survive, including Arthur Houghton's copy sold at Christie's in 1979. Courtesy of the Lilly Library, Indiana University, Bloomington, Indiana.

Fig. 5.3.
*London Almanack for the Year of Christ, 1790.* London, for the Company of Stationers, [1789], 48mo, goatskin with vellum onlays partially stained blue, elaborately gilt-tooled, in matching slipcase, a typical deluxe almanac binding. Almanacs were a staple of the retail trade in gift books and can be seen in various sizes and bindings from the

Restoration onwards, those in larger formats often featuring royal and other coats of arms. A similar binding on an 1800 edition of this almanac is shown in the frontispiece of Louis Bondy, *Miniature Books* (1994).

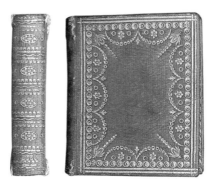
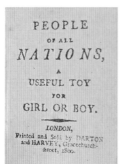

PEOPLE
OF ALL
NATIONS,
A
USEFUL TOY
FOR
GIRL OR BOY.

LONDON,
Printed and Sold by DARTON
and HARVEY, Gracechurch-
street, 1800.

a Chinese.

Fig. 5.4.
*People of all Nations, a Useful Toy for Girl or Boy.*
London, Darton and Harvey, 1800, 64mo, in elegant gilt-tooled goatskin, the engravings with publisher's hand-coloring, a *very* special present. Courtesy of Department of Special Collections, Charles E. Young Research Library, University of California, Los Angeles.

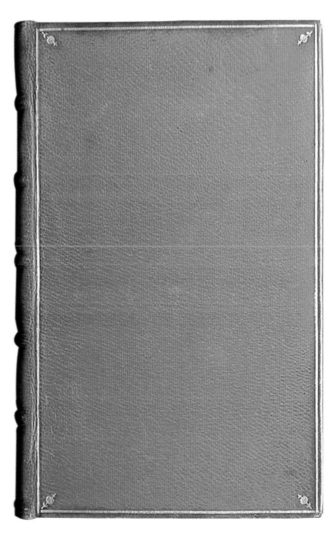

Bound by
C. KALTHOEBER,
London.

Fig. 5.5.
Samuel Egerton Brydges, *Sonnets and Other Poems.* London, for B. and J. White, 1795, foolscap 8vo, goatskin. After Baumgarten's death in 1782, Christian Kalthoeber succeeded to the business. Benjamin White, whose later imprint this is, continued to use the firm for his deluxe bindings. Sometime around 1790, Kalthoeber began to insert printed tickets in his work, always on the upper corner of the front free end-paper verso.

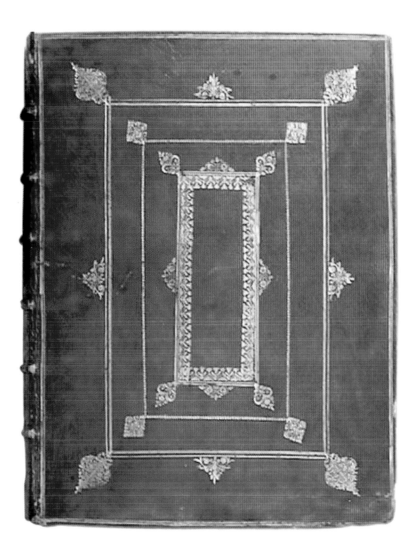

Fig. 5.6.
Nicolas Fatio de Duillier,
*Fruit-Walls Improved,*
*by Inclining them to the*
*Horizon. . . . By a Member of*
*the Royal Society.* London,
R. Everingham . . . to be
sold by John Taylor, 1699,
4to, goatskin. A large and
thick paper copy, finely
bound, the kind presented
to other members of the
Royal Society—Samuel
Pepys was one—or the
aristocracy. Taylor probably also kept some for sale
in his shop. Courtesy of
the William Andrews
Clark Memorial Library,
University of California,
Los Angeles.

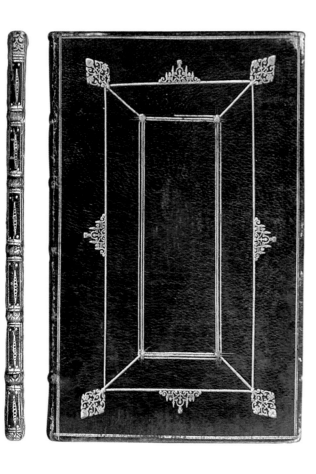

Fig. 5.7.
*A Companion to the Altar: shewing the Nature and Necessity of a Sacramental Preparation . . . unto which are Added, Prayers and Meditations.* London, for Edward Parker, 1723, 8vo, gilt paneled goatskin typical of devotional books of the period, the spine unlettered, with a gilt edge-roll and inside borders, and marbled endpapers. The title-page imprint concludes, "This Book is Bound up with the Common-Prayers of several Sorts: And to be had at the Place abovesaid." Parker must have catered to different congregations and had copies bound to suit each of them: this one contains only the order for Holy Communion, extracted from an unidentified edition of the *Book of Common Prayer.* Were it not for Parker's statement on the title-page, one might assume this to be a bespoke binding. For a similar binding on George Herbert's devotional poems, see figure 4.14.

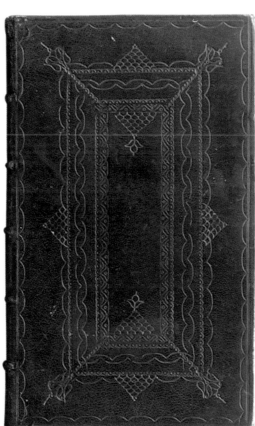

Fig. 5.8.
John Playford, *The Whole Book of Psalmes: with the Usual Hymns . . . Composed in Three Parts.* London, J. Heptinstall, for the Company of Stationers, 1707, 8vo, black goatskin in "somber" style. Somber bindings began to appear in the 1670s and remained in vogue until about 1720. Booksellers probably laid in stocks of them before Lent, when more ostentatious bindings may have seemed inappropriate, but they would also have kept them on hand year-round for mourners. This is a typical example: elaborately tooled in blind, entirely without gilt. Even the edges of the leaves are stained black. Many binders probably worked in this style, and a wide range of tool variations can be found.

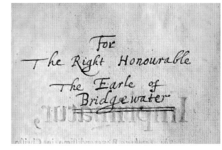

Fig. 5.9.
Isaac Basire, *Deo & Ecclesiae
Sacrum. Sacriledge Arraigned
and Condemned by St. Paul.*
London, by W.G. for
W. Wells and R. Scot,
1668, second edition, 8vo,
goatskin, a presentation
binding, inscribed by the
author or publisher on the
recto of the imprimatur leaf.
Courtesy of the William
Andrews Clark Memorial
Library, University of
California, Los Angeles.

5.7–5.8), deluxe bindings show respect for the Almighty, and when carried to church can also be admired by one's neighbors. As objects of beauty, fine bindings have appealed to collectors since antiquity.

Most deluxe bindings were probably purchased as gifts. Even Samuel Pepys, as famously indulgent as he was with most of his pleasures, seems to have bought few of his books in fancy goatskin bindings. He bought devotional books that way, and some elegant books secondhand. With only a few exceptions, such as the well-known commission to William Nott, Pepys purchased new books in calf and ordered calf when rebinding. Though his library contains many fine goatskin bindings, Pepys received most of them as presents.[7]

Pepys, like many modern book-buyers, had to make budgetary decisions, whether to buy a few deluxe bindings (comparable to today's limited editions) or a larger number of books in cheaper, albeit decorated, calf. Only the grandest of royal and aristocratic libraries consistently ordered their books delivered or rebound in fine bindings.

The wealthy and powerful received many finely-bound books from those expecting preferment or money in return (fig. 5.9). When authors and booksellers gave deluxe copies of their publications, they were "presentation bindings." Alexander Pope's friend Charles Jervas makes it clear there was a hierarchy of presentation bindings, else he would not have lamented that "one of the best" was given to a knight instead of a duke.[8]

Some cataloguers describe certain pre-1800 fine bindings as "presentation" even in the absence of any mark of provenance (figs. 5.10–5.11). Others use the term when there is a match of an aristocratic bookplate to a name in a list of subscribers. But book buyers, both shop customers and subscription patrons, may simply have paid a higher price to receive a better copy (fig. 5.12). Without an inscription, the name of the recipient on the binding itself, or some other determinative point (figs.

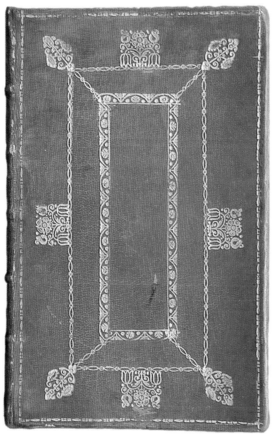
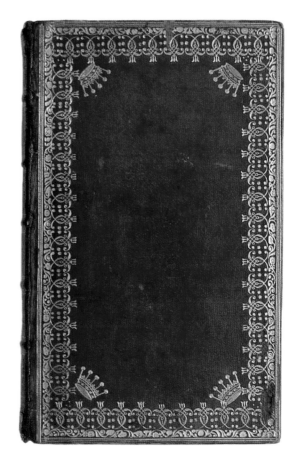

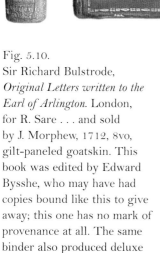

Fig. 5.10.
Sir Richard Bulstrode,
*Original Letters written to the
Earl of Arlington.* London,
for R. Sare . . . and sold
by J. Morphew, 1712, 8vo,
gilt-paneled goatskin. This
book was edited by Edward
Bysshe, who may have had
copies bound like this to give
away; this one has no mark of
provenance at all. The same
binder also produced deluxe
bindings for Egbert Sanger

and Edmund Curll. One
such, black goatskin on what
appears to be the dedication
copy of John Ozell's translation of Nicolas Boileau-
Despreaux's *Works,* 2 vols.,
1712–11, was illustrated in
my Catalogue XII, *English
Literature 1600–1850* (Bath,
1986), item 9.

Fig. 5.11.
 Jonathan Swift, *Works.*
Dublin, George Faulkner,
1744, 6 vols., 8vo. This
is the second volume of a
special issue, with passages
suppressed in the printed
text of the poems sepa-
rately copied in manu-
script and bound in.
Several copies of this
issue have survived, all in
deluxe goatskin. It seems
likely that some were for
sale in Faulkner's shop,

although many were
certainly for aristocratic
patrons. By 1744 Swift's
mental state had deterio-
rated to a point where
he could not have been
personally involved,
either with the manuscript
additions or with the
distribution of copies.
Courtesy of the William
Andrews Clark Memorial
Library, University of
California, Los Angeles.

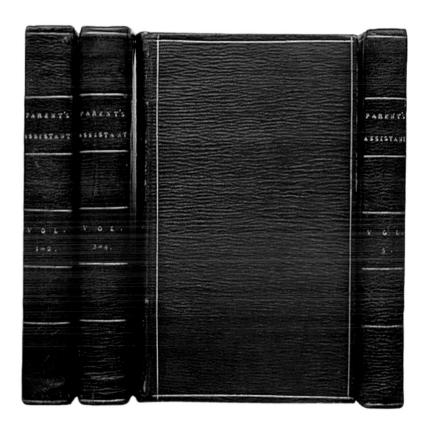

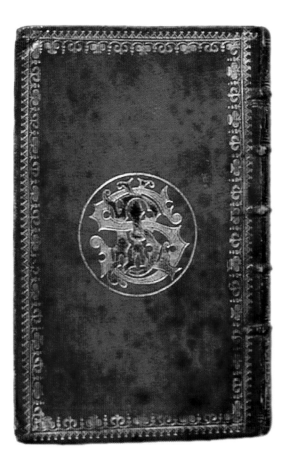

Fig. 5.14.
James Mackenzie, *Treatise concerning the Origin and Progress of Fees*. Edinburgh, 1734, 8vo, goatskin, a Scottish presentation binding with a note by the recipient "Ex Dono Jacobi Mckenzie" dated 1735. The binding has later ownership markings of the Birmingham Law Society; their gilt monogram on this lower cover is only slightly less obtrusive than the large capital letters on the upper.

IT is humbly defired, that what you or any of you, moft noble Ladies, Gentlewomen, or others, are pleafed to beftow or give towards this good and great defign, that you would be pleaf- ed to take a receipt on the back- fide of Time, or Charity, fealed with three feales, namely, the Treafurers, Houfkeepers, and Regifters, and it fhall be fairly recorded, and hung up in the School-houfe to be read of all from Time to Time, to the world's end we hope.

Fig. 5.15.
William Blake, *The Ladies Charity School-house Roll of Highgate: or, a Subscription of Many Noble, Well-Disposed Ladies for the Easie Carrying of it on.* [London, 1670], pot 8vo, goatskin, one of a number of bindings in similar style, often described as the work of the "Charity School Binder." Some bore the names of donors to the school stamped on the upper covers and are unquestionably presentation bindings; others, like this one, were probably kept on hand to encourage donations, and sent when one was received. There may have been more than one binder working for the school, as a variety of tool-impressions are seen on surviving examples. See, *e.g.*, Maggs Bros. Ltd. *Bookbinding in the British Isles*, Catalogue 1075 (1987), item 75, and Mirjam M. Foot, "English and Foreign Bookbindings," in *The Book Collector* (Spring 1983), p. 78. Courtesy of the Brick Row Book Shop.

Fig. 5.16.
Elkanah Settle, *Carmen
Irenicum. The Union of the
Imperial Crowns of Great
Britain. An Heroick Poem.*
London, for the Author,
1708, folio,goatskin gilt,
with the arms of the Earl of
Manchester. Settle employed
a trade binder to produce
presentation bindings in what
Howard Nixon has described
as "a successful racket." *Five
Centuries of English Bookbinding*
(1978), p. 130. Settle composed
short poems which were printed in folio, bound in goatskin,
and gilt-stamped with the
coats of arms of different aristocratic families on the covers.
He sent these unsolicited offer-
ings to the families, and if he
received money in return, his
object was achieved. But if
the book was sent back (and
many were), Settle simply
had another prospect's coat of
arms stamped on a leather
overlay and tried again. This
copy had the desired effect
first time around. The gilt
arms are original and the front
endpaper bears the library
label and engraved bookplate
of the recipient's family.

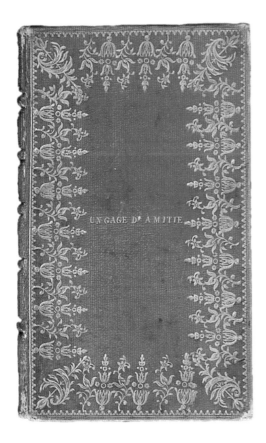

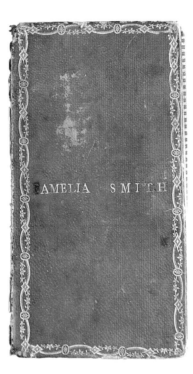

Fig. 5.17.
Oliver Goldsmith, *Poetical Works*. London, for J. Osborne and T. Griffin, 1785, 12mo, goatskin, spine with floral ornaments but unlettered. The sentiment "Un Gage d'Amitie" is so generic that it may well have been lettered before the book was offered for sale, but the binding is clearly fully finished without it. Collection of William Zachs.

Fig. 5.18.
*The Book of Common Prayer.* Oxford, 1783, pot 12mo, goatskin, the spine fully gilt but unlettered, a typical example of a book that would have been personalized while the purchaser waited. The name, "Amelia Smith," gilt on the upper cover shows distinct signs of being a rushed job: the workman lettered a "B" to begin with, and had to black it out and start over. The mistake is visible just to the left of the initial "A."

5.13–5.16), referring to a deluxe binding as "presentation" is, at best, overly optimistic. Without such evidence, the term "presentation" should be eliminated from the cataloguer's vocabulary. "Deluxe binding" is less problematic, and may encompass all goatskin, russia, and vellum bindings as well as elaborately decorated calf and sheep.

In the days when bookshops and bookbinderies were on the same premises or nearby, deluxe bindings could be personalized in short order. This is clear from the correspondence of the bookbinder William Hall, a journeyman working for John Bell:

> Mr. John Bell came down from the front shop with a small book in his hand to be lettered, which was sold to a gentleman who was waiting for it. . . . Mr. Bell, looking along the row of men, about eight or nine of them, seemed to challenge the whole lot, saying: 'Not one of you capable of lettering a book?' I felt much hurt, knowing that I had some practice in lettering. I stepped forward, saying: 'If you please, Sir, I will letter it.' . . . It pleased the gentleman very well."[9]

On that day, head finisher Thomas Fairbairn was on an errand, and there was no one but Hall capable of handling the single-letter tools required for personalizing a book. Some bindings may already have had generic messages on them, such as "Un gage d'amitie" (fig. 5.17), but anyone wanting a name or a special message had to wait for the lettering to be done (fig. 5.18).

Well before Bell's time, gilt tooling could be applied to a book while the customer waited. An early example is this goatskin binding on works by Richard Allestree, personalized for Jane Wynne (fig.

5.19). This shows every sign of being a ready-bound copy with the name added, in a form identical to many printed book-labels of the period. Remove it, along with the double fillet and small corner acorns above and below (which match no other tools on the binding), and what is left is standard trade goatskin. Another personalized Allestree binding (fig. 5.20) is less likely to have been a short-order job: Ann Green's name is carefully integrated, and the circlets above and below it are repeated elsewhere on the spine.

As the eighteenth century progressed, more and more literature appeared in fine bindings (fig. 5.21). Wars brought the publication of rousing patriotic poems (fig. 5.22), which authors gave to prospective patrons and well-to-do customers purchased as gifts or for show. By the latter half of the century, the craze for novels meant that the more respectable ones (those unlike, *e.g.* fig. 5.23) often appeared in deluxe bindings (fig. 5.24). From 1770 onwards, however, the increasing issue of books in boards and wrappers created a larger market for bespoke rebinding of recent publications. Fine examples are, in effect, identical to high-end trade bindings (fig. 5.25).[10]

From about 1660 to 1730 the works of Richard Allestree were much in demand, and often given as gifts. The sheer quantity of surviving examples in similar fine bindings demonstrates that they must have been a staple of retail bookshops. Allestree was a Royalist and clergyman whose writings emphasized sound morality. In the anti-Puritan, anti-sectarian mood of the post-Restoration, his books were "perhaps the favourite reading of many devout Anglicans."[11] *The Whole Duty of Man*, first published in 1659, appeared in at least fifty different editions by 1700; *The Gentleman's Calling* (1660), twenty; *The Causes of the Decay of Christian Piety* (1667), fifteen or more; and *The Ladies Calling* (1673), a dozen. Because the books were reprinted so frequently, almost all bindings on any edition are certain to have been executed within a few months of publication, which provides an excellent opportunity to study the development of binding styles. Figure 5.26 shows the trend towards spine lettering on four editions of *The Causes of the Decay of Christian Piety.* The two editions from the 1670s are unlettered, but those of 1694 and 1704 have the titles in the second spine panel, which has remained the standard placement ever since. Lettering was not universally adopted, however, as can be seen in figure 5.27, five editions of Allestree's *The Government of the Tongue.* Three of these, from 1677–1702, are lettered. The first edition of 1674 in calf is unlettered, as one would expect, but so is the seventh edition of 1721 in red goatskin. The development of lettering styles is also clearly visible in figures 5.26 and 5.27, from the crowded form of the 1670s—"Gouer/ nmt./ of/ Tongu"—through the progressively tidier work of the early eighteenth century. One binder determined to get as much of the title as possible on the spine by lettering up instead of across. His work on a matching set of four titles by Allestree appears in figure 5.28. Were Allestree's and other works only lettered when part of a set, or was lettering simply an additional expense, purchased at the discretion of the bookseller or private customer? The latter seems more likely, and is further indicated by the inclusion of lettering as a separate cost in the 1743 Dublin bookbinders' price list.

Spine decoration and lettering evolved between 1670 and 1720, yet there is little evolution of the standard cover panel on ordinary deluxe goatskin during the same period. The decoration on the 1694 *The Causes of the Decay of Christian Piety* (fig. 5.26(c)) would look entirely at home on the red cover of the 1721 edition of *The Government of the Tongue* (fig. 5.29). The covers of elaborately gilt bindings took many different forms during the same period, however, from all-over tooling (fig. 5.30) to more

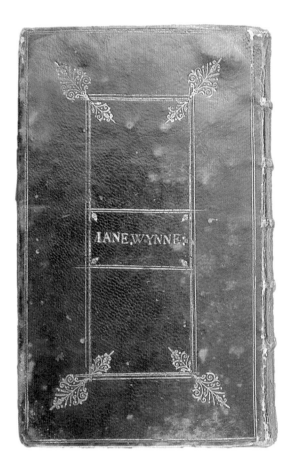

Fig. 5.19.
Richard Allestree, *The Gentleman's Calling*. London, R. Norton for Robert Pawlet, 1676, bound with *The Ladies Calling* and two other works by Allestree, the latter three printed in Oxford in 1676 and 1675, 8vo, goatskin gilt, spine with French corners and a repeated central fleuron, unlettered. Ordinarily one would assume that a volume with multiple works bound together would be bespoke, but Allestree's works were so popular that this was just one of many ways they were offered ready-bound. Courtesy of Department of Special Collections, Stanford University Libraries.

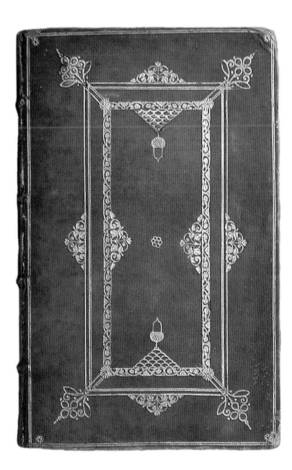

Fig. 5.20.
Richard Allestree, *The Ladies Calling*. Oxford, At the Theater, 1693, 8vo, gilt-paneled goatskin. Was this binding bespoke, as seems likely, or were examples like this produced with a blank space on the spine and personalized later? Courtesy of the William Andrews Clark Memorial Library, University of California, Los Angeles.

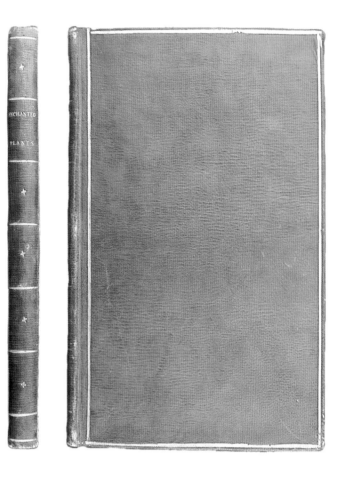

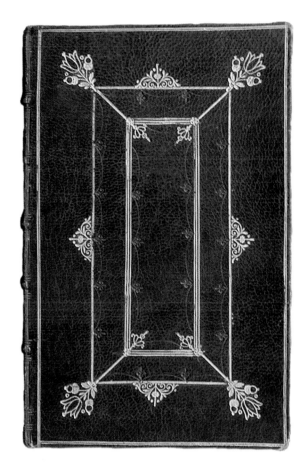

Fig. 5.21.
Maria Henrietta Montolieu, *The Enchanted Plants, Fables in Verse*. London, Thomas Bensley, 1800, 8vo, straight-grained goatskin. Books by aristocratic ladies regularly turn up in fine bindings. As early as the 1660s, folio editions of Katherine Philips's poems were bound in gilt-paneled turkey, and so were early eighteenth-century octavos by Lady Mary Chudleigh and the Countess of Winchelsea, among others. Courtesy of Department of Special Collections, Stanford University Libraries.

Fig. 5.22.
John Dennis, *Britannia Triumphans: or the Empire Sav'd, and Europe Deliver'd.* London, for J. Nutt, 1704, 8vo, gilt-paneled goatskin, spine gilt but unlettered, all edges gilt. The poem celebrates the Duke of Marlborough's victory at the battle of Blenheim in August of the same year: "Up, rouse your selves, ye nations, praise the lord." Courtesy of the William Andrews Clark Memorial Library, University of California, Los Angeles.

Fig. 5.23.
A surprising number of novels had racy title-pages: clearly they sold well. But they were unlikely to have been put in fine bindings for gifts, and this example survives as issued, in wrappers, all edges untrimmed. Courtesy of Department of Special Collections, Charles E. Young Research Library, University of California, Los Angeles.

DID YOU EVER SEE SUCH DAMNED STUFF?

OR,

SO-MUCH-THE-BETTER.

A STORY

Without Head or Tail,

Wit or Humor.

*Rantum-skantum* is the Word,
And *Nonsense* shall ensue.

LONDON:

Printed for C. G. SEYFFERT in Pall-mall. 1760.

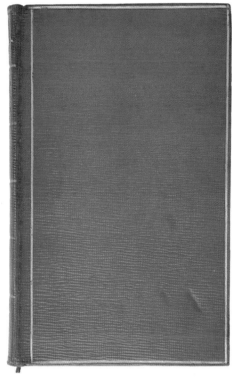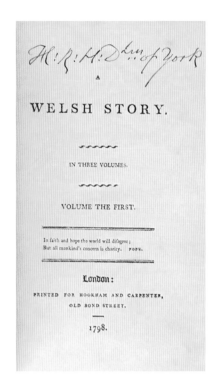

Fig. 5.24.
Mary Barker, *A Welsh Story. In Three Volumes.* London, for Hookham and Carpenter, 1798, 3 vols., 12mo, goatskin. This is the dedication copy to the Duchess of York, specially bound; the printed dedication to the Duchess comprises pp. iii–iv of the preliminaries in the first volume. Publication details for the book survive, and show that, although the title states that the printing was "for" the booksellers Hookham and Carpenter, the 750-copy edition was underwritten by the authoress and cost £120. She ended with a loss of some £48. James Raven et al., *The English Novel 1770–1829*, Vol. I, 1798:15. Collection of William Zachs.

Fig. 5.25.
Charlotte Smith, *Montalbert. A Novel.* London, for E. Booker, 1795, 3 vols., 12mo, a half binding of goatskin over marbled boards, spines gilt. The novel was advertised at 12s. sewed or in boards, and 15s. "neatly bound." This elegant half binding is not easy to categorize. It is probably too fine to be the kind of binding contemplated at 15s. It could be a bespoke rebinding of a copy purchased in boards or wrappers, or the kind of binding for which a well-to-do customer might have left a standing order. Collection of William Zachs.

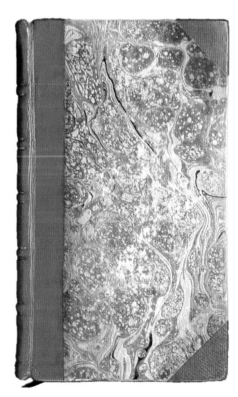

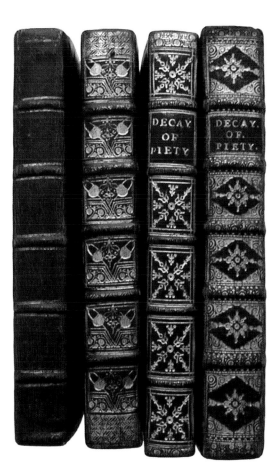

Fig. 5.26.
Richard Allestree, *The Causes of the Decay of Christian Piety.* Four editions, all printed in London, 8vo, and bound in goatskin. The spines are shown from left to right, and the covers (facing page) are shown clockwise: (a) R. Norton, 1675; (b) R. Norton, 1679; (c) Edward Pawlet, 1694; (d) J.H. for E. and R. Pawlet, 1704. Courtesy of the William Andrews Clark Memorial Library, University of California, Los Angeles.

austere geometric and mosaic styles. Only the Harleian style, whose origins can be seen in earlier work by Robert Steel's bindery, showed staying power. Introduced in 1718 or 1719, it slowly displaced paneled covers on ordinary deluxe work by the 1730s. So named because Thomas Elliott and Christopher Chapman used it on books they bound for Lord Harley, this style features an elaborate, but usually fairly narrow, perimeter border of multiple rolls enclosing a central lozenge-shaped ornament built up with small tools. The Harleian influence can be seen in the borders of Vincent Bourne's *Poematia* (fig. 5.31), and in the Scottish binding on Mackenzie's *Treatise*, 1735 (fig. 5.14). It remained in widespread use for the remainder of the century (fig. 5.32).

Harleian elements and panels, some of the latter with cottage-roof designs, were magnificently combined in the lost Irish parliamentary bindings, among the finest executed anywhere in this period, beginning around 1740. The 149 volumes of the manuscript records of the Irish Lords and Commons featured an almost incredible variety of ornament, but all were destroyed by fire during the 1922 siege of the Four Courts.[12] These Irish Parliamentary binders also worked in more modest Harleian styles. Maggs Bros. Ltd. have catalogued a volume, bound circa 1740, from a set of the ubiquitous Richard Allestree works. It shows a very narrow double fillet and trefoil roll border, and a large central diamond filled with small floral and other ornaments.[13]

The reference literature of British bookbinding illustrates many elaborate bindings, not only goatskin, but calf, vellum, and russia (fig. 5.33). It is reasonable to assume that many of these deluxe bindings graced the shelves and windows of bookshops and were sold retail. Would anyone but a bookseller have commissioned Richard Balley's extraordinary "backless" bindings, where spine and fore-edge were

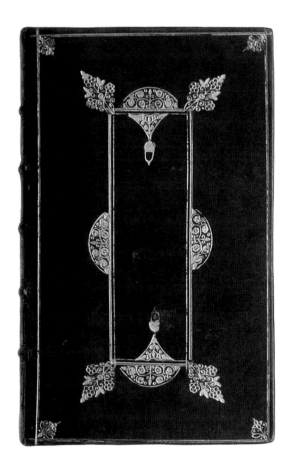

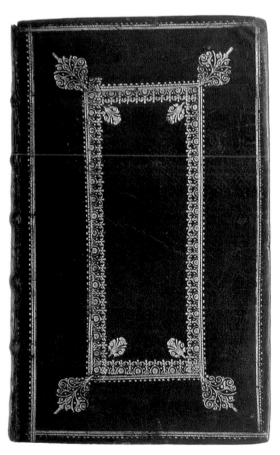

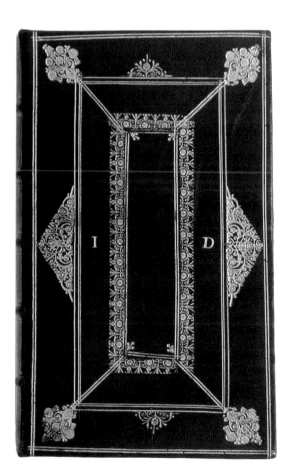

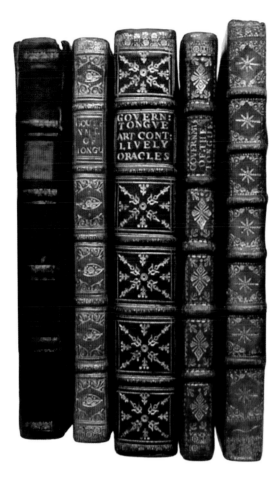

Fig. 5.27.
Richard Allestree, *The Government of the Tongue.* Five editions, all printed "Oxford, At the Theatre," 8vo, and all but the first bound in goatskin. From left to right the dates are 1674; "MDCLXVII" (but 1677); 1693 (bound with two other works); 1702; and 1721. Courtesy of the William Andrews Clark Memorial Library, University of California, Los Angeles.

Fig. 5.28.
Richard Allestree, four works, 8vo, uniformly bound in goatskin. From left to right: *The Gentleman's Calling.* London, Eliz. Pawlet, 1705; *The Art of Contentment.* Oxford, At the Theatre, 1705; *The Government of the Tongue.* Oxford, At the Theatre, 1702 (also shown in fig. 5.27); and *The Government of the Thoughts.* London, John Marshall ⌈no date, but circa 1705⌉. Courtesy of the William Andrews Clark Memorial Library, University of California, Los Angeles.

Fig. 5.29.
Richard Allestree, *The Government of the Tongue.* Oxford, At the Theatre, 1721, seventh impression, 8vo, goatskin. The unlettered spine is shown in figure 5.27. Courtesy of the William Andrews Clark Memorial Library, University of California, Los Angeles.

Fig. 5.30.
Hermann Hugo, *Pia Desideria: or, Divine Addresses . . . Englished by Edm. Arwaker.* London, for Henry Bonwicke, 1686, foolscap 8vo, black goatskin with applied silver paint, gilt-tooled with an all-over pattern of drawer-handle and small tools in the style of Queen's Binder A (possibly William Nott, Pepys's "famous bookbinder.") Queen's Binder A probably created the pattern; one of his bindings is on a 1675 edition of Allestree's *Government of the Tongue.* Imitators, both toolcutters and binders, took it up, and for the next fifteen years similar bindings—in effect knockoffs—were available throughout the trade. Nott's binding is Howard M. Nixon, *English Restoration Bookbindings* (1974), plate 61; for a calf binding on the 1690 edition of this translation, see figure 2.14.

Fig. 5.31.
Vincent Bourne, *Poematia.* London, Sumptibus Authoris, Typis J. Watts, 1734, 12mo, goatskin. An erased ownership inscription on the endpaper has left the date 1736 still visible (there is a facing signature dated Balliol College, 1748).

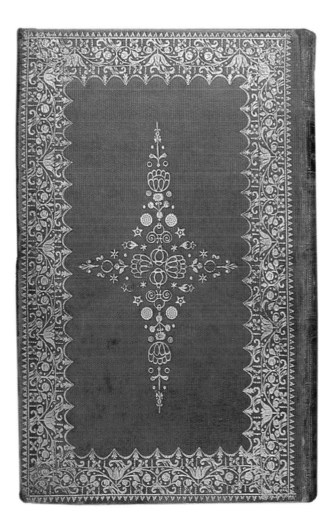

Fig. 5.32.
Marcus Hieronymus Vida,
*Christiad, a Poem*, translated by
J. Cranwell. Cambridge, Sold
by J. Woodyer, and T. & J.
Merrill [et al.], 1768, demy
8vo, goatskin, by Ed. Moor in
Harleian style, with a presentation inscription, "from the
translator's Daughter." The
binding of presentation copies
like this was probably arranged
by one of the two Cambridge
booksellers named in the
imprint, either Thomas
Merrill, who had a binding
business of his own and doubtless knew the fine binders in
town, or John Woodyer. Moor
was probably the finest of the
Cambridge binders of the
period; for his distinctive tools
see Howard M. Nixon, *Five
Centuries of English Bookbinding*
(1978), plate 65, and Mirjam
M. Foot, *The Henry Davis
Gift*, Vol. I (1978), pp. 76–86.
Courtesy of Department of
Special Collections, Stanford
University Libraries.

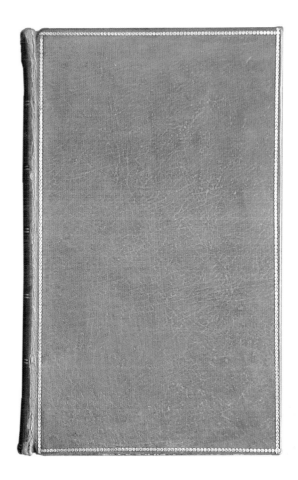

Fig. 5.33.
Edward Capel, *Prolusions; or,
select Pieces of antient Poetry*.
London, for J. and R. Tonson,
1760, 8vo, russia. This elegant
book anticipates the nineteenth
century in its typography and
paper, and its austere binding
is similarly advanced. Russia
was made by treating calfskin
or cowhide with birch bark
oil, which gave it the lustrous
honey color visible in the photograph. The material was first
seen in England circa 1730 and
was at its most popular around
1780, but it fell out of favor in
the early nineteenth century,
probably because purchasers
had learned by then that it was
unusually fragile and tended
to fall apart even with moder-
ate use.

Fig. 5.34.
Jeremy Taylor, *The Golden Grove. . . . Composed for the Use of the Devout; especially of Younger Persons.* London, J.L. for John Meredith, 1703, 12mo, "the One and Twentieth Edition," goatskin with a cottage roof panel and four circles stained black. Was this exuberant binding a gift for a "younger person?" There is a contemporary signature "Ann Gardner" on the title-page that does not look especially childlike, but it may be her very best penmanship. Courtesy of the William Andrews Clark Memorial Library, University of California, Los Angeles.

indistinguishable, on multiple copies of the same book?[14] Balley also produced conventional bindings, and the pattern shown in figure 5.34, with its cottage roof panel and central circles stained black, is very similar to a known Balley binding—except the tools do not match.[15] Did this binder receive a bespoke commission for something in Balley's style, or was he simply imitating Balley on his own initiative or at the behest of a bookseller? The latter two explanations seem more likely, since the book, the twenty-first edition of Jeremy Taylor's devotional *The Golden Grove*, is just the kind that might be purchased in an attractive binding as a gift, but is less likely to have been singled out for a special bespoke binding.

Sometimes purchasers' annotations demonstrate that books and their bindings were separate purchases, although such detailed inscriptions appear far less frequently than owners' notes showing the prices they paid for ready-bound books. A census of price-annotated books ought to be possible one day, and the correlation of dates and other information in these annotations, when present, should allow scholars to distinguish between books bought new and second-hand. Unfortunately, the percentage of such notes in deluxe bindings will be small: devotional books were meant to be above mercenary considerations, and prices are almost never found in books given as presents. In time, however, we should have a better idea of retail prices for seventeenth- and early eighteenth-century books in deluxe bindings, as well as what binders charged for such work. Matching bindings will also be identified in greater numbers, more clearly defining the styles developed by bookbinders for specific booksellers. Such matches—the three illustrated in figures 5.35–5.37 are a near-random sample—will further support the presumption that deluxe bindings were as much a part of the wholesale and retail book trade from 1660–1800 as their counterparts in calf and sheep.

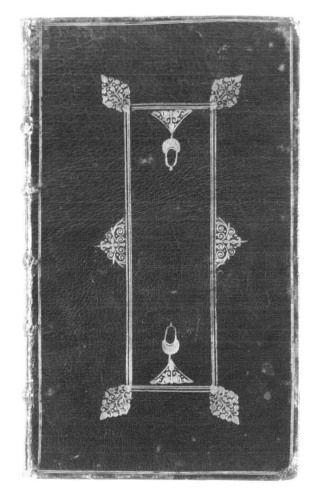

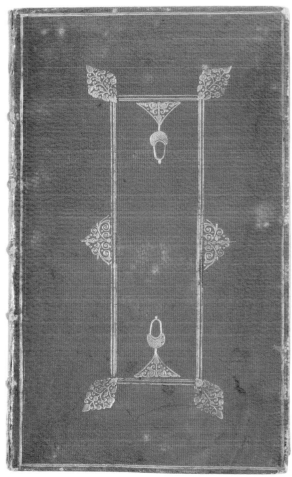

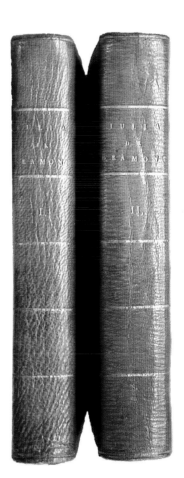

Fig. 5.35.
Charles Goodall, *Poems and Translations . . . by a late Scholar of Eaton.* London: for Henry Bonwicke, 1689, 8vo, two copies, identically-tooled, one in black and one in red goatskin, typical of the multiple copies in deluxe bindings produced for authors and booksellers around this time. They were purchased separately by John R.B. Brett-Smith, whose collection was sold at Sotheby's in 2004. He recognized them for the twins they are, and reunited them after three hundred years. Reproduced by courtesy of Sotheby's, London.

Fig. 5.36.
Lady Cassandra Hawke, *Julia de Gramont. By the Right Honourable Lady H\*\*\*\*.* London, for B. White and Son, 1788, 2 vols., foolscap 8vo, goatskin, probably for the publisher, Benjamin White, and

the author. At least two other copies of this novel are identically bound. This and the other copies may be Kalthoeber bindings—the austere elegance is typical of his work—or the work of another binder working for White in similar style. Collection of William Zachs.

Fig. 5.37.
John Hatsell (ed.), *Select Poems.* London, 1795, royal 8vo, two copies, each with a presentation inscription from the editor, identically bound in half stained sheep. Courtesy of the William Andrews Clark Memorial Library, University of California, Los Angeles.

# CONCLUSION

This book's primary purpose has been to show the interdependence of the bookselling and bookbinding trades, and the ways in which bookbinders worked to fill the shelves, stalls, and saddlebags of established and itinerant booksellers. As a result, retail book buyers could pick and choose their books ready-bound in the form that pleased them best and that best suited their pocketbooks.

That most books were sold ready-bound makes far more intuitive sense than the notion that retail customers had to buy their books in sheets, or, as Michael Sadleir put it, "at most in a plain paper wrapper," and then wait for them to be bound. The concept has firm factual support: Starkey and Clavell were advertising as ready-bound over eighty per cent of the books they listed in the late 1660s and '70s, and general catalogues continued to treat leather-bound copies as standard until the beginning of the nineteenth century, when boards and wrappers became predominant.

When I suggest the possibility that such-and-such a binding may have been executed for a particular bookseller—James Woodward, for example, or Jacob Tonson—I may be wrong about a specific book, but the evidence presented here conclusively supports the *principle* of wholesale and retail binding by and for booksellers. Samuel and Charles Mearne, Francis and John Noble, the Newberys, and John Bell are only a few of the hundreds of booksellers employing binders between 1660 and 1800. John Stockdale's and Benjamin White's catalogues confirm the range of bindings commissioned for upmarket bookshops; bindings on their books will certainly prove fruitful subjects for further investigation. Thomas Payne and the Robinsons were also successful, high-end booksellers during the latter part of the eighteenth century whose bindings sometimes show distinctive features, and William Zachs's *The First John Murray*, a biographical study with a check-list of editions from 1768 to 1795, provides an ideal basis for researching bindings produced for that publisher. For the Restoration and Augustan periods, further examination of prayer-books and other works published by the Mearnes, father and son, will bring to light more of their deluxe and other publishers' bindings, as should a detailed examination of the books printed for the major literary publishers, Henry Herringman, Jacob Tonson, and Bernard Lintot. These last will require the most patience, as many of their editions were large and widely subscribed through the booksellers' syndicates.

Can, or should, the present study significantly change the way rare book collectors and professionals approach earlier English, Irish, and Scottish bindings? There are three points on which this book provides assistance. First, the illustrated binding chronologies in Chapter 2, "The Bookbinders' Price Lists," and Chapter 4, "Common Trade Bindings: a Sampler," are comprehensive enough that cataloguers should be able to declare a binding to be contemporary with the date of its book's publication, or at least to suggest an approximate date, *e.g.*, "early to mid-eighteenth century," or "late seventeenth or early eighteenth century." Second, the term "trade" may properly be applied at least to calf and sheep bindings in the styles described in the bookbinders' price lists, provided, of course, that the bindings are contemporary with their books. Third, with respect to fine bindings, especially in goatskin, the term "presentation binding" should only be used where there is clear evidence, specific to the copy described, that it was given by the author, bookseller, or sponsor of the publication. "Deluxe binding" is, I believe, a more appropriate general term, describing the many fine bindings that may reasonably be assumed to have been part of booksellers' retail stock. When there is clear evidence, from advertisements and multiple surviving copies, that part of an edition was issued in a special binding, "gift" may properly be applied, just as it would in connection with a nineteenth-century publisher's gift binding.

Bookbinding research has come a long way since 1918, when Gordon Duff debunked the idea that all fine Restoration goatskin bindings were by Samuel Mearne. Scholars later matched tool impressions with biographical and other data to reveal a number of previously unrecognized bookbinders. Although most of these were fine binders, writers like Howard Nixon and David Pearson have shown that the same techniques could be used to reveal the work of ordinary craftsmen working with simpler patterns on calf and sheep.

It is now possible to look ahead to the next generation of bookbinding scholarship. A combination of digital imagery and telecommunications technology will allow a small digital camera to transmit images of bindings to a central database, to be sorted by tool impressions and matched with other work by the same binders. Names of original owners, prices paid, and even the occasional binder's identity, together with information from the archives of bookbinders and book-traders, may be correlated in such a database. Among other things, this information will help to establish the number of binders working for individual wholesale and retail booksellers. We will discover to what extent binders specialized in the materials they used, the different styles in which they worked, the number of tools they owned, and which tools were passed from one generation to the next. This research will expand our knowledge of book trade history in general, and help us to appreciate the range of work by individual binders. It will also confirm the primacy of trade bookbinding during a period when expanding readership and competition between booksellers propelled the economic and technical developments which led to the mechanization of book production.

# NOTES

## INTRODUCTION

1. Graham Pollard, "Changes in the Style of Book-binding," in Geoffrey Wakeman and Graham Pollard, *Functional Developments in Bookbinding* (1993), p. 40. Pollard's article first appeared in *The Library*, Fifth Series, Vol. XI, No. 2 (1956), pp. 71–94, but page references throughout this book are to the 1993 volume. The consensus view is quoted from Mirjam Foot, *Studies in the History of Bookbinding* (1993), p. 303, and it can also be found at the beginning of P.J.M. Marks, *The British Library Guide to Bookbinding* (1998), p. 7: "Until the nineteenth century, most books were not sold ready bound. . . ." John Carter, writing a few years before Pollard, anticipated the consensus view: books sold unbound were a "majority till the 17th century and a steadily decreasing majority till the early 18th." John Carter, *ABC for Book-Collectors* (1952), p. 177. This is the first edition of the *ABC*, but the quotations in this book are unchanged in subsequent revised editions.

2. Carter, *ABC*, pp. 176–77. Carter goes on to note that "such bindings are always difficult and often impossible to identify with absolute certainty," and that it is even more difficult to prove such an identification: "perhaps once in fifty times to someone who is either ignorant or skeptical (or both)."

3 J.H. Loudon, *James Scott and William Scott, Bookbinders* (1980), pp. 325–26. Evidence of such edition binding can be found in the earlier eighteenth century as well, and demonstrates that Carter is wrong in stating that "the analogy between a boarded book of 1750 and an 1850 book in publisher's cloth is a false analogy." John Carter, *ABC*, p. 176.

4. R.B. McKerrow, *An Introduction to Bibliography* (1928), p. 125, n. 1, quoting a communication from R.W. Chapman.

5. Pepys's entry is dated 12 March 1669. He went to "Nott's, the famous bookbinder that bound for my Lord Chancellor's library. And here I did take occasion for curiosity to bespeak a book to be bound. . . ." *Diary*, ed. Latham and Matthews (1970–1983), VIII, 237–38. Pepys also bought many books ready bound (the term as indexed by Latham and Matthews, XI, 23); these purchases are discussed in Chapter 1.

6. Michael Sadleir, *The Evolution of Publishers' Binding Styles 1770–1900* (1930, reprint 1990), p. 6.

7. It is no accident that the bookbinding scholar Charles Ramsden began his study of bookbinders outside London with the year 1780, and that with the possible exception of a Cambridge binding, every illustration of a provincial English binding in that study dates after 1800. *Bookbinders of the United Kingdom (Outside London) 1780–1840* (1954, reprint 1987), *passim*. The work of several pre-1780 fine Oxford and Cambridge bookbinders has been identified, and examples appear in the standard illustrated studies, as does that of some binders working in more modest trade styles. See, *e.g.*, Howard M. Nixon, *Five Centuries of English Bookbinding* (1978), pp. 143–45, identifying tools used by William Bonnor of Cambridge circa 1736, and David Pearson, *Durham Bookbinders and Booksellers, 1660–1760* (1986), *passim*, for tools used by several Durham bookbinders from 1660–1760.

## CHAPTER ONE

1. "From 1760–1780 or 90 Bookbinding was as well paid a Trade as any other." John Jaffray MS p. 225, quoted in Esther Potter, "The London Bookbinding Trade," in *The Library*, Sixth Series, Vol. 15, No. 4 (1993), p. 263, n. 19. The Jaffray manuscripts are the most important source for bookbinding trade anecdotes of the last twenty years of the eighteenth century; they have been authoritatively dealt with by Ellic Howe, *The London Bookbinders 1780–1806* (1950, reprint 1988).

2. Howe provides one piece of evidence for this comparison in the form of the premiums paid by families to have their sons enter the trade. Bookbinders generally received less than half the premiums paid to printers (£5–10 as opposed to £20–30), and one-fifth to one-tenth the premiums received by booksellers and stationers. Howe goes on to note that this low rate for bookbinders was "probably because the prospects of financial advancement were small. I suspect that during the eighteenth century the majority of master bookbinders made very poor livings, and frequently failed in business." Ellic Howe, *A List of London Bookbinders 1648–1815* (1950), p. xvi.

3. The statement comes from the bookseller Christopher Barker, writing in 1582: "In the tyme of King Henry the eighte there were . . . Stationers, which have, and partly to this daye do use to buy their bookes in grosse of the . . . printers, to bynde them up, and sell them in their shops, whereby they well maytayned their families." *Ibid.*, p. xxiii, quoting Arber, *Transcript of the Stationers' Company Registers*, I, 114.

4. George Wither, *The Schollers Purgatory* (ca. 1625), quoted in Stephen Parks, *John Dunton and the English Book Trade* (1976), pp. 182–83.

5. Robert Campbell, *The London Tradesman. Being a Compendious View of all the Trades now practiced in . . . London and Westminster* (1747), p. 135. I am grateful to David Pearson for this citation, which differs from the discussion of "Book-Binders" in another 1747 publication quoted by Bernard C. Middleton, *A History of English Craft Bookbinding Technique*, second ed. (1978), pp. 259–60.

6. This quotation is taken from the first edition of 1675 (Wing H1272), pp. 259–60. John Dunton confirms that this was the upward mobility binders sought, and notes that Mr. Dancer "was formerly a Binder, but is now a noted Bookseller in Fleet-street." Similarly Mr. Gifford, having worked as a binder, "now keeps a Shop in Old Bedlam; and, having printed several Copies that have sold well, he will, if he continues Fair-keeping, get a lumping portion for his Daughters." John Dunton, *The Life and Errors* (1705), quoted throughout this book in John Nichols's edition of 1818, pp. 228 and 260.

7. *A generall note of the prises for binding all sorts of bookes*, folio broadside, "Imprinted at London. 1619." This and other price lists are transcribed, three of them with fac-similes, in Mirjam M. Foot, "Some Bookbinders' Price Lists of the Seventeenth and Eighteenth Centuries," in *Studies in the History of Bookbinding* (1993), pp. 15–67.

8. Graham Pollard suggests that these price lists were in fact regulations imposed by the Stationers' Company. Graham Pollard, "Changes in the Style of Bookbinding," in Geoffrey Wakeman and Graham Pollard, *Functional Developments in Bookbinding* (1993), p. 40. This seems unlikely, and indeed the 1695 list specifically states that the prices were "agreed on by the Bookbinders, Freemen of the City of London, And by them Presented to the Master, Wardens and Assistants of the Worshipful Company of Stationers, at a Court holden March, 1694/5." These rate increases were brought to the Stationers' Company "beging their Approbation," but the increases were clearly calculated by the binders themselves. Nor do binders failing to abide by the price lists seem to have incurred any penalty beyond their own economic disadvantage. One such binder was Caleb Swinnock, who bound for Dunton. "[H]ad he not by working at under-rates turned himself out of doors, perhaps he had rode out the storm of Wiving. Caleb Swinnock was the only man that could ever tempt me to take Sheep's-leather Books at 14s. the hundred." Dunton, *Life and Errors*, ed. Nichols, p. 261.

9. *A generall note . . .* 1619, in Foot, *Studies in the History of Bookbinding*, p. 26. The price comparisons are taken from the 1625 statement of Hugh May, Clerk of the Markets to his Majesty's Household. The eh.net (Economic History Services) website states that 2d. in 1625 is the approximate equivalent of 97 new pence in 2002, or about $1.50.

10. The regulations originated in 1586, the result of buyers complaining that larger stab-sewn books broke apart after comparatively little use. For details of the limitations, see David Foxon, "Stitched Books," in *The Book Collector*, Vol. 24, No. 1 (1975), pp. 111–124.

11. The Dublin bookbinders' price list of 1743 states that "All Dictionaries . . . and all Octavo Bibles, bound plain are to be Ten-pence, and no Quarter Book of any Sort whatsoever is to be allowed," which of course implies that with other books the quarterly rule applied. This practice corresponded to the time-honored Station-ers' Company custom of the free quarterly book, and

meant that a bookseller purchasing unbound sheets and placing the entire lot with one binder would get his quarterly binding free of charge.

12. Cyprian Blagden, "The Memorandum Book of Henry Rhodes, 1695–1720. Part II," in *The Book Collector*, (Summer 1954), p. 108: "They delivered books to authors and customers; they acted as bill-collectors. Mr. Stiles [a bookbinder] spent two days in September 1717 sorting waste paper in Rhodes's warehouse and the same man is called by Bowyer [the printer] sometimes a porter and sometimes a binder."

13. Howe found bookbinders named in the 1669 price list who were apprenticed or employed by masters including not only printers, scriveners, stationers, letter founders, writing masters, and clasp makers, but also linen drapers, tallow chandlers, glovers, cutlers, dis-tillers, and even—shades of Ben Jonson—a bricklayer. Howe, *List*, pp. xii–xiii. No doubt with such diverse backgrounds some bookbinders were able to manage diverse businesses of their own. Other bookbinders remained in the employ of booksellers. Whether they received the kind of piecework rates established by the price lists, or earned wages comparable to the book-sellers' other employees, is unclear. Arrangements may have varied from one business to another, and also according to whether a bookbinder had served his apprenticeship with that particular business.

14. Many surviving eighteenth-century bookbinders' trade cards are intended to appeal to the gentry. Thomas Edlin's, circa 1745, declares that he "Bindes all sorts of Books in Turkey, Morrocco, Russia and Calves Leather, Right Shagreen & Vellum Extraordinary." Heal Collec-tion, British Museum Print Department, no. 17.45; also quoted in Howe, *List*, p. 33. For a later, similar, trade card, circa 1790, see *ibid.*, p. 38, the entry for the West End binder James Fraser, who offered "moroco, Russia and all other curious and elegant bindings at most rea-sonable rates. Likewise gilds and marbles leaves after the neatest and best manner. Gentlemen's libraries repaired and beautified."

15. Middleton, *History of English Craft Bookbinding*, pp. 258–60, supplies the basis for this hypothesis. The 9d. bindings used as an example provide a gross weekly income (based on the usual six-day week) of between £5 and £6. The comparatively few successful special-ized binders could earn two or three times as much; the cheapest bulk binders rather less. J.C. Hüttner, a German visitor to London in 1802, comments that by that time a single English binder could produce "25–30 books a day from sewing frame to leather," which is a startlingly high number even though it excludes sewing and finish-ing. J.C. Hüttner, *Englische Miscellen*. Band 6 (1802), translated and summarized in Middleton, *History of English Craft Bookbinding*, p. 255. I am not sure that Hüttner's figure is correct (he gets at least one other number demonstrably wrong elsewhere in the same account), but clearly productivity was on the upswing towards the end of the eighteenth century.

16. One of these was the bindery attached to John Bell's bookshop, and a story in the Jaffray manuscripts suggests that there may have been as many as ten finishers working for Bell. Howe, *London Bookbinders*, pp. 68–9.

17. Dunton, *Life and Errors*, ed. Nichols, pp. 257 and 262.

18. Howe remarks an "I. Baker" in Bagford's notes, and a "John Baker" in the Stationers' Records. Howe says this Mr. Baker's exact identity is uncertain. Howe, *List*, p. 5. But "I." was a standard initial for "Iohn" or "John" at that time. Baker, wrote Dunton, "binds so extraordinarily well, that two of my customers gave particular charge that no man in London should bind the books they bought of me but Mr. *Baker* and Mr. *Steel*." *Life and Errors*, ed. Nichols, p. 258. Knowles, "an ingenious and constant man at his Trade," executed special bindings for Dunton on "that 'History of Living Men' and 'Athenian Oracle' which I lately dedicated and presented to the Prince of Denmark and Duke of Ormond with my own hand." *Ibid.*, p. 260. Robert Steel, the best-known of the three, was apprenticed to Samuel Mearne, and in his turn had Lord Harley's binder Thomas Elliott as his apprentice. Dunton called Steel "my occasional Binder; for, when I met with a nice Customer, no binding would serve him but Mr. Steel's; which, for the fineness of it, might vie with the Cambridge Binding." *Ibid.*, p. 262.

19. E. Gordon Duff, "The Great Mearne Myth," *Papers of the Edinburgh Bibliographical Society* 11 (1918), p. 62 describes an octavo *Life of St. Francis Xavier*, London, 1688, "in an elaborately gilt red morocco binding. Written on the last fly-leaf was . . . 'Payd Mr. Jacob Tonson for this Booke in sheets 2. 6. Payd Mr. Daniel Search for the binding it, 6. 6.'" The 1669 and 1695 bookbinders' price lists respectively allowed 9d. and 10d. for an ordinary calf binding in this format.

20. In 1691, John Dunton wrote that "a poor *Fly* can't stir upon the water, but—pop, he's [*i.e.* the conger's] at him." The 1700 *Dictionary of the Canting Crew* described the conger as "a Set or Knot of Topping Book-sellers of London who agree . . . that whoever of them Buys a good Copy, the rest are to take off such a particular number . . . in Quires, on easy Terms." Both these references are from Norma Hodgson and Cyprian Blagden, "The Notebook of Thomas Bennet and Henry Clements," in *Oxford Bibliographical Society Publications*, New Series, Vol. VI, 1953 (1956), pp. 76 and 67 respectively. A later, more specific definition of "conger" makes clear that the "knot" referred to in the 1700 canting dictionary meant something on the order of "ten or more" booksellers. *Ibid.*, p. 86, quoting the 1730 edition of Bailey's *Dictionary*.

21. Sometimes these title-pages were press variants, and sometimes cancels. Among the press-variant titles were "some copies of Robert Clavell's London printings," which gave "a Dublin bookseller's name." M. Pollard, *Dublin's Trade in Books 1550–1800* (1989) p. 93. Such practices continued throughout the eighteenth century.

22. Hodgson and Blagden, "Notebook of Thomas Bennet," *passim*. The authors give a succinct account of the workings of various kinds of syndicates. A typical example, given in one of Bennet's notes, involved Bates's *Pharmacopea*, of which Samuel Smith was the commissioning bookseller. Bennet was a major shareholder, and bought 1500 copies at the partners' subscription rate of 9d. per copy, which would have given Smith a modest profit on his investment. In the event that another partner ran out of copies, he could acquire additional copies from syndicate members willing to sell at an agreed price of 1s., but the trade price to non-participating booksellers was 1s. 4d. These prices were for copies in sheets.

23. As if this weren't complicated enough, there is an additional problem of old and modern terminology. Bookbinders who ran their own warehouses were, in effect, wholesale distributors. Their delivery services were a menial job, taking books to, and collecting money from, retail or "public" bookshops. These services earned them the name "publisher," a meaning that has entirely disappeared from modern usage.

24. Hodgson and Blagden, "Notebook of Thomas Bennet," p. 97. One binder they mention (see note 12) is Edward Styles or Stiles. "Nearly all the sheets which Bowyer printed for the . . . Congers between 1717 and 1735 were delivered to a man called Styles." *Ibid*, p. 96.

25. Bowyer's ledger refers to this as "Abstract of the Book of Moses." *The Bowyer Ledgers . . . Reproduced on Microfiche*, ed. Keith Maslen and John Lancaster (1991), P869–70. The printing and delivery references here quoted are also from these two fiche pages.

26. "Super Royal" paper made a very grand octavo, even larger than the usual royal octavo format, which in its turn was close to twice the size of a pot octavo. See the Appendix at the end of this book for descriptions and measurements of paper sizes and formats.

27. I have so far been unable to trace a copy in an Elliott binding. ESTC does not distinguish large paper copies, and the New York Public Library copy, stated in OCLC WorldCat to be "Large paper copy. Signatures and pagination continuous. . . . Bound in blue morocco, tooled, with edges gilt over red," is a mid-nineteenth century binding by Riviere. Thomas Elliott was, of course, binder to another Edward Harley, Earl of Oxford and one of the great collectors of the Harleian Library. There may well have been a connection between these two Harleys and their binder, but I don't know what it is.

28. "Mr. Chulmley" gets us back to Cyprian Blagden's bookseller Henry Rhodes, who used nearly twenty different bookbinders, one of whom was "Mr. Cholmley." Both were doubtless the same Philip Cholmondeley profiled in Howe, *List*, p. 21, and who is referred to as "ye Binder & Porter" in 1698. Blagden, "Memorandum Book of Henry Rhodes, Part II," p. 108. Among Rhodes's other employees were the bookseller/bookbinders Francis Fayram and James Woodward. Maslen and Lancaster index Cholmondeley under "Chulmley," also suggesting Philip. "Mr. Matthews" is more elusive; their indexed "Matthews," for whom no first name is ventured, appears in the Bowyer ledgers from 1730–1760.

This is one of his earliest appearances, which makes the only overlapping Howe entry, Emanuel Matthews, unlikely, as he died in 1734. Thomas Matthews was turned over as an apprentice in 1754, and had a son who was a bookbinder; if this family's bookbinding went back one generation before Thomas (could Emanuel have been Thomas's grandfather?) we would probably have our man. See Howe, *List*, p. 67.

29. The last Bowyer entry for this title, dated June 16, 1734, is for copies given "to Mr. Elliott for Watts." The only likely candidate is John Watts, who not only printed for himself and others, but had books printed for him.

30. Only a single copy of the reissue is recorded in the on-line *English Short-Title Catalogue* (T88814), at the British Library.

31. For an example of the first part of this argument, see, *e.g.*, Nicholas Pickwood, "Onward and downward: how binders coped with the printing press before 1800," in *A Millennium of the Book*, ed. Robin Myers and Michael Harris (1994), p. 63: "By selling in sheets, [booksellers] could save themselves not only the cost of the binding, which would have increased the bookseller's investment in a title. . . ." Pepys's *Diary* records his irritation at having to wait for a binding, though on a book he already owned and which he was having bound by the bookbinder/bookseller John Martin. The book was Athanasius Kircher's *Musurgia Universalis* (Rome, 1650), for which Pepys paid 35s. on 22 February 1668, and which the next day he left at Martin's for binding. On the 29th Pepys went to Martin's "expecting to have had my Kercher's *Musurgia*, but to my trouble and loss of time, it was not done." *Diary*, ed. Latham and Matthews (1970–1983), IX, 97. It was finished by 4 March, and Pepys recorded his satisfaction: "very well bound." *Ibid*, IX, 102. He also noted the total cost, book and binding, of £3. 0. 0, which means the binding worked out at 12s. 6d. per folio volume. For an illustration of this binding, see Howard M. Nixon, *Catalogue of the Pepys Library at Magdalene College, Cambridge*, Vol. VI (1984), plate 12.

32. Pollard, "Changes," p. 59. Even if the Comenius engraving did depict normal English booksellers' practice, which I argue it does not, this suggestion seems highly speculative. Vertical half-titles were not normal practice in the London printing trade, and in my experience are about as rare as a preliminary leaf with only a signature mark, which clearly was no use to a bookseller filing books. Although the vertical half-title disappears after the turn of the eighteenth century, normal horizontal half-titles continued, usually filling a leaf left over after a preliminary signature was set up, a leaf which would otherwise be blank. Functionally, half-titles helped protect title leaves from wear and tear as gathered and folded sheets were handled, and quite often they ended up being used by binders as additional pastedowns, underneath endpapers, which process helped align and secure a book's sheets during forwarding.

33. Wakeman, *Functional Developments*, p. 13. Wakeman's is a comparatively recent view. Earlier scholars like R.W.

Chapman and R.B. McKerrow were more influenced by at least some of the evidence, such as Starkey and Clavell's catalogues, discussed in this book. McKerrow offers the unsupported but interesting statement that "at the end of the sixteenth century I think that a person wishing to buy a new book would generally find at the booksellers copies of it ready bound, if it was large or thick in leather, if it was small or thin in forel." McKerrow, *An Introduction to Bibliography*, pp. 123–24. McKerrow also briefly discusses seventeenth- and eighteenth-century binding, in sections headed "early forms of issue" and "publishers' bindings," at pp. 124–26.

34. The copying of the Nuremberg engravings for the 1659 English edition was in keeping with normal seventeenth century practice. At that time there were few English artists capable of producing the kind of original work needed, and in any case an English bookseller or syndicate would have been unlikely to commission original copperplates for a children's book.

35. Henry R. Plomer, et al. *A Dictionary of the Printers and Booksellers who were at Work in England, Scotland and Ireland from 1726 to 1775* (1968), p. 139, suggests that figure 1.7 depicts James's circulating library, which is quite possible, but nowhere stated on the card itself. Illustrations of book trade premises are few and far between, as so often is the case with unremarkable places and activities. More turn up after 1780, as can be seen in Sigfred Taubert, *Bibliopola* (Hamburg, 1966). See, *e.g.*, Taubert, Vol. II, plate 84, a charming mezzotint of a pretty young woman outside a bookshop/circulating library, circa 1782; plate 88, Wigstead's aquatint of an author in a bookshop, 1784, anticipating Rowlandson's later engraving of Dr. Syntax; plate 99, Hamilton & Co.'s Wholesale and Retail "Shakspeare Library" circa 1790; and plate 103, Lackington's "Temple of the Muses." Plate 3 in the same volume shows what may be the earliest illustration of a European bookshop: an interior view of English premises, circa 1350, with a female bookseller offering manuscripts—all of which, it may be noted, are ready-bound.

36. Hüttner, *Englische Miscellen.* Band 6 (1802), translated and summarized in Middleton, *History of English Craft Bookbinding*, p. 257.

37. David Pearson, "Book Collectors in Oxford, 1550–1650," in *Antiquaries, Book Collectors, and the Circles of Learning*, ed. Robin Myers and Michael Harris (1996), p. 18. Pearson notes that John Dorne's day-book for 1520 describes the form in which books were sold: "ligatus" for bound and "in quaterniis" for sheets. Of books that would normally be bound, as opposed to "pamphlets and broadsheets which sold for 6d. or less . . . just over 400 items" are described as sold "in leather, in parchment, or just 'bound,'" and there are 71 items sold . . . in sheets." Pearson concludes that "the books sold bound were ready-bound before purchase, and that the books sold in sheets were being sold that way for independent binding." Pearson offers other valuable evidence for the widespread use of trade binding at that time, all of which is equally applicable 150 years later: identical bindings

on the same book, indicating they were "stocked by the booksellers ready bound in anticipation of customer demand," and dated ownership inscriptions "observably later than the likely date of binding . . . [suggesting] that these . . . waited several years to find a purchasing customer." *Ibid*, p. 19.

38. I am no expert on Continental bindings, trade or otherwise, but to the extent that the present is any guide to the past, I suggest that the differences still visible in the organization of the Continental and British book trades provide some valuable clues. In almost any sizable French town, for example, one can find a street-level bookbindery ready to bind not only antiquarian books but also the many French books published unopened and untrimmed in wrappers. I am told the same is still true in other European countries, especially in Southern Europe, and to some degree in Germany as well, which would explain the Comenius illustration from Nuremberg.

39. Graham Pollard gives an account of the Russhe lawsuit in "The English Market for Printed Books," in *Publishing History*, 4 (1978), p. 12. Garrett Godfrey's accounts are described by David Pearson as "rather more fragmentary" than Dorne's. David Pearson, *Oxford Bookbinding 1500–1640* (2000), p. 12.

40. The academic was Joseph Mede and the country gentleman Sir Martin Stuteville. Among the books sent in 1628 was the just-published George Wither poem *Britain's Remembrancer*. If Mede were commissioning a binding for it, or any of the other books listed in the correspondence, there would no doubt somewhere be a reference to or a question about the binding style or cost. That no such reference appears is a pretty good indication that Mede was buying these books ready bound. This correspondence is quoted by David McKitterick, "Customer, Reader, and Bookbinder: Buying a Bible in 1630," in *The Book Collector*. Vol. XL, No. 3 (1991), pp. 382–406, and the reference to *Britain's Remembrancer* is on p. 391. I refer to the bespoke Bible in the next chapter, and I should add that my inferences about the extent of ready binding are taken from the Mede-Stuteville correspondence itself, and are not suggested by Dr. McKitterick.

41. The statement appears in the Dublin price list of 1743: "Octavos shall be charg'd Ten Pence, Twelves Eight Pence (at least) . . . to all Gentlemen, Authors, or others." This and the other price lists are discussed in the next chapter; for the quotation see "Some Bookbinders' Price Lists of the Seventeenth and Eighteenth Centuries," in Mirjam M. Foot, *Studies in the History of Bookbinding* (1993), p. 52.

42. "I am told . . . that Mr. Kirton is utterly undone, and made 2 or 3000*l* worse than nothing, from being worth 7 or 8000*l*." *Diary*, VII, 309, 5 October 1666. Pepys also heard of "the great loss of books in St. Pauls churchyard, and at their hall also—which they value at about 150000*l*." *Ibid.*, p. 297.

43. Edward Hyde, Earl of Clarendon, *The Life* (1759), p. 354, quoted in Edward Arber, *The Term Catalogues*, *1668–1709 A.D.* (1903–06), I, vii–viii. E.S. de Beer, *The Diary of John Evelyn* (1955), III, 459, n. 3 suggests "the stationers [*i.e.* members of the Stationers' Company] probably suffered greater losses through the Fire than any other traders."

44. I examined Andrew Maunsell, *Catalogue of English Printed Books* (1595); William London, *Catalogue of the Most Vendible Books in England* (1657–1660); and George Tokefield, *Catalogue of Such Books as have been Entered in the Register of the Company of Stationers: and Printed from the 25. of December, 1662. to the 25. of December, 1663* (1664).

45. In response to the seventh number of *Mercurius Librarius*, a rival *Catalogue of Books* appeared at about the same time. Both contained publications for Easter Term, 1670. The rival catalogue was declared to be "Collected by, and printed for, the Booksellers of London," and the complaint was that "the Publishers of Mercurius Librarius" made "unreasonable demands for inserting the Titles of Books," and also that they omitted many, and refused "all under 1sh. Price." By including books under a shilling, the rival catalogue contained "forty-six more titles than the corresponding Number 7 of Mercurius Librarius." Arber, *Term Catalogues*, I, ix.

46. The edition advertised in *Mercurius Librarius* is probably Wing B3637A, the imprint of which is "Excudit Rogerus Nortonus, vaeneuntque apud Sam. Mearne, 1670." The two copies in figure 1.10 are Wing B3664A "Apud Sam. Mearne, Bibliopolam Regium," and Wing B3675C, "Apud Car. Mearne, Bibliopolam." I suspect Mearne's "Price bound" of 4s. bought (at least in his shop) a decorated binding befitting both a Mearne publication and a devotional book in Latin, but goatskin must have commanded an additional premium.

47. Wing C4598. The catalogue was printed by Samuel Simmons, who famously bought the copyright and printed the first edition of Milton's *Paradise Lost* in 1667. Both this catalogue and its successor of 1675 are distinct from the periodicals (including *Mercurius Librarius*) Edward Arber collected as *The Term Catalogues*. For this reason I avoid the use of "term catalogue" throughout this book.

48. In the *Mercurius Librarius* for Michaelmas Term 1670, *Paradise Regain'd* was offered by its publisher John Starkey at 4s. bound. Clearly sales did not go well, as the 1673 price shows a reduction of 40%. The second edition of the poem did not appear until 1680.

49. Robert Clavell, *The General Catalogue of Books Printed in England Since the Dreadful Fire . . . to . . . Trinity Term, 1674* (1675).

50. See, *e.g.*, Crook's unpriced list at the end of the 1678 edition of Thomas Hobbes's *De Mirabilibus Pecci*, Wing H2224.

51. Cyprian Blagden advances the argument that the waxing and waning was according to the bookbinders' adherence to the prices in their lists. Cyprian Blagden, "The Memorandum Book of Henry Rhodes, 1695–1720," in *The Book Collector* (Spring 1954), p. 38. He also

remarks that, at the beginning of the eighteenth century, there appeared to be two groups of booksellers, one who believed in "published prices," and another group who did not. *Ibid.*, p. 35. Robert Clavell and Henry Rhodes were among the former, and from Clavell's 1673 catalogue one might infer that Henry Herringman was among the latter. My impression is that many grand booksellers tended not to price their lists, at least not before 1750, and that the less grand did, if only to impress upon their customers how cheap their books could be. Booksellers who did not price their catalogues, like Robert Dodsley, still made it clear to customers that their books were "neatly bound and at the lowest prices." This statement appears on Dodsley's unpriced list on the wrappers of Lord Lyttelton's *Observations on the conversion and apostleship of St. Paul. In a letter to Gilbert West*, 1747. I am grateful to Mr. Stephen Weissman of Ximenes Rare Books for communicating this description. Folios continued to be offered in sheets much more consistently than books in smaller formats, and price statements emphasized this fact, as *e.g.*, John Wilford, *Memorials and Characters, Together with the Lives of divers Eminent and Worthy Persons*, 1747, the title-page of which declares "Price One Pound Six Shillings and Six Pence in Sheets."

52. Robert Clavell, *The General Catalogue of Books Printed in England . . . to the End of Trinity-Term MDCLXXX* (1680), "To the Reader." Clavell was more than a little depressed: he went on to condemn book auctions: "more probable for the Buyer to gain advantage by a Lottery, than in this way," and also "the imposing of old Rubbish out of Shops." All of these, he mourned, "may in a little time put an end" to his catalogues, the reputation of them "now growing weak and faint."

53. Nixon, *Catalogue of the Pepys Library*, VI, xiii. These standard patterns are stated by Nixon to be the "house" styles bespoke by Pepys. Mirjam Foot goes further: "[I]t is clear that Pepys himself specified the way the spines of his books were to be tooled." "Scholar-collectors and their Bindings," in *Antiquaries, Book Collectors, and the Circles of Learning*, ed. Robin Myers and Michael Harris (1996), p. 38. Pepys's taste is by definition evident on bindings bespoke by him, some of which Nixon illustrates, but Pepys's options, as David Pearson puts it, "were directed very much by the standard fare of the day," and even his bespoke bindings are typical of the gilt calf of the period. David Pearson, *English Bookbinding Styles 1450–1800: A Handbook* (forthcoming), Chapter I, "Owners and Bindings." A good example is Kircher's *Musurgia* (Rome, 1650) bound at the bookseller John Martin's bindery in Nixon's style "F" (see note 31, above, in this chapter). Martin was active in the trade at least until 1680, the period during which the "F" style bindings were executed. But Nixon also groups under the "F" style a number of different bindings executed to similar patterns with different tools, as can be seen in figure 1.14, which also appears in Nixon, *Catalogue of the Pepys Library*, VI, plate 11. In cases where the specific tools on the Kircher binding can be seen to reappear on other books in Pepys's library, it is logical to infer that

those books were bound in, or for, Martin's shop. If they were second-hand books Pepys already owned, they were bespoke bindings, but new books in Martin bindings, just as with all the other books printed in London during this period and bound by other booksellers in similar styles with different tools, were bought ready-bound.

54. *Diary*, VI, 32, 5 February 1665.

55. *Diary*, VI, 2, 2 January 1664/5, also quoted in Nixon, *Catalogue of the Pepys Library*, VI, xvi. I follow both Nixon and the editors of the *Diary* in assigning the purchase of Hooke's *Micrographia*, and the commission "for the new binding of a great many of my old books," recorded by Pepys on 18 January 1664/5, to Kirton's shop. *Diary*, VI, 14–15 and n. 1, where Kirton is referred to as "Joseph." At this time, Pepys generally referred to Kirton as "my bookseller," and so it is with these entries. Kirton, of course, would have had copies of Hooke's *Micrographia*, but I cannot resist pointing out that it was published by a bookseller who was also in St. Paul's Churchyard, John Martin, and who was also known to be a bookbinder. After the Great Fire, Martin became Pepys's principal bookseller—is it conceivable that they were doing business as early as 1665?

56. The closest we get to such an entry is one from the later *Diary* from which Howard Nixon infers that Pepys bought a book, Kircher's *Musurgia* (Rome, 1650) in sheets. *Diary*, IX, 102 n. 1, 4 March 1668. The book is a folio, the size most likely to be left unbound for bespoke binding. But Pepys himself makes no reference to the book's being unbound; it was an eighteen year-old Italian import when he bought it, and was likely at the very least to have found its way into a vellum wrapper. Whether such a book should be considered "new" or "second-hand" I leave to the reader's determination. Either way, it was a book Pepys bought, and then ordered bound, just as in all the other references in the *Diary* to binding projects. For a discussion of the Kircher binding itself, see notes 31 and 53, above, in this chapter. For perhaps the best-known of the references to rebinding, see *Diary*, IX, 480 and n. 2, 12 March 1669, Pepys's visit to William Nott, "the famous bookbinder that bound for my Lord Chancellor's library." Pepys was so impressed that he "did take occasion for curiosity to bespeak a book to be bound, only that I might have one of his binding." The book was "almost certainly . . . *A conference about the next succession to the crown of Ingland* (1594)."

57. *Diary*, IX, 57–59, 8–9 February 1668.

58. Nixon, *Catalogue of the Pepys Library*, VI, xiv, quoting *Letters and Second Diary of Samuel Pepys*, ed. R.G. Howarth, 1933, p. 344. The Le Cène volume is illustrated as Plate 17a in Nixon's catalogue. It is absolutely typical trade calf with extra gilt.

59. Pearson, *English Bookbinding Styles*, Chapter 1.

60. Much of this later binding work was carried out by John Berresford for Pepys, beginning possibly as early as 1685. Some of Pepys's ready-bound books have been uniformly labeled or relabeled, and Berresford may have had a hand in this. One of these labelers, conceivably

Berresford, used two sizes of type in his lettering, and his work is sufficiently distinctive to stand out on a number of different binding styles. This distinctive labeling style can be seen on, *e.g.* Osborn's *Works*, Nixon, *Catalogue of the Pepys Library*, VI, plate 16a. One highly Pepysian label has "Rochester's Life," which all viewers would assume to be the famously pious account of the rake's deathbed conversion by Bishop Burnet, but is in fact a volume of Rochester's amorous and other poems.

61. Pearson, "Book Collectors in Oxford," p. 19. Of course one can go on and on listing exceptions, from the royal bindings by the Mearnes in Pepys's time, through Humfrey Wanley's commissioning Thomas Elliott and Christopher Chapman to bind the Earl of Oxford's special books and manuscripts in morocco in the 1720s, to the special bindings commissioned by Jonas Hanway and Thomas Hollis in the 1760s and '70s. Itinerant finishers were also employed by the gentry throughout the eighteenth century to make the spines of their libraries uniform. But creating this kind of uniformity was as much a luxury as ordering a bespoke binding in the first place, and collectively these processes applied to no more than the 1520 Dorne proportion of one book in six, if that many.

## CHAPTER TWO

1. Mirjam M. Foot, "Some Bookbinders' Price Lists of the Seventeenth and Eighteenth Centuries," in *Studies in the History of Bookbinding* (1993), pp. 15–67. The 1743, 1744, and 1760 lists transcribed in this article survive only in the bookbinder James Coghlan's memorandum book, which in 1970 belonged to Mr. P. Radcliffe Evans. Howard M. Nixon, "The Memorandum Book of James Coghlan. The Stock of an 18th-Century Printer and Binder," in *Journal of the Printing Historical Society*, No. 6 (1970), p. 33. The 1766 Dublin list is known to have been published, but no copy has been found. The 1791 list, tantalizingly stated to be "work done for booksellers," is in a private collection in England. A brief description appears in M. Pollard, *Dublin's Trade in Books 1550–1800* (1989), p. 128.

2. Foot, "Some Bookbinders' Price Lists," p. 15.

3. David McKitterick tells the full story, although without mentioning the bookbinders' price list, in "Customer, Reader, and Bookbinder: Buying a Bible in 1630," in *The Book Collector*. Vol. XL, No. 3 (1991), pp. 382–406.

4. Cyprian Blagden, "The Memorandum Book of Henry Rhodes, 1695–1720," in *The Book Collector*, (Spring 1954), p. 38. Blagden says the operative date for Clavell's victory was 1670. *Mercurius Librarius*, the predecessor of Clavell's catalogues, listed prices bound as early as 1668, so clearly binders had some kind of agreement in effect then, probably based on an earlier price list. There may have been at least one other list between 1646 and 1669; Mirjam Foot is surely correct in saying that "there must have been a great many more lists than the eight or nine we know now." Foot, "Some Bookbinders' Price Lists," p. 15.

5. William S. Mitchell in *The Book Collector* (Spring 1968), p. 82. The copy attracted Mitchell's notice because of its contemporary Newcastle bookseller's ticket. Although that ticket states "Books Bound after what manner you please," Mitchell remarks that "there is nothing to indicate that the volume was not bound in London." *Ibid.*

6. Foot, "Some Bookbinders' Price Lists," p. 25.

7. *Ibid.*

8. Mirjam Foot explains these two terms as referring to "a difference in sewing technique, one more expensive than the other . . . referring most probably to sewing on raised bands for which four or five cords were used and sewing on sawn-in or recessed bands for which two thongs or cords were sufficient." *Ibid.*, p. 18. This seems logical but for one thing: the term is applied only to Bibles, from folios right down to duodecimos, never to any other books, and the price differential is significant: an entire 3s. for a folio (11s. for "Gilt over, or double lac'd," and 8s. for "Corners, or single lac'd"), and a differential of 6d. for a duodecimo. This is much too much for sewing, which was paid at miniscule rates—at most "three half pence" per hundred sheets (a halfpenny or less for a typical octavo) according to the 1744 London price list—in view of its being carried out by bookbinders' wives. Double and single laced must refer to a degree of gilding, and perhaps also edge-gilding, on books, as in Shakespeare's "cloth a gold, and cuts, and lac'd with siluer." Probably "double lac'd" means two, quite elaborate, panels enclosing a large center ornament, "single lac'd" an outer panel, probably less elaborate, with correspondingly simpler gilding on the spine.

9. Sheep was not allowed to be used on especially large and thick volumes, by express order of the Stationers' Company. The 1644 price list, the first specifically to refer to sheep, gives the largest size allowed as "smale Follio pot paper" (when folded about 15 x 12½ inches), and this limitation continues throughout the English lists. (The 1743 Dublin list allows the largest folio in sheep to be based on the size of the "Coasting Pilot," and also "Royal, Medium, Demy, and Propatria" folios.) The 1760 list limits the size for sheep bindings still further, giving octavo as the largest. For the Stationers' Company limitation on the use of sheep, see Foot, "Some Bookbinders' Price Lists," p. 16 and n. 5.

10. *The Shorter Oxford Dictionary* takes an example from the writings of John Evelyn: "A balustrade which edges it quite round."

11. Mirjam Foot's suggestion that "extraordinary" may mean "decorated with a lot of gold tooling as in the modern 'extra' binding" is surely correct. Foot, "Some Bookbinders' Price Lists," p. 19.

12. Howard M. Nixon and Mirjam M. Foot, *The History of Decorated Bookbinding in England* (1992), plate 56, illustrates an example by Mearne on a 1662 *Book of Common Prayer*. This binding includes the cypher of Charles II at the corners of the central gilt panel, but the basic style was a popular one through the end of the century and beyond.

13. "Pot" in this context is a reference to the type of paper. It was Dutch, and had a pot as a watermark. Pot paper was good quality, and the sheet size was a little smaller than "Fools-Cap" (another watermark). For descriptions of these and other papers, see the Appendix at the end of this book.

14. Foot, "Some Bookbinders' Price Lists," pp. 48–52, and fig. 2.3. All subsequent quotations from this price list are taken from these five pages, and are not separately noted. Similarly inclusive notes are given for subsequent price lists cited in this chapter.

15. For further details of Baker, see Chapter 1, note 18. The definitive account of this broadside is given by Bernard C. Middleton, "The Bookbinders Case Unfolded," in *The Library*, Fifth Series, Vol. XVII, No. 1, March 1962, pp. 66–76, who also suggests some other, less likely, identifications for Bagford's "Mr I. Baker."

16. *Ibid.*, p. 66.

17. *Ibid.*, p. 67. Middleton goes on to note that "all that can safely be said is the Pepys bound it up later than April 1684 . . . and that it was printed before March 1695." *Ibid.*, p. 68. The April 1684 date is determinable from the fact that the broadside was bound with Moxon's *Mechanick Exercises*, the last part of which appeared in that month.

18. *Ibid.*, quoting from S.T. Prideaux, *An Historical Sketch of Bookbinding* (1893), p. 243.

19. *Ibid.*, p. 76.

20. See, *e.g.*, John Hannett, *Bibliopegia* (1865), p. 381. In preparation for the gilding, the binder first applied egg white, or glaire, in a process the broadside calls "Glearing the Book," after which the gold itself was applied, heating the roll or other tool to make the gilt foil bond with the glaire.

21. Middleton, "The Bookbinders Case Unfolded," p. 76.

22. Foot, "Some Bookbinders' Price Lists," pp. 21 and 52–56. The unique copy, in James Coghlan's memorandum book, is cut up and mounted

23. Foot, "Some Bookbinders' Price Lists," p. 21. In note 17 on p. 66, she notes one significant variation: "a Bible, 'Quarto, without Cuts' is 5s., the same as that for 'Edges Extraordinary' for the same size Bible in 1669 and 1695." She also suggests that these prices include "a certain amount, but not a great deal, of gold tooling." *Ibid.*, p. 21.

24. Nixon, "Memorandum Book of James Coghlan," p. 41.

25. Joseph McDonnell and Patrick Healy, *Gold Tooled Bookbindings Commissioned by Trinity College Dublin* (1987), plates G, and XIII–XX. McDonnell and Healy categorically state that both the "blew Turky" and the "Red Lether" are goatskin, so the "Turky" must have had some additional attribute. What that is is explained by Hannett: "The turkey grain is formed by steeping the cover in water, rubbing it from corner to corner, and then contrary way, till the grain is brought up full and square." Hannett, *Bibliopegia*, p. 264. In 1732 Leathley

also supplied Trinity College with a list of his standard charges for binding various sizes of books; these are consistent with the prices in the 1743 Dublin list, especially when one allows for the fact that the price rises in that list were declared to be the result of the increasing cost of calf. McDonnell and Healy, *Gold Tooled Bookbindings*, p. 46. If Leathley had bound the royal octavo Platos in calf according to the 1743 list, they would have been at most 2s. 6d. each in "the Gilt Work," or 1s. 9d. in calf with gilt backs.

26. The term "roan" came into use in the early nineteenth century (*The Oxford English Dictionary* says 1818), and appears to have meant either the outer or inner split of sumach-treated sheepskin, with "skiver" specifically referring to the inner, less coarse, split.

27. Foot, "Some Bookbinders' Price Lists," p. 23. "Perfect" bindings are entirely without sewing, and were so called because of the enthusiastic greeting they received in the 1830s and '40s, when inventors introduced new kinds of adhesives (caoutchouc, gutta-percha, etc.) which were supposed to be, but definitely were not, permanent.

28. *Ibid.*

29. Foot, "Some Bookbinders' Price Lists," pp. 57–60.

30. *Ibid.*, pp. 60–64.

31. Nixon, "Memorandum Book of James Coghlan," pp. 41 and 44. Mirjam Foot quotes Nixon, and the definition of red basil from Hannett's *Bibliopegia*, in "Some Bookbinders' Price Lists," pp. 24–25.

32. Foot, "Some Bookbinders' Price Lists," p. 25 and note 28.

33. James Watson, quoted in Ellic Howe, *The London Bookbinders 1780–1806* (1950, reprint 1988), p. 114. It may be that some binding techniques evolved in the latter part of the eighteenth century which allowed binders to produce these "immense numbers" faster and hence earn the better pay referred to in the Jaffray manuscripts. The Jaffray reference appears in Chapter 1, note 1, and the techniques are discussed in Chapter 1, note 15.

## CHAPTER THREE

1. Edward Arber. *The Term Catalogues, 1668–1709 A.D.* (1903–06) I, xii.

2. "[I]n those days wholesaling and publishing were usually done by the same firms." Graham Pollard, "Changes in the Style of Bookbinding," in Geoffrey Wakeman and Graham Pollard, *Functional Developments in Bookbinding* (1993), p. 61. There are, however, some interesting cases where, for geographical or other reasons, the wholesaler and publisher are not readily identifiable as the same firm.

3. Michael Sadleir, *The Evolution of Publishers' Binding Styles 1770–1900* (1930, reprint 1990), pp. 8–9.

4. John Dunton, *The Life and Errors*, ed. John Nichols (1818), p. 261. But Dunton's binder, Swinnock, worked at "under-rates," *i.e.* undercutting those in the book-

binders' price-lists, so his prices were a little lower than those of the trade generally. Bulk binding rates were memorialized in the Dublin 1743 and London 1744 price lists, as discussed in the previous chapter.

5 James E. Tierney, *The Correspondence of Robert Dodsley* (1988), p. xiv.

6. Thomas Dyche and William Pardon, *A New General English Dictionary*, quoted in Cyprian Blagden, "The Memorandum Book of Henry Rhodes, 1695–1720. Part II," in *The Book Collector* (Summer 1954), p. 115. Some modern authors, such as John Feather, have avoided the term "publisher" altogether when writing about the pre-1800 book trade. A modern publisher, writes Feather, is "the financier and organizer with the legal right to issue the book. But in the eighteenth century . . . the 'publisher'. . . distributed, or 'published', the book, in the sense in which, in legal terminology, a libel can be 'published' by the distributor or seller as well as the author, the printer, or the financier/organizer." John Feather, *The Provincial Book Trade in Eighteenth-Century England* (1985), p. 153, n. 56.

7. Such incentives included the "quarterly book" (discussed in note 17 below), which was so well-established throughout the Stationers' Company that it apparently carried over to bookbinders. See Chapter 1, note 11 and accompanying text. Much of the preceding discussion is indebted to Cyprian Blagden and his analysis of Rhodes's memoranda; see, especially, "The Memorandum Book of Henry Rhodes," pp. 114–16.

8. Dunton, *Life and Errors*, ed. Nichols, p. 204. Dunton complains of "all that pride and arrogance that is found in the carriage of some Publishers." *Ibid.*, p. 220. Cyprian Blagden suggests the Churchills as "perhaps the arrogant ones to whom Dunton referred." Blagden, "Memorandum Book of Henry Rhodes," pp. 115–16.

9. William Zachs, *The First John Murray and the Late Eighteenth-Century London Book Trade* (1998), p. 35.

10. David Pearson, *Durham Bookbinders and Booksellers 1660–1760* (1986), p. 4, noting about 550 of 700 books received ready-bound; the rest were "bound or rebound in Durham." Clavell's earlier catalogues were priced, which made it simpler to place orders, but also made it easy for retail customers to bypass their own local booksellers. By the time of Clavell's 1696 catalogue, which was largely unpriced, the preface made it clear that it was "in the Interest of all the *Booksellers* in *England* to have this *General Catalogue* in their Shops," and it was assumed, as John Feather writes, "that orders for books would reach London through the country booksellers." Feather, *Provincial Book Trade*, pp. 45–46. One can therefore see two reasons for the discontinuation of prices in Clavell's catalogues: (1) protests from country booksellers that the priced catalogue enabled customers to bypass them and deal directly with London (assuming such customers could make the necessary financial arrangements, not always easy at that time), and (2) priced catalogues limited the country bookseller's mark-up.

11. *Ibid.*, p. 64.

12. *Ibid.* Feather gives a number of examples for various parts of the country, with samples of the imprints used on some of the books involved. Some of these imprints also included Scottish and Irish booksellers.

13. William Hall was one such binder. He recounted stories of his contemporaries in the 1780s and '90s, many of whom served their apprenticeships in the provinces. Ellic Howe, *The London Bookbinders 1780–1806* (1950, reprint 1988), *passim*. John Feather's study of the provincial book trade contains little on bookbinders, but their trade must have grown in tandem with provincial booksellers' wholesale and retail businesses. Esther Potter writes that, apart from London, the University towns, Edinburgh, and Dublin, binders elsewhere "were producing only simple serviceable bindings until about 1700." Esther Potter, "To Paul's Churchyard to Treat with a Bookbinder," in *Property of a Gentleman*, ed. Robin Myers and Michael Harris (1991), p. 34. I would put the date a half-century later, by which time the provincial book trade had expanded sufficiently to support more upmarket bookbinders. Potter cites in support of her thesis Charles Ramsden's work on provincial bookbinders, but Ramsden's book begins at 1780, and few earlier examples have been conclusively identified. Potter goes on to note: "Binding, like printing, came very late to Wales and most collectors had their binding done in London, Dublin, Shrewsbury or Chester." *Ibid.*, p. 35.

14. Warren McDougall kindly communicated some statistics from the perspective of Scottish booksellers. David Hall of Philadelphia received Bibles (with clasps) from Adrian Watkins of Edinburgh from 1750–56, and in 1758 and 1760 Hall insisted to Hamilton & Balfour, also of Edinburgh, that they should not send books in sheets because binding costs were very high in America. Charles Elliot, active in Edinburgh in the 1770s and later, and sufficiently prosperous to open a shop in London in 1784, sent his first large shipment to Philadelphia at the end of that year. It was worth nearly £2,000, and consisted entirely of books bound in Scotland. The Scottish Customs export statistics to America, on those occasions when bindings are specified, refer far more to bound books than unbound. I suspect the figures for ready-bound Irish books were similar, based on my own experience of finding copies with early American provenances. Both Scottish and Irish printings were cheaper than those from London.

15. John Feather gives a succinct summary of the situation, quoting a London bookseller in 1759 (John Whiston) who listed some of the most commonly-printed texts, *e.g.* "Spectators, Tatlers, Guardians, Shakespear, Gay's poems and fables, Swift's works. . . ." Feather, *Provincial Book Trade*, p. 9, and more generally pp. 6–11. The whole matter of pirated editions is complex and often misunderstood. Irish editions of English texts were not covered by English copyright laws, and so were not piracies *per se* unless imported into England or her colonies. Mary Pollard suggests that "before 1780 illegal [Irish] exports to the plantations may have been more lucrative and more universally attempted" than those to

Britain. M. Pollard, *Dublin's Trade in Books 1550–1800* (1989), p. 108. Scottish editions were covered by English copyright laws, and there were, of course, also pirated editions printed in the provinces. In their vain attempt to hang on to perpetual copyright of profitable texts, the London booksellers displayed one of these, Thomas Luckman of Coventry's edition of *The Pilgrim's Progress*, in Parliament.

16. Examples are too numerous to discuss in detail, but J.W. Egerer notes the agreeable one of Thomas Cadell's accommodation of the Edinburgh bookseller William Creech. Creech had taken five hundred copies of Robert Burns's subscription edition of *Poems in the Scottish Dialect*, 1787. Cadell and his younger partner Andrew Strahan were ready to print their own edition of Burns's poems in the spring of that year, but Egerer shows from contemporary advertisements that they delayed printing in order to take on some of Creech's Edinburgh copies which he had been unable to sell. For Creech to ship copies of his Edinburgh printings to "his London agents [was] a not unusual thing for him to do." J.W. Egerer, *A Bibliography of Robert Burns* (1964), pp. 13–14.

17. Johnson's account of the practice includes the "quarterly book," or, as Johnson puts it, "for every hundred books so charged we must deliver a hundred and four." R.W. Chapman, *The Letters of Samuel Johnson* (1952), II, 114. The quarterly book was well established by the end of the sixteenth century, with booksellers allowing any fellow member of the Stationers' Company "that buye a quarterne of the same together, one Booke freely and without demaundinge anythinge for the same one booke." Marjorie Plant, *The English Book Trade*, third ed. (1974), p. 257, quoting Greg and Boswell, *Records of the Court of the Stationers' Company, 1576–1602*, p. 22. Plant's discussion of trade discounts generally confirms Johnson's account, which she also cites, incorrectly giving the date of his letter as 1766. Plant, *English Book Trade*, p. 258. Graham Pollard notes that trade discounts "remained relatively constant from the sixteenth to the nineteenth century." Graham Pollard, "The English Market for Printed Books," in *Publishing History*, 4 (1978), p. 15.

18. Johnson's account has the retailer buying for 16s. 6d. a book which he will sell at retail for £1.0.0, a discount from the retail price of 17½ percent. But in Johnson's day the total discount given by the bookseller issuing a book was between 30–35 percent, and John Feather suggests that a retailer buying directly from the commissioning bookseller might have received the full discount. Feather, *Provincial Book Trade*, pp. 56–59. Plant notes that Christopher Barker offered his large Bible at discounts to London companies willing to buy in quantity, at 24s. bound or 20s. unbound, although "if it were prised at XXXs. it were scarce sufficient." Plant, *English Book Trade*, p. 257. Later booksellers, especially those selling educational books or religious tracts, offered quantity discounts of fifteen or so percent to *any* purchaser of a dozen or more copies. I suspect discounts to booksellers were also determined by the quantity purchased.

19. There is a detailed example in Chapter 1, note 22.

20. This is more than a theoretical construct: since 1774 Thomas Cadell had been the Clarendon Press's London "Warehouse-keeper or publisher" for books other than those "in the learned languages." Chapman, *Letters of Johnson*, II, 112, discussing letter no. 463. Cadell was also one of the London booksellers named in the imprint of Blackstone's *Commentaries on the Laws of England*, printed at the Clarendon Press between 1765–69.

21. Probably Charles Dilly, or possibly his brother Edward. Both the Dillys and Cadell were important London booksellers with active wholesale and retail businesses; Johnson is limiting their roles to those they played specifically in relation to the Clarendon Press.

22. Chapman accurately notes that Johnson does not mean "there were no retailers in London; but the position of the London retailer as such was the same as the country bookseller's." *Ibid.*, II, 114, n. 463–2. Johnson presumably tells the story as he does to avoid the question "why should there be three different agents involved in selling a single book in London?"

23. *Ibid.*, II, 114–15. The ellipses omit Johnson's discussion of the quarterly book, and its inclusion in the discounts offered through the trade. The quotation is long enough as it is, and there is a summary of the quarterly book in note 17 to this chapter. Johnson's letter also appears in Boswell's *Life*, under Tuesday 12 March 1776, where Boswell describes this passage as "of great importance."

24. Pollard, "Changes in the Style of Bookbinding," p. 61 and n. 118.

25. Cadell employed William Craig, "supposed to have conducted a thriving business," and Dilly was a primary employer of John Lovejoy, who "had a great business and kept a great many hands at one time." Howe, *London Bookbinders*, pp. 32 and 45. Both Craig and Lovejoy operated high-class binderies, which were probably used for the booksellers' best work. The two may also have taken larger, edition-sized orders for putting books into wrappers and boards, most of which was done by women and apprentices anyway, but the larger bookselling firms could save money by employing their own hands for this work as well as the simpler leather bindings.

26 Murray commissioned "a few thousand" bindings each year. "By 1781 he was handling enough new books to set up a bindery and employ a full-time binder. He paid this man sixteen shillings a week. At busy periods journeymen binders would be hired to complete jobs." William Zachs, *The First John Murray and the Late Eighteenth-Century London Book Trade* (1998), p. 35. It seems unlikely that for 16s. Murray got a binder capable of doing fine work. It was not uncommon for a good finisher in the 1780s to make a pound or even a guinea per week.

27. R.B. McKerrow, *An Introduction to Bibliography* (1928), p. 125, n. 1. John Feather confirms "the variable price of books which was a consequence of simultaneous issue in different forms of binding, and that "the 'usual Allowance' was made on the basis of the price for a

particular form of binding," with "more or less fixed prices for each form; prices are often quoted for 'sheets', 'stitched', 'wrappers', or 'boards'." Feather, *Provincial Book Trade*, p. 57. Whether a retail bookseller ordering a total of twenty-five copies in a variety of bindings received his quarterly copy is nowhere recorded, but most likely he did. No doubt he and the wholesaler had a good time negotiating in which binding it would come.

28. Sadleir, *Evolution*, p. 2.

29. Feather, *Provincial Book Trade*, p. 57, quoted above in note 27. Before 1750, of course, "boards" would hardly have signified as an alternative form of binding.

30. As part of my initial research for this book, I identified a half-dozen booksellers who were known to have bookbinderies, including Richard Janeway, Ralph Simpson, and Francis Fayram, and examined several dozen copies of books containing their imprints. Fayram was particularly interesting because he probably acted as a warehouseman/bookbinder as well as a bookseller, and he collected subscriptions for Henry Rhodes on at least one occasion. Blagden, "Memorandum Book of Henry Rhodes, Part II," p. 113. I had hoped to find some distinctive and recurring binding features, and to begin a file of prospective publishers' bindings from the early eighteenth century. The attempt was a notable failure. Most of these booksellers belonged to syndicates, sometimes large ones, and their names appeared with several others in books' imprints. These books probably had several bookbinder/warehousemen, as well as the usual wide variety of retail bindings. I do not doubt that a wider sampling of copies will turn up some consistent features, however.

31. John Jaffray's manuscripts, quoted in Mirjam M. Foot, "Some Bookbinders' Price Lists of the Seventeenth and Eighteenth Centuries," in *Studies in the History of Bookbinding* (1993), p. 25 and n. 28. My earlier reference is in Chapter 2, note 32 and accompanying text.

32. James Raven, "The Novel Comes of Age," in James Raven and Antonia Forster, *The English Novel 1770–1829: A Bibliographical Survey. . . . Volume I: 1770–1799* (2000), p. 88.

33. Bell's trade card appears in facsimile in Stanley Morison, *John Bell, 1745–1831* (1930), opposite pp. xii. Bell's circulating library was also highly successful, and the profits of his operations aroused envy among the older established elements of the book trade, so much so that at one point Bell was prompted to issue an engraved advertisement headed "Opposition Defeated By Spirit, Perseverance and Elegance, Exemplified in Bell's Publications." The text of the advertisement gives details of "a Subscription of near Ten Thousand Pounds . . . raised by forty-two of the most powerful of the London Booksellers . . . not only meanly to suppress, but vainly attempting to rival the superior execution of the above-mentioned works." *Ibid.*, p. 96.

34. Howe, *London Bookbinders*, p. 19. Fairbairn's activity, however, gave the booksellers their opportunity for revenge on Bell: they and the prosecuting bookbinders indicted Fairbairn as one of the strikers anyway.

35. Bell's use of pallets for lettering is known from the correspondence of the bookbinder William Hall. Howe, *London Bookbinders*, pp. 68–69.

36. Sadleir, *Evolution*, pp. 10–11. What persuaded Sadleir to accept these bindings as publisher's was the combination of the unusual binding material (the vellum spines), the printed paper labels, and Newbery's extensive advertisements. S. Roscoe, *John Newbery and his Successors, 1740–1814* (1973), pp. 393–96, discusses the first appearance of the "Vellum manner," and corrects Sadleir's dating of the innovation, noting its probable introduction around 1768. Roscoe quotes one of Newbery's advertisements, dated 1773, which states that "In the course of five Years, upwards of Fourteen Thousand Volumes have been sold bound in this Manner." Roscoe cites additional evidence supporting 1768 as the year in which these bindings were introduced; his discussion of them is, I think, definitive.

37. Esther Potter, "To Paul's Churchyard to Treat with a Bookbinder," in *Property of a Gentleman*, ed. Robin Myers and Michael Harris (1991), p. 28.

38. Roubiquet is mentioned in the same sentence as Roger Payne and Baumgarten in a 1781 pamphlet declaring the "Degree of Perfection" to which bookbinding had arrived "in the Course of the last sixteen Years." Tierney, *Correspondence of Robert Dodsley*, p. 393 and n. 12.

39. Dunton, *Life and Errors*, ed. Nichols, p. 260.

40. Howard M. Nixon, "English Bookbindings XLIII," in *The Book Collector* (Winter 1962), p. 466. Nixon illustrates a fine example of a Brindley publisher's binding in this article, on the Duke of Newcastle's *General System of Horsemanship*, 1743.

41. Philip Gaskell, *A Bibliography of the Foulis Press* (1964), p. 54–55. Gaskell illustrates some Foulis bindings with "a certain design involving crosses in spine panels . . . commonly used at the Foulis bindery" in the first part of his "The Early Work of the Foulis Press and the Wilson Foundry," in *The Library*, Fifth Series, Vol. VII (1952), pp. 77–110.

42. I have also seen matching sheep bindings on three different copies of the 1669 Thomas Helder issue of *Paradise Lost*, and consider these to be publisher's bindings as well. Helder advertised the book in Starkey and Clavell's catalogues "price bound 3s," and Helder had a bookbindery as part of his business.

43. "Advertisement to the Public," in *The Rational Lovers: or, the History of Sir Charles Leusum, and Mrs. Francis Fermor*, 1769.

44. James Raven, "From promotion to proscription: arrangements for reading and eighteenth-century libraries," in *The Practice and Representation of Reading in England*, ed. James Raven et al. (1996), p. 178. The Nobles were early library proprietors, beginning in the 1740s, the period when "commercial circulating libraries . . . were first established" in England. *Ibid.*, p. 175.

45. The "more than fourteen percent" teaser is probably for the booksellers: if they are already getting a fifteen percent discount, *i.e.* are paying 17s. in the pound, it can be argued that the further 2s. is a percentage of the 17s., which makes it more like eleven+ percent than ten. Either way, if the country bookseller pays 15s. in the pound, he is getting both the retailer's and the distributor's discount in Johnson's hypothetical case, cited earlier in this chapter, paying the same percentage as Dilly, the "wholesale bookseller."

46. I did not find consistent binding features on 1740s Noble publications. Other booksellers were involved in most of them, and different groups of binders may have been employed. Or maybe I was just unlucky.

47. The Noble publications cited here are so rare that anyone wishing to compare copies may readily find these examples by searching the titles in library databases, without fear of getting anything other than the bindings under discussion. For this reason shelf marks and call numbers are not added to locations.

48. Both of these books from the Beinecke Library have been rebacked, but the covers appear to be original. What appears to be the same edge-roll also appears on the Beinecke copy of *The Rival Mother: or, The History of the Countess of Salens*, 2 vols. (1755), and on the four volumes of the British Library copy of *Love at Cross Purposes, Exemplified in Two Sentimental and Connected Histories from Real Life* (1769). It is the most generic of the three edge-rolls illustrated, however, and the binding features on this latter title especially are not persuasively similar, although one must remember that more than a decade separates it from the other four. This copy of *Love at Cross Purposes* raises another significant question about publishers' bindings of this period. Many binders discarded half-titles and advertisements, or pasted endpapers over them, so often that the bookseller David McGee in *A Course in Correct Cataloguing* (1977) offers as one of his tongue-in-cheek definitions "Half-Titles: Very important when your item happens to possess them." Every other example suggested as a possible publisher's binding in this chapter is complete with its half-titles and advertisements; one would think that a publisher's binder would be under orders to preserve the latter, especially. But in the second volume of this copy of *Love at Cross Purposes*, the entire publishers' catalogue at the end has been discarded. Does this disqualify the binding, and any binding with these leaves missing, as publisher's? Probably so, but it might not if the novel had been published by a syndicate. Less powerful members of syndicates received books in sheets with more powerful members' advertisements in them; not surprisingly, the binders of such copies often cancelled these advertisement leaves.

49. Longe had an especially large collection of novels. His library was sold around 1910; the Dobell firm was the primary purchaser. See Hugh Amory, *New Books by Fielding: An Exhibition of the Hyde Collection* (1987), p. 53. Other Longe copies of novels published by the Nobles include Katherine Maxwell, *The History of Miss Katty N——*, [1757], and *The Adventures and Amours of the Marquis de Noailles, and Mademoiselle Tencin*, 2 vols. (1761), both at the Beinecke Library.

50. This is a large folio somber binding (black with all-over blind tooling), British Library call number C.66.k.10. The binding is quite well-preserved, but whatever evidence there was of Woodward's having bound it has disappeared as of June 2003. Yet this evidence must have been there when Howe transcribed it sometime before 1950. See Ellic Howe, *List of London Bookbinders 1648–1815* (1950), p. 103. Howe says the binder's name and address were "stamped," presumably on a printed ticket of some kind.

51. David Pearson, "Who, or What, is I W?," in *The Book Collector*, Vol. 50, No. 2 (2001), pp. 235–38: "I W might stand for a phrase or motto, although this seems less likely." *Ibid.*, p. 238. Pearson has noted over ninety examples on books with imprints from 1675 to 1729. He remarks the strong Cambridge association of many of them, concluding that "accumulated evidence from a number of these books makes it clear that the tool belonged to a Cambridge bindery." *Ibid.*, p. 237. The two University towns had the largest concentration of bookbinders in England outside London, and were thus more likely to receive books in sheets from London booksellers, especially standard academic and theological texts like those "I.W." bound.

52. The copy in contemporary paneled sheep is at the Folger Shakespeare Library, that in calf which I suggest is circa 1720–1730 at the Brotherton Collection, University of Leeds, and that in marbled boards, rebacked, at the National Library of Scotland. I am grateful to curators at all three of these libraries for supplying descriptions and photographs in response to my inquiries.

53. Jacob Tonson Jr.'s will makes it clear that a bookbindery was part of the business at the time of his death in 1735. Because Jacob Jr. was not the businessman his uncle was, I have no doubt that the bookbindery was part of the empire built by the elder Jacob, who took over his brother's business premises around 1698, made the substantial acquisition of a printing house by 1703, and bought the rich literary copyrights of the bookseller Henry Herringman in 1707. See Kathleen Lynch, *Jacob Tonson, Kit-Cat Publisher* (1971), p. 108. (Lynch relies on Septimus Rivington for her assignment of the Herringman purchase to Jacob Jr., which I believe is a mistake).

54. The phrase "pompous Folio Edition" was coined by Jonathan Richardson in *Explanatory Notes and Remarks on Milton's Paradise Lost* (1734), and is quoted in Helen Darbishire, *The Early Lives of Milton* (1932), p. 294. For Tonson's role in the syndicate (or conger), see Norma Hodgson and Cyprian Blagden, "The Notebook of Thomas Bennet and Henry Clements," in *Oxford Bibliographical Society Publications*, New Series, Vol. VI, 1953 (1956), p. 81: "Tonson's domination was, I believe, more complete than that of any of the others." The reference is to transactions around 1715, but Tonson's power was established well before that.

55. This hypothesis is extrapolated from the procedures described in Henry Rhodes's memorandum book. Rhodes's bookbinder/warehouseman delivered bound copies not only to Rhodes, but also to other members of the trade. Rhodes's various editions of *The Young Secretary's Guide*, extensively advertised at "1s., 12mo., bound," are one example, and his binders included "Mr. Cholmly," previously discussed. As Rhodes's business grew "there must have come a stage . . . when it paid him to make use of a binder and of the binder's back-street premises." Blagden, "Memorandum Book of Henry Rhodes, Part II," pp. 110–11. It is also possible, of course, that these are bindings executed for Tonson's retail shop rather than for wholesale distribution.

56. Jonathan E. Hill, "From Provisional to Permanent: Books in Boards 1790–1840," in *The Library*, Sixth Series, Vol. 21, No. 3 (1999), p. 252, n. 20.

57. Circulating libraries commissioned uniform bindings for their books—easily done as practically all such libraries were run by booksellers. A 1797 pamphlet, *The Use of Circulating Libraries Considered*, confirms the practice, advising libraries to put their books "into the hands of a good binder, to be half bound uniform, and uncut" [i.e. with the edges untrimmed]. The reason "for advising that they should be uncut, must be obvious to every person in the trade, but my wish here is to inform the public in general. Many valuable publications are put in boards, or half bound, which, at a future time, the purchaser may want to put into better binding or new covers, then, if the edges are cut and coloured, the book will have every appearance of being new." Quoted in Pollard, "Changes in the Style of Bookbinding," p. 42 and n. 20.

58. Quoted in Roscoe, *John Newbery*, p. 394.

59. More detail, including some specific binding prices, and costs of labor and materials, is given in M. Pollard, *Dublin's Trade in Books*, p. 127.

60. *A General Catalogue of Books in all Languages, Arts, and Sciences, that have been Printed in Great Britain, and published in London, since the Year M.DCC to the Present Time* (1779).

61. Zachs, *The First John Murray*, plate 25.

62. William Bent, quoted in Pollard, "Changes in the Style of Bookbinding," p. 66, n. 18.

63. "The advance in price will be, in general, as follows: A volume of 18mo or 12mo, 6d. more in sheep, and 1s. in calf letd.—common 8vo, 1s. more in sheep, and 1s. 6d. in calf letd.—royal 8vo, 2s. more in calf letd.—4to, 4s. to 6s., and folio 5s. to 7s. and upward, according to size, in calf and lettered. December 7, 1803." Bent, quoted in Pollard. *Ibid*.

64. An excellent account of the transition in the 1790s is given by Jonathan E. Hill :

> The proportionate increase in the use of board bindings is reflected in advertisements put out by publishers and booksellers. At the beginning of the decade [i.e. 1790] John Stockdale offered a wide variety of texts and bindings in a sixteen-page advertisement which he inserted into a copy of James Andrew's *Anecdotes, &c. Antient and Modern* (John Stockdale, 1790). Of the works offered, only a few are described as being 'in boards.' Some are offered without any binding. Others are for sale 'Bound', that is, bound in leather; russia or morocco are listed, with 'gilt', or 'extra gilt'. By the middle of the decade, the choice has not changed much. In an advertisement leaf inserted into the twelfth volume of Robert Henry's *The History of Great Britain* (Strahan & Cadell, 1795), only one of ten items listed is offered 'in boards'. A year later, of some 160 titles in a sixteen-page advertisement inserted into a copy of James Andrews's *History of Great Britain* (T. Cadell Jr. and W. Davies, 1796), only ten are described as 'in boards'. But five years after that, in 1801, nine out of ten titles are being offered in boards in a three-page advertisement bound into a copy of L.P. de Ségur's *History of the Principal Events of the Reign of Frederic William II* (Longman & Rees, 1801).

Hill, "From Provisional to Permanent," p. 252.

65. The letter is undated, but from internal references must have been written at the end of 1786. Fordyce requested "that Two or Three Dozen may be *Bound* against Wednesday or Thursday next, that I may carry a few with me into the country. . . . I should like them to be finished in the manner of Dr. Price's *Sermons* which you sent me. I think it very elegant, in every respect. The *Green* Ground of the Title on the back I prefer much to the *Blue*, & the *Yellow* on the edges of the leaves to the *Green*." I am grateful to Robert Harding of Maggs Bros. Ltd. for bringing this letter to my attention, and to Stephen Parks, Curator of the Osborn Collection at the Beinecke Library, Yale University, for supplying a photocopy of the original (Osborn Files Folder 19249).

66. Raven, "The Novel Comes of Age," p. 90. Raven discusses the increased number of bankruptcies in the book trade after 1774, and concludes that "for every ostentatious success-story, from the eminence of Cadell to the audacity of Lane's Minerva Press and Lackington's Temple of the Muses, there were dozens of miserable or wildly fluctuating returns."

67. James Raven's entries and reports of advertisements confirm this pricing. See James Raven, *British Fiction 1750–1770* (1987) and Raven and Forster, *The English Novel. . . . Volume I: 1770–1799*. He also discusses the potential profitability of editions in "The Novel Comes of Age," p. 95. Further confirmation of prices can be found in catalogues of the period; *The General Catalogue* for 1779, cited above, has a thirteen-page section of "Novels and Romances," with a few duodecimo novels "sewed" at 2s. 6d. per volume, and the rest with no specifications and therefore bound, 3s. per volume. As far as I can tell, early editions of *Pamela* were not advertised sewed, but only at 3s. per volume "bound." William Sale, Jr., *Samuel Richardson. A Bibliographical Record* (1936), pp. 15–24. Three shillings was the per-volume price for bound copies of the first edition of 1741 and also for the eighth editon of 1762. The various volumes of the

duodecimo edition of *Sir Charles Grandison* were advertised in 1753 and 1754 at 2s. 6d. sewed or in boards, although the first four volumes were once advertised together at 10s. 6d. in boards. *Ibid.*, p. 76. George Faulkner advertised his Irish edition of *Pamela*, 1741, at a slightly lower price, as one would expect, 5s. 5d. for the first two volumes, bound. *Ibid*, p. 16.

68. These figures are taken from Raven, *British Fiction 1750–1770*, and Raven and Forster, *The English Novel. . . . Volume I: 1770–1799*. Advertised prices are also quoted from the entries for individual novels in these two works, which are chronological and fully indexed. Because these entries are readily accessible to readers wishing to confirm or expand upon them, and because this book has plenty of endnotes already, Raven and Forster item numbers are not cited for each novel. Raven's introductory survey in the latter work, "The Novel Comes of Age," combines, as can be seen in the preceding notes and text, statistical analysis with social and cultural history, and provides a wealth of information about the workings of the book trade of that time, excepting, alas, bookbinding. His research and compilations were essential to this study, but are in no way to blame for its analyses and inferences concerning bound copies, and the motivations and actions of booksellers.

69. What is certain is that wrappered and boarded popular literature was not part of the visual landscape of country house libraries. In my experience these books, when kept, found their way into cupboards underneath the display bookcases, or into the passages or rooms used by servants. In my days at Christie's I once spent hours in the pantry cupboards of a Scottish country house, searching through stacks of wrappered and boarded books among which I had found, virtually as new, Volume III of the first edition of Jane Austen's *Sense and Sensibility*. When I finally found the other two volumes I remarked to the aristocratic owners that this was one of the most valuable books in the house, an exceptional survival in original condition, and doubtless so because one of their ancestors had bought Jane Austen's first novel, read it, hadn't cared for it enough to send it for rebinding, and never bought another. My ebullience was arrested by an icy stare from the Countess, who replied, "I am sure, Mr. Bennett, that *our* ancestors would never have felt that way about Jane Austen."

70. Jonathan E. Hill's study adds support to this account of the transition to boards. Warren McDougall also sent details of a sample of the largely medical publications of Charles Elliot of Edinburgh from 1771–1790. Some one hundred titles have a note of the binding state, taken mainly from newspaper advertisements but sometimes from advertisements in the books. Sixty-nine titles were advertised as either sewed or (more often) in boards, twenty-one titles as sold both sewed/boards or bound, one title sold sewed or half-bound, one title half bound, and eight titles bound. Taking into account the occasions where there is a choice, the total comes to ninety-one books/titles sold sewed or in boards, two sold half bound, twenty-nine sold bound.

There were, of course, readers fond enough of their popular literature to have it bespoke bound, as there were in preceding decades. Several elegantly-bound collections of eighteenth and early nineteenth century novels have survived: the Chawton House Library in Hampshire has a large percentage of that formed by Lady Vane Stewart, for example. The higher survival figures for bound copies should not blind us to the prevalence of sewn and boarded copies as issued. If an ordinary novel of the 1790s, for example one by a little-known or anonymous Minerva author, was published in an edition of five hundred copies, at least four hundred of those were probably sewn or in boards. If twenty of the five hundred copies survived—a very high rate for a popular novel—several might be in later bindings, and no more than three or four still sewn or in boards.

71. Letter of William Hall to John Jaffray, quoted in Howe, *The London Bookbinders*, p. 10.

72. Most novels of this period, including those discussed here, were issued in duodecimo (or, less often, foolscap octavo) format. Novels were, however, occasionally issued in other formats, among them crown octavo, a grander production altogether. A good example is William Beckford's *Vathek*, published by Joseph Johnson in 1786 under the title *An Arabian Tale* at 4s. sewed. Another from the same year is Thomas Holcroft's translation of Billardon de Sauvigny's *Amourous Tale of the Chaste Loves of Peter the Long*, published by the Robinsons and "beautifully printed upon a fine Writing Paper," advertised at 3s. 6d. sewed.

73. Henry R. Plomer et al., *Dictionary of Printers and Booksellers . . . from 1726–1775* (1968), p. 215. A fuller account of the Robinsons and novel publishers is given by Raven in "The Novel Comes of Age," pp. 71 et seq., and especially pp. 76–77, where Robinson's is described as "the most remarkable establishment" in Paternoster Row, and a "scene of renowned entertainment. Mrs. Radcliffe, Mrs. Thrale, and Mrs. Inchbald were frequent visitors."

74. There are a few exceptions, but the shift is quite dramatic: in 1789 Lane published eighteen novels, fifteen of them at 2s. 6d. per volume sewed; in 1790 the total output was twenty-two novels, nine of them at 2s. 6d., and another eight advertised at both 2s. 6d. and 3s. Lane added "Minerva" to the name at the end of 1790, and in 1791, published twenty-two novels, of which only one was advertised at 2s. 6d. per volume, and three at both 2s. 6d. and 3s. All the rest were advertised at 3s., and one two-decker in octavo was advertised at both 3s. and 3s. 6d.

75. Even Francis Noble, who had published novels at 3s. per volume bound since the 1740s, tried the new price with one of his very last publications, Phebe Gibbes's *The Niece*, 3 vols. (1788). It was variously advertised at 9s. with no binding given, 9s. (and also the old price of 7s.6d.) sewed, and 10s. 6d. in "calf lettered."

76. Pollard, "Changes in the Style of Bookbinding," pp. 59–61. Pollard supports his argument by pointing

out that the labels are set "in Caslon and not in Baskerville type." Since Pollard's article was written, however, Philip Gaskell has recorded Baskerville's use of Caslon type, so the type alone does not conclusively prove the label was by another printer. Philip Gaskell, *John Baskerville a Bibliography* (1973), p. xx. Whoever printed the labels, I agree with Pollard that they were for copies handled by a wholesale distributor.

77. In the *Public Advertiser* of 5 April 1766. See Gaskell, *John Baskerville*, p. xxix. Such a binding would have been sheep or calf, not boards. A few bindings are known to have been executed for Baskerville himself, although I am not aware of one on this title. These seem to have been special bindings for presentation, an entirely different proposition to, say, the full-time commercial bindery in the Foulises' printing-house. I am grateful to William Barlow for telling me about these Baskerville bindings.

78. Gaskell, *John Baskerville*, p. 48.

79 Pollard, "Changes in the Style of Bookbinding," p. 61 and n. 118.

80. It must continue to be emphasized, however, that boards and paper labels are not the only publisher's binding on books such as Blackstone's *Commentaries*. There were probably substantial numbers of copies issued in calf, and in calf-backed boards—one copy in the latter binding, untrimmed, is no. 407 in *The Rothschild Library* (1954), p. 77. Boards and paper labels for this period are simply the most *identifiable* publisher's binding.

81. Pollard, "Changes in the Style of Bookbinding," p. 61.

82. If printing a half-title on a leftover leaf makes sense as a way both to protect and to label copies of books in folded sheets, it is probably wise to look for a similar logic in the integral printing of paper spine labels, uncommon as they are. These leaves are almost always excised in leather-bound copies. Binderies probably worked on leather bindings first, since they took longer and were more profitable. Perhaps the labels excised from these copies were given to the journeymen and apprentices responsible for putting up copies in boards. These integral labels continued to appear, albeit infrequently, until the 1840s.

83. Sadleir, "Eleventh-Hour Notes," *Evolution*, p. 96.

84. William A. Jackson, "Printed Wrappers of the Fifteenth to the Eighteenth Centuries," in *Harvard Library Bulletin*, Vol. VI, No. 3 (1952), p. 313.

85. The parody would be meaningless if there were not an established convention of such wrappers, but few examples survive, and those that do are unlettered. Roger Stoddard, who describes the unique copy of *Rome Excis'd* at Harvard, notes "a collection of poems published by Cambridge University on the deaths of Prince Henry and Princess Mary of Orange: *Threni Cantabrigeienses in funere duorum principum, Henrici Glocestrensis* . . . (Cambridge, by John Field, 1661; Wing C354). Its limp vellum wrappers have been swabbed with printer's ink, its endpapers have been swabbed black —perhaps after they were pasted in—and its edges are

stained black." Roger E. Stoddard, "The Use of Mourning Wrappers in New England, with a Note on Mourning Papers in English Books at Harvard," in *Harvard Library Bulletin*, Vol. XXX, No. 1 (1982), p. 98. Stoddard refers to two other examples cited by D.F. Foxon, *English Verse 1701–1750* (1976): William Hogg, *In obitum augustissimi invictissimique Magnae Britanniae* (London, 1702, Foxon H278), and Samuel Wesley, *The parish priest . . . upon a clergyman lately deceas'd* (London, 1731, Foxon W345), this last recorded in the printer William Bowyer's ledgers as twelve copies "stitcht in black." Hogg's pamphlet survives in its original wrappers at Yale, and Stephen Parks was kind enough to look at it for me, reporting that "in this case [mourning wrappers] are simply plain black paper pasted to paper similar to that on which the pamphlet is printed, making them a bit stiffer."

86. This photograph shows a left-over wrapper from No. XXIV being used for No. 42, with the change made in manuscript. This slightly compromises Jackson's definition, but clearly does not reduce the status of this wrapper to a "binder's wrapper."

87. In November 2002, Stephen Weissman of Ximenes Rare Books kindly sent me a note of early printed magazine wrappers he has handled. They included (1) an issue of the *Gentleman's Magazine* for April 1743, in pale blue wrappers; (2) 14 numbers of the *London Magazine*, from 1739–1742, in pale blue wrappers; and (3) A single number of the *Historical Register* for 1724, in grey wrappers.

88. One example of Dodsley's printed wrappers, dated 1747, was previously discussed in Chapter 1, note 51; an even earlier example, pointed out to me by William Zachs, is the Cambridge University Library copy of the first part of Edward Young's *The Complaint . . . Night the First* (1742).

89. Jackson warns that these integrated wrappers "should not be confused with 'wrap-arounds,' which are common on pamphlets of the eighteenth century and which . . . contain . . . title or half-title on the recto of the first leaf [and] text, table, index or advertisements which is continuous with matter which is an integral part of the book." Jackson, "Printed Wrappers of the Fifteenth to the Eighteenth Centuries," pp. 313–14. Jackson notes integrated wrappers on surviving English editions of *The Schoole of Vertue*, beginning in 1593, with editions of 1621 and 1642 having "a domestic scene" on the wrappers. He was also aware of the Irish edition illustrated here: "the 1698 Dublin edition has . . . a cut of a schoolmaster surrounded by pupils." *Ibid.*, p. 319. As this copy is unique (see Wing S2412F), the description was probably communicated to him by Arnold Muirhead, who purchased it from Bernard Quaritch Ltd. in 1949. The Quaritch catalogue description remarked the woodcuts, but did not describe them as wrappers.

90. An excellent summary of their origin and use is given by Roscoe, *John Newbery*, pp. 396–7. They were mostly manufactured in Germany, but came to England

via Holland, hence their name. It has been suggested that "Dutch" is a corruption of "Deutsch."

91. Harvey Darton saw the British Library copy in its original boards, but it was rebound in the 1930s. F.J. Harvey Darton, *Children's Books in England*, third ed., revised by Brian Alderson (1982), p. 101.

92. Roscoe, *John Newbery*, p. 396.

93. Other examples are described in Roscoe, *John Newbery*, especially item J253 (13) and Plate 11, a 1784 edition of *The Museum for Young Gentlemen and Ladies*. Harvey Darton, *Children's Books in England*, p. 128, illustrates the covers of a 1783 edition of *The History of Little Goody Two Shoes*. *The Rothschild Library* (1954), p. 138, no. 608, describes a 1777 edition of the same title in "black and white printed paper boards, decorated with vignette illustrations of the story." The Rothschild copy has printed at the foot of the title-page "Price Six-pence, bound and gilt." It was no doubt a warehoused copy intended to be bound in Dutch gilt boards, caught by the shortages of the early 1780s.

94. Roscoe, *John Newbery*, p. 397, suggests it began to be used around 1767; Bernard C. Middleton, *A History of English Craft Bookbinding Technique*, second ed. (1978), p. 132, says "about 1770."

95. Middleton, *History of English Craft Bookbinding*, p. 132. Douglas Leighton notes several examples of canvas bindings, one on *Geography for Children*, 1791, which was advertised in William Bent's catalogue that year as "Bound in the Common Manner." "Common" in this context meant the simplest possible binding, usually sheep, for which canvas was here offered as a substitute. Douglas Leighton, "Canvas and Bookcloth. An Essay on Beginnings," Bibliographical Society offprint (1948), p. 41.

96. The latest example of vellum-backed marbled boards with printed paper labels I have seen is on the tenth edition of John Aikin and Anna Letitia Barbauld, *Evenings at Home*, 6 vols., 18mo, for J. Johnson, 1814. The spines are stained green *à la* Newbery; only the more modern setting of the printed paper labels suggests the actual date.

97. The earliest recorded use of "roan" in connection with bookbinding is 1818. See Chapter 2, notes 26 and 31, and accompanying text. I have not discovered any special term for it from the 1790s.

98. Mary Elliott, "The Book-Case," in *Flowers of Instruction: or, Familiar Subjects in Verse* (1820), p. 5.

### CHAPTER FOUR

1. Caxton's binder was using a form of panel decoration as early as the 1480s, and a distinct precursor of the Restoration paneled style is on a velvet binding by the Cambridge binder Daniel Boyse circa 1627. Howard M. Nixon, *Five Centuries of English Bookbinding* (1978), plates 1 and 29. For an early cottage-roof design on a Mearne binding, see, *e.g.*, Howard M. Nixon, *English Restoration Bookbindings* (1974), plate 29, showing red goatskin on a 1662 *Book of Common Prayer*.

2. For William Bonnor, see Nixon, *Five Centuries of English Bookbinding*, pp. 143–45; the illustrations include impressions of Bonnor's tools. In Chapters 2 and 3, I discuss some London binders, including John Brindley. Giles Barber has extrapolated from a binding stamped "Dymott fecit" to identify other examples of the work of this mid-eighteenth century London binder. "Richard Dymott, Bookbinder," in *The Library*, Fifth Series, XIX (1964), pp. 250–53. David Pearson's pioneering archival research in *Durham Bookbinders and Booksellers* (1986) and *Oxford Bookbinding 1500–1640* (2000) has expanded our knowledge of individual bookbinders in those cities. Other binders are discussed in Howard M. Nixon and Mirjam M. Foot, *The History of Decorated Bookbinding in England* (1992), Chapters 4 and 5.

3. Ellic Howe, *A List of London Bookbinders 1648–1815* (1950), p. 89. See also Nixon and Foot, *History of Decorated Bookbinding in England*, p. 82, and P.J.M. Marks, *The British Library Guide to Bookbinding* (1998), p. 20. There is also evidence that Steel's apprentice Thomas Elliott acquired some of the Steels' tools after 1717, about the same time he began to work for perhaps their best customer, Lord Harley.

4. G.D. Hobson, *Bindings in Cambridge Libraries* (1929), p. 164.

5. Specialized studies of Irish and Scottish bindings have had little to say, or illustrate, from the period 1660–1720, nor does the rich British Library on-line *Database of Bookbindings* contain any examples at this time. No doubt the growing prosperity of Dublin, Glasgow, and Edinburgh; the new college library at Trinity, Dublin; the increasing national character of Irish and Scottish literature exemplified in authors like Jonathan Swift and Allan Ramsay; and booksellers like George Faulkner and James Watson had much to do with new and distinctive binding styles after about 1720.

6. Maurice Craig, *Irish Bookbindings 1600–1800* (1954), pp. 2–3.

7. Richard J. Wolfe, *Marbled Paper* (1990) is the essential guide to the origin and date of most of these papers.

8. Trade card of John Wilson, bookbinder in Norwich, reproduced in David Pearson, *English Bookbinding Styles 1450–1800: A Handbook* (forthcoming), Chapter 7. Other advertisements offer the same service in slightly different terms: William Gray in Canon-Alley, St. Paul's, London "Gilds and Letters Gentlemens Studies, at reasonable Rates," and William Wiginton in Elliot's Court, Little Old Bailey, London, declares "Gentlemens Libraries refitted on the lowest Terms." *Ibid.*

### CHAPTER FIVE

1. David Pearson, *Oxford Bookbinding 1500–1640* (2000), pp. 42–43.

2. John Carter, *ABC for Book Collectors* (1952), pp. 71–72, quotes W. Carew Hazlitt's 1904 remark that "the édition de luxe was 'dilettantism *in extremis*.'" The days when

the term "édition de luxe" was used, in Carter's words, as "bait for suckers" are sufficiently past for its pejorative implication to have faded. "Gift binding" in its usual bibliographical sense suggests *wholesale* fine binding, and is normally used to describe a nineteenth century special, more expensive, publisher's issue. Nineteenth-century gift bindings were inspired by the range of such bindings sold in eighteenth century shops, which in turn were inspired by those of the seventeenth century. The edition bindings of thumb Bibles and almanacs included a separate "gift" issue in decorated goatskin, but if gift bindings had been a major part of the wholesale book business before 1760, some description of them would probably have found its way into the bookbinders' price lists. Pre-1760 publisher/bookbinders like Samuel Mearne and John Brindley produced early gift bindings in their own workshops, and some devotional and courtesy books, such as Richard Allestree's, were sufficiently popular that wholesale distributors might have had part of an edition specially bound in goatskin. James Raven notes that by the end of the eighteenth century some upmarket publishers offered "*De luxe* subscription and special editions . . . to specific custom and to those who had the money to aspire to learning, position and gentility," a use of "deluxe" parallel to that suggested in this chapter. James Raven, "From promotion to proscription: arrangements for reading and eighteenth-century libraries," in *The Practice and Representation of Reading in England*, ed. James Raven et al. (1996), p. 178. But the majority of such bindings, like those in calf and sheep, were probably executed for retail traders. This chapter needs a term without specifically wholesale connotations.

3. Printed at the end of Brindley's 1744 edition of Cornelius Nepos and quoted by Esther Potter, "To Paul's Churchyard to Treat with a Bookbinder," in *Property of a Gentleman*, ed. Robin Myers and Michael Harris (1991), p. 32.

4. *Ibid.*, p. 26. Donaldson's business was widespread: he declared that his books were sold at his shops in Edinburgh and London, and also "by the booksellers of Great Britain, Ireland, and America." *Ibid.*

5. Quoted by A.N.L. Munby, reviewing Ellic Howe, *A List of London Bookbinders 1648–1815*, in *The Book Collector* (Winter, 1952), p. 271. It may well have been a Benjamin White catalogue to which Robert Skipwith referred Thomas Jefferson in 1771. Jefferson noted: "These books if bound quite plain will cost the prices affixed in this catalogue. If bound elegantly, gilt, lettered, and marbled on the leaves, they will cost 20 p. cent more. If bound by Bumgarden in fine marbled bindings, they will cost 50 p. cent more." Quoted in Ellic Howe, *A List of London Bookbinders 1648–1815* (1950), p. xxvii.

6. In some ways accumulating such evidence seems especially daunting because fine binders worked for many different booksellers, and also actively sought and received private commissions. Without a dated inscription including a separate note of the binding price, or extrinsic records, such those showing binding orders

placed by Charles II and Lord Harley with, respectively, the Mearnes and Jane Steel, there is no way to prove whether a single deluxe binding is trade or bespoke. But these are the same problems that confront researchers into ordinary trade bindings. The presence of more distinctive tool impressions on deluxe bindings should allow increasing numbers of them to be associated with individual booksellers, and allow the inference of trade, rather than bespoke, commissions. See figure 3.13 and accompanying text.

7. Howard M. Nixon, *Catalogue of the Pepys Library at Magdalene College, Cambridge*, Vol. VI (1984), pp. xxiii–xxiv. Other exceptions, noted by Nixon, include the goatskin bindings commissioned from John Berresford on some very important books and manuscripts, including Pepys's illustrated roll of Henry VIII's ships.

8. Jervas's note was in a receipt for copies received from the bookseller Bernard Lintot. George Sherburn, *The Correspondence of Alexander Pope* (1956), I, 296. The copy in question went to the King's physician, Sir John Shadwell, instead of to the Duke of Montagu.

9. Ellic Howe, *The London Bookbinders 1780–1806* (1950, reprint 1988), pp. 68–69. Hall may simply have been lettering a spine label as an extra for a cheaper calf or sheep binding, but the principle is the same.

10. Differentiation is made even more difficult by the dispersal of private libraries. A large run of novels, or any other form of literature, uniformly bound suggests bespoke rebinding, but taken one title at a time there is no basis on which to draw such a conclusion.

11. James Sutherland, *English Literature of the Late Seventeenth Century* (1969), p. 30.

12. Maurice Craig, *Irish Bookbindings 1600–1800* (1954), p. 3, frontispiece, and plates 1–17. It appears from the surviving records that all volumes up to the mid- or late-1730s were bound at about the same time, and subsequent volumes were bound upon publication.

13. Maggs Bros. Ltd., *Bookbinding in the British Isles*, Catalogue 1212 (1996), item 101.

14. At least seven of these backless bindings are recorded, no fewer than three of them on the same 1701 edition of *The Book of Common Prayer*. Balley's contemporary John Bagford remarked that "you could not know the fore-edge from the back, both being cut and gilded alike." Quoted in Howard M. Nixon, *Five Centuries of English Bookbinding* (1978), p. 126.

15. The known Balley binding is Maggs Bros. Ltd., *Bookbinding in the British Isles*, Catalogue 1212, item 76; the binding depicted in figure 5.34 is item 79 in the same catalogue, and a superb specimen of a backless Balley binding, on *The Book of Common Prayer*, 1699, is item 75.

# APPENDIX OF SIZES AND FORMATS

Paper sizes and printing formats were crucial to bookbinders, determining their costs of labor and materials. Common paper sizes such as crown, foolscap, and pot (so called because of their watermarks) appear in the earlier bookbinders' price lists. The 1760 list includes other paper names, from the largest "imperial" size down through royal, demy, and crown, but not the smaller foolscap and pot sizes.

This book does not specify a paper size for every binding it illustrates. Instead, it takes the simplest possible approach, avoiding technical terms and, like the earlier price lists, associating different paper sizes with well-known publications. Within the most common octavo (8vo) and duodecimo (12mo) formats, the absence of a specified paper means that the size is post or crown, the latter roughly 7½ x 5 inches in octavo, and 6⅔ x 3¾ inches in duodecimo, with large post paper slightly bigger (at most three-quarters of an inch in height), and small post a little smaller—these are not easy to tell apart when trimmed and neither post-horn nor crown watermark is evident.

Other paper sizes and formats mentioned in this book—foolscap and pot most frequently—follow, from largest to smallest. The dimensions refer to untrimmed folded sheets; trimmed leaves in normal bound copies are up to ten percent smaller (see fig. 4.5). This is not a comprehensive list.

IMPERIAL: folio 30 x 22 inches, sometimes seen in quarto, rarely in smaller formats.

ROYAL: folio 20 x 12½, octavo 10 x 6¼ inches. "Super-Royal" was a bit bigger.

DEMY: octavo 8¾ x 5⅝, duodecimo 7½ x 4⅞ inches.

FOOLSCAP: quarto 8½ x 6½, octavo 6¾ x 4¼, duodecimo 5⅔ x 3¼ inches.

POT: quarto 7½ x 6, octavo 6¼ x 3¾ , duodecimo 5 x 3⅛ inches.

Booksellers also commissioned smaller formats, especially for children's and devotional books, and usually employing post, crown, or smaller papers. Octodecimo (18mo), which this book uses to describe one of the most common sizes of late eighteenth- and early nineteenth-century children's books (about 5½ x 3½ inches when trimmed), is not accepted as a format for English books by all scholars. R.B. McKerrow states in *An Introduction to Bibliography for Literary Students* (1928), p. 173, that he has "not met with it in English printing," but more recently Philip Gaskell, in *A New Introduction to Bibliography* (1972), pp. 107, 329, and fig. 61, has acknowledged it, citing sources as early as 1755 and providing diagrams of its imposition. It is regularly referred to by booksellers of the period (see, *e.g.* William Bent's statement quoted in Chapter 3, note 64). English 18mos are usually signed in sixes, or alternating twelves and sixes. Figure 1.8 illustrates what must be a pot 8vo, typeset and trimmed to the exact size of the usual children's books of the period—clearly intended to fit right into their serried ranks.

Other small formats include, with their most common measurements (which can vary somewhat according to paper size):

16MO: 4 x 3½ inches.      48MO: 2¼ x 1½ inches.

24MO: 4 x 2½ inches.      64MO: 1⅝ x 1 inches.

32MO: 3½ x 2¼ inches.

More complete tables of paper sizes can be found in J.D. Fleeman, *A Bibliography of the Works of Samuel Johnson*, Vol. I (2000), p. xxxvii, and in Philip Gaskell, *A New Introduction to Bibliography* (1972), pp. 73–75.

# ACKNOWLEDGMENTS

This book would never have been written without the encouragement and advice of scholars on both sides of the Atlantic. Bruce Whiteman at the Clark Library was one of its initial and most enthusiastic supporters. Both he and Suzanne Tatian took time to tour the Clark stacks with me, and allowed me to assemble carts of material to photograph. Equal courtesy and support were given by Joel Silver at the Lilly Library, John Mustain at Stanford, and Daniel J. Slive at UCLA Special Collections. Joel not only arranged for photographs to be taken of the bindings I selected on our library tour, he also pointed me to books, like Milton's 1667 *Paradise Lost*, which I would otherwise have left unconsidered. Later he found and sent a surprise photograph of Speechly's *Treatise on the Culture of the Pineapple* with its price "One Guinea" on the spine. John Mustain took me through the Stanford stacks, conjured books and articles at what seemed a moment's notice, checked references, scanned illustrations, and within hours of my panicking about not being able to find George Tokefield's 1664 catalogue, faxed me a copy of the entire text. He and his wife Kate also took time from their summer to read and offer detailed critiques of the typescript. Dan Slive donated what I think would otherwise have been a day off in order to guide me through the rare book stacks at UCLA. Without him, the illustrations of eighteenth century literature, and especially children's books, would be much the poorer.

Bill Zachs read several different chapter drafts and offered indispensable advice for their improvement. He shared his knowledge of the eighteenth century book trade and his editorial expertise in equal measure, and when necessary he was ruthless in cutting my paragraphs and sentences down to size. David Pearson read the book both in typescript and proof, and his sharp eye and vast knowledge of English bookbinders were equally invaluable. He also shared the typescript for his forthcoming *English Bookbinding Styles 1450–1800: a Handbook*, which I have cited several times in the course of this study. Mirjam Foot kindly took time from her busy teaching schedule to read page proofs, and offered a detailed critique. Although we disagree on some important points, I am grateful for her generous and expert advice, and for a number of corrections.

As a bookbinder Philip Dusel is increasingly recognized as one of the consummate craftsmen of our generation. He has worked tirelessly to discover and replicate the techniques used by seventeenth- and eighteenth-century binders, and shared his thoughts on many of the topics in this book, consistently providing both inspiration and practical information. Among his many suggestions was the possibility that edge-rolls might be one way to identify the otherwise generic work of individual trade binders.

Stephen Parks made it possible for me to look at Francis and John Noble novels at the Beinecke Library. He sent details of the Fordyce letter quoted in Chapter 3, and generously gave of his time tracking down an elusive set of printed wrappers. Roger Stoddard at the Houghton Library kindly gave me permission to reproduce the 1669 bookbinders' price list, and the cover of the 1733 pamphlet *Rome Excis'd*. Giles Mandelbrote located several Noble novels at the British Library I would otherwise have missed, and he and James Raven met me in London in November 2002, offering advice and encouragement. Philippa Marks took the trouble to send call numbers for early bindings, and facilitated my use of the two "edges" bindings reproduced in Chapter 2. In Oxford, Clive Hurst at the Bodleian looked at the notes John Carter and Graham Pollard made in the early 1930s for a study of wholesale bookbinding, and enabled me to conclude (I hope not too arrogantly) that this book could proceed without reference to them. When I visited the Bodleian, Geoffrey Groom and Cherry Robertson retrieved still more Francis and John Noble publications, on a day when many of the library stacks were closed.

Robin de Beaumont provided illustrations, read early drafts, and suggested parallels with the work of some nineteenth century binders. Ian Jackson was a mine of information and references, lending me books and journals, and pointing me towards others. He introduced in conversation the names of several books of which I had never before heard, so gracefully that my ignorance was never exposed. Steve Weissman of Ximenes Rare Books wrote me a letter about publisher's wrappers, which I quote in Chapter 3. Robert Harding of Maggs Bros Ltd. challenged some of my assumptions, supplied illustrations, and quoted the Fordyce letter, now at the Beinecke Library, of which I would otherwise have been unaware. Warren McDougall shared statistics and insights about the Scottish book trade, and especially its exports. Alaina Sloo and Karla Knight saw the manuscript of this book through the sticky operations of, respectively, copy-editing and indexing, and I am grateful for their patience and thoroughness.

Katy Homans was both graphic designer and mastermind. There is a lot to be said for having a great book designer as an old and dear friend, and Katy made all the problems about which I might easily have obsessed seem matters of course. I am grateful to my publishers Robert Fleck and John von Hoelle at Oak Knoll Press for allowing me to work with Katy, and for their steadfast support of this project from the outset.

Most of the illustrations in this book come from four major university libraries—the William Andrews Clark Memorial Library, the Lilly Library at Indiana University, and the Special Collections Departments at Stanford University and the University of California at Los Angeles—and one private collection, that of William Zachs. Francis Lapka took the fine digital photographs of the Lilly Library's books; the author is responsible for the others, except for those provided by, respectively, the British Library, Trustees of the British Museum, Cambridge University Press, the Houghton Library at Harvard University, Maggs Bros. Ltd., the Pepys Library at Magdalen College, Cambridge, Bernard Quaritch Ltd., and Sotheby's.

I end this long list of acknowledgements with a salute to my old friend and mentor Noel King, who for thirty-five years has gently reminded me that those of us lucky enough to live in the world of learning need to try to give something back. And I conclude with this book's dedication: to my wife Valerie Andrews and my son Adrian Bennett. Valerie has been an editor since her days with *Time/Life*, but she has never had to live with any other editorial project quite so long, or so intimately. She read and revised each version of every chapter, endnote, and caption, for a year and a half, and she kept her sense of humor when mine was out the window and long gone. She and Adrian both had faith that this book would someday be finished, and I am glad to say they were right.